Strategy, Organization Design, and Human Resource Management

STRATEGIC MANAGEMENT POLICY PLANNING:
A Multivolume Treatise, VOLUME 3

General Editors: *Howard Thomas,* Department of Business Administration,
University of Illinois, Urbana-Champaign, and *Dan E. Schendel,*
Krannert Graduate School of Management, Purdue University

Strategic Management Policy and Planning

A Multivolume Treatise

General Editors:

Howard Thomas
Department of Business Administration
University of Illinois at Urbana-Champaign

and

Dan E. Schendel
Krannert Graduate School of Management
Purdue University

Strategy, Organization Design, and Human Resource Management

Edited by: CHARLES C. SNOW
College of Business Administration
The Pennsylvania State University

 JAI PRESS INC.

Greenwich, Connecticut   *London, England*

Library of Congress Cataloging-in-Publication Data

Strategy, organization design, and human resource management / edited
   by Charles C. Snow.
        p.   cm — (Strategic management policy and planning : v. 3)
     Includes bibliographies.
     ISBN 0-89232-807-X :
     1. Strategic planning.   2. Organization.   3. Personnel management.
   I. Snow, Charles C. (Charles Curtis), 1945-   . II. Series.
   HD30.28.S739 1988
   658.4′012—dc19   88-8549

Copyright © 1989 JAI PRESS INC.
55 Old Post Road, No. 2
Greenwich, Connecticut 06830

JAI PRESS LTD.
3 Henrietta Street
London WC2E 8LU
England

Library of Congress Catalog Number: 88-8549

ISBN: 0-89232-807-X

Manufactured in the United States of America

CONTENTS

PART III.   HUMAN RESOURCE MANAGEMENT

LIST OF CONTRIBUTORS

W. Graham Astley	University of Colorado, Denver
David E. Bowen	University of Southern California
Richard A. Brahm	University of California, Irvine
Richard B. Chase	University of Southern California
James W. Dean, Jr.	The Pennsylvania State University
Jane E. Dutton	University of Michigan
Donald C. Hambrick	Columbia University
Lawrence G. Hrebiniak	University of Pennsylvania
Vijay K. Jolly	International Management Institute Geneva
William F. Joyce	Dartmouth College
Richard Normann	The Service Management Group Paris
Edward J. Ottensmeyer	Clark University
John E. Prescott	University of Pittsburgh

Rafael Ramirez	The Service Management Group Paris
Daniel C. Smith	University of Wisconsin, Madison
Charles C. Snow	The Pennsylvania State University
Gerald I. Susman	The Pennsylvania State University
N. Venkatraman	Massachusetts Institute of Technology

PREFACE

The chapters in this volume address current issues in competitive strategy, organization design, and human resource management. The book's sweeping title is intended to suggest that an organization's strategy, design, and human resource practices form an integrated system. Each of the authors who was invited to write a chapter was given the considerable challenge of discussing the strategic, organizational, and managerial implications of his or her topic. Also, the authors were asked to write a technically sound chapter that would appeal to academic readers and to use language that would make the material accessible by practitioners. I hope you find their efforts to be successful.

The volume is divided into three main parts. Part I focuses primarily on strategy. It includes a chapter that reviews the strategy literature, a chapter on global competitive strategies, and a chapter on competitive strategy in service businesses. The overall goal of this part of the book is to provide a current assessment of the literature on organizational strategy and discussions of the rapidly evolving research on global and service strategies.

The focus of Part II is organization design. Three topics of current research interest are addressed—information technology, competitor intelligence, and strategic issue management—and each chapter discusses how organizations can be designed to take advantage of developments in these important areas. The fourth chapter in this section discusses the design issues associated with emerging post-industrial strategies, especially the requirements for interorganizational collaboration.

Part III deals with key aspects of human resource management. One chapter discusses the management of service employees, a second traces the organizational and managerial implications of the adoption of advanced manufacturing technology, and the concluding chapter describes reward systems appropriate for general managers.

I want to publicly thank the authors for their contributions to this volume, and I specifically want to acknowledge the help and support of two superb secretaries, Shirley Rider and Mary Towner.

Charles C. Snow

PART I

STRATEGY

_____

STRATEGY, STRUCTURE, AND PERFORMANCE:

PAST AND FUTURE RESEARCH

Lawrence G. Hrebiniak, William F. Joyce,
and Charles C. Snow

What type of competitive strategy will be most successful in a particular industry? Are managers responsible for strategic success, or is success primarily determined by the environment? What kind of organization structure is needed to implement a chosen strategy? What actions are taken when organizations do not perform well?

Over the past four decades, an increasing amount of theory and research has been aimed at these and similar questions. Traditionally, this research area has been referred to as *strategy, structure, and performance,* and in the 1980s it has become a topic of central interest to scholars in Strategic Management. The overall purpose of this chapter is to take stock of the strategy-structure-performance literature to this point and offer some recommendations about how future research might proceed.

The first section of the chapter presents a broad overview of strategy-structure-performance theory and research. The second section is an historical review of the key concepts and theoretical perspectives associated with this literature. The third section summarizes and assesses the major empirical studies. In the fourth section, a number of substantive and methodological recommendations are offered for conducting research in this area. The chapter closes with some general observations and conclusions.

OVERVIEW OF THE STRATEGY-STRUCTURE-PERFORMANCE LITERATURE

A broad conceptual framework that encompasses research on strategy, structure, and performance is shown in Figure 1. A representation of the seminal approaches developed by Coase (1937), Mason (1939), Bain (1956, 1968), and Learned, Christensen, Andrews, and Guth (1965), this conceptual scheme has four major components: environment, strategy, structure, and performance. The *environment* consists of the general social, economic, political, legal, and cultural factors affecting aggregate organizational activity (macroeconomic conditions, sociocultural values, government regulatory philosophy, and so forth), as well as factors associated with a specific industry (rate of growth, entry and mobility barriers, cost structures, and so forth). *Strategy* refers to a set of decisions and objectives regarding the nature and range of businesses a firm chooses to operate (corporate strategy) and the basic competitive approaches used in each of the businesses (business strategy). *Structure* is a broad concept that encompasses an organization's basic design or anatomy as well as the management processes used to coordinate and control its operations. Finally, *performance* is a multidimensional outcome of organizational behavior. Organizations develop strategies and structures to achieve various purposes; performance refers to the degree of fulfillment of these purposes. Any organization's performance can be assessed from several different levels and perspectives, at different times, and using different indicators. Therefore, gauging organizational performance is no simple matter. Nevertheless, it is widely believed that performance information is the prime stimulus for changing strategy, structure, and/or the environment.

In the following sections, we will use this broad conceptual scheme to organize a discussion of the literature. However, before doing so, it may be helpful to review some of the characteristics and issues associated with the literature and this overarching theoretical framework.

First, the strategy-structure-performance literature is fraught with *imprecise terminology*. For example, the concept of "structure" is used by industrial economists to refer to characteristics of an industry or market. Organization theorists, on the other hand, use structure to refer to an organization's fundamental shape or configuration. Similarly, organization theorists use the phrase "strategy and structure" to refer to an organization

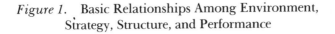

Figure 1. Basic Relationships Among Environment,
Strategy, Structure, and Performance

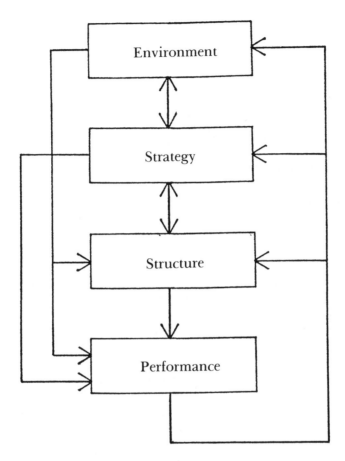

as a complete system whereas industrial economists characterize the design and behavior of an organization as "firm conduct." In order to be consistent in our discussion, we will treat strategic decisions as commitments to action that serve to substantially define an organization's environment. These commitments are carried out by developing organization structures and management processes to utilize resources. Finally, the success of these actions is measured by adopting the perspective of various stakeholders and using appropriate performance indicators. This approach is not intended to be normative; it does not describe a purposive, sequential decision making and action process. Rather, it is simply a means of classifying relevant theory and research.

6 L. G. HREBINIAK, W. F. JOYCE, and C. C. SNOW

Second, the strategy-structure-performance framework can be viewed as either *static* or *dynamic*. In the Strategic Management literature, the "content" of strategy often is differentiated from the "process" of strategy. That is, some researchers have focused on actual strategic decisions and their outcomes (content), essentially searching for relationships among strategy, structure, and performance. Often, these investigations have taken the form of static correlational studies. Other researchers have focused on the people and activities associated with formulating and/or implementing a strategic decision (process). By their very nature, process studies tend to be longitudinal (at least having traced events back in time). Thus, there is an implicit presumption that research can lead to improvements in the *kinds* of decisions managers make as well as the *means* used to make them, so both static and dynamic analyses play a role in strategy-structure-performance research.

Third, the framework does not specify the *direction of causality* among its components. Does the environment determine the appropriate strategy? Or can a given strategy alter the environment? Does the environment essentially determine performance? Or is the impact of the environment on performance moderated by strategy and structure? Is causality even a meaningful concept in trying to explain such complex relationships? Current thinking in the strategy-structure-performance area seems to be that none of these basic relationships is unidirectional and that it is most useful to examine the *individual* and *joint* effects of certain factors on others; *types* and *ranges* of feasible relationships; and so forth.

Fourth, the framework *has not been completely tested*. The strategy-structure-performance literature is interdisciplinary, and though there are areas of overlap and consistency, there are many other areas where the empirical evidence is missing, incomplete, or contradictory. Generally speaking, the database supporting this literature overrepresents large, private manufacturing enterprises and underrepresents international companies, service organizations, and not-for-profit organizations. Therefore, as the U.S. economy continues to become more service-oriented and international in scope, the theory of strategy, structure, and performance will become increasingly less relevant and applicable unless steps are taken to make the database more representative of all organizations.

HISTORICAL DEVELOPMENT OF KEY CONCEPTS AND PERSPECTIVES

As indicated in Figure 1, the strategy-structure-performance framework is composed of four main elements: environment, strategy, structure, and performance. The discussion of the literature is organized around these concepts, and it emphasizes historical developments in each area.

Environment

Early Conceptions of the Environment. For the first half of this century, management and organization theorists tended to ignore the environment, or at least to hold it constant, as they sought universalistic principles of planning, organizing, controlling, and the like. Weber (1947), who first articulated the characteristics of a bureaucracy (clearly defined hierarchy, positions, rules, and so forth), was concerned with the reciprocal effects of bureaucracy and the larger sociocultural environment, but he ignored the immediate task environment in his writings (Hrebiniak, 1978). He implied, in effect, that bureaucracy was appropriate for all organizational settings. Similarly, Taylor (1911) viewed his principles of scientific management as universally applicable, and he treated environmental demands and organizational strategies as fixed in his search for the "one best way" to manage. Later proponents of administrative principles, such as Gulick and Urwick (1937), Barnard (1938), Brown (1945), Mooney (1947), and Fayol (1949), expanded the focus to include the upper reaches of the organization. However, these theorists also paid little attention to environmental differences even though they were attempting to integrate experiences from the church, the military, and business into a common set of recommendations for the design and management of organizations.

Economists were concerned with environmental characteristics, but their conception of an organization was abstract and simplistic. In early economic theories of the firm, market forces set the prices for goods and services, and the entire firm was characterized as a production function whose blend of capital and labor was dictated by the quest for cost minimization. Moreover, all firms within an industry were assumed to be identical (except for their size). Entrepreneurial and marketing decisions sometimes were acknowledged, but little effort was made to specify the impact of the environment on organizational strategy and structure.

Disenchantment with universalistic organization and management principles grew in the 1950s. Two developments occurred during this period that thrust the environment into a more prominent role in organizational analysis. The first, prompted by work in general systems theory by von Bertalanffy (1950, 1956), was the idea that an organization was an *open system*. As such, the organization drew resources from its environment. An influential article by Dill (1958) articulated specific features of an organization's *task environment,* and, along similar lines, Thompson (1967) developed a relatively comprehensive framework that portrayed an organization as an intendedly-rational system embedded in a network of environmental actors and influences. The role of management in such a system was to coalign the organization with its general environment as well as with its ever-changing task environment.

A second important development was the introduction of *contingency theory*. The phenomenon that produced this concept can be traced most directly to the research of Woodward (1958) and Burns and Stalker (1961), whose studies of organization structure under different market and technological conditions dramatically changed the conventional view of the universality of management principles. Later, Lawrence and Lorsch (1967) coined the term "contingency theory" as a way of describing the organizational differentiation required to match environmental variation. Essentially, the contingency approach argued that "it depends," and research quickly moved toward the identification and description of the major contingency variables upon which organizational behavior depends. Unlike the early theorists, who tended to view structure and process as independent variables that could be manipulated by managers, contingency theorists viewed many internal aspects of the organization as dependent variables, whose form was largely determined by forces originating in the organization's environment.

Through the late 1950s and the 1960s, a series of increasingly elaborate contingency models portraying the links among environment, technology, size, structure, and process were developed. Over time, these models became quite fragmented and deterministic, prompting Child (1972) to call for a *strategic choice* perspective in which organization-environment relations were viewed as resulting primarily from choices made by managers. Elaborating upon this perspective, Miles and Snow (1978) urged researchers to develop a "neocontingency" perspective that (a) recognized managerial or strategic choice as the primary link between the organization and its environment; (b) focused on management's ability to define, learn about, and manage the environment; and (c) encompassed the multiple ways that organizations can respond to similar environmental conditions.

Current Conceptions of the Environment. Current theory portrays an organization's environment in either of two basic ways: as a set of evolutionary, largely deterministic influences or as a dynamic context enacted by managers. The first view is called *organizational ecology,* and it has been pursued at three levels of analysis (Carroll, 1984). At the organizational level, organizations are seen as developing and adapting over time. The forms they assume are based on both internal and external factors, but this evolutionary perspective tends to emphasize the deterministic and noncognitive aspects of adaptation. A second level of analysis is referred to as "population ecology" (Hannan and Freeman, 1977, 1984), and it employs a selection approach to evolution. In this view, organizations usually are characterized as more inertial than adaptive. Groups or populations of organizations are seen as moving through an evolutionary process characterized by variation (the presence of many organizational forms), selection (the elimination of certain forms by the environment), and retention (the preservation of advantageous structural traits). The population ecology approach focuses on environments, either industrial or geographic, and examines the characteristics of *groups* of organizations such as restaurants, newspaper firms, and so forth. The third level of analysis is the community level that uses a macroevolutionary approach to investigate the behavior of entire communities of organizations (e.g., within a city or across several urban areas). This emerging approach, currently only tangentially related to conventional modes of organizational analysis, seems to have promise for explaining the adaptive responses of large, heterogeneous groups of organizations to major historical transformations.

The organizational ecology perspective tends to treat the environment as concrete, objective, and independent from the organization (Smircich and Stubbart, 1985). Conversely, the *enactment* perspective says that organizational environments are acts of managerial invention rather than discovery (Weick, 1977), and thus the theorist's basic task is to investigate how and why managers focus their attention on a particular portion of the environment, how they gather information about this area of concern, and how they interpret this information for decision-making purposes. The process of enacting the environment is a never-ending one, involving the alignment of the organization with a continually evolving network of opportunities, threats, and constraints. Clearly, the enactment perspective places a great deal of emphasis on the strategic choices managers make to position their organizations within selected environments.

The ecological and enactment perspectives now appear to be converging somewhat (Hrebiniak and Joyce, 1985; Wholey and Brittain, 1986). Scholars representing the different perspectives are beginning to focus on the same phenomena (e.g., entrepreneurship, adaptation and development, performance) albeit with different concepts and often with different research goals. Industrial economists, historically more closely associated with the ecological perspective, are also beginning to acknowledge the role of enactment or strategic choice in their characterizations of firm behavior (Caves, 1980; Porter, 1981).

Strategy

The concept of strategy began to appear in the organizational literature at approximately the same time as the open system and contingency concepts. Strategy was introduced as a conceptual decision-making aid and advanced most notably by faculty members at the Harvard Business School (see Learned, et al. [1965] for an early statement). The Harvard view of strategy was (and is) *normative,* in that strategy was treated as a managerial art, an imaginative act of integrating numerous complex decisions about a firm's opportunities, risks, and resources. As such, strategy was viewed as the primary means by which an organization aligned itself with its environment, but early emphasis on the uniqueness of strategy, documented by countless case studies, pushed the contingency idea to its logical limit.

In contrast to the normative approach, Chandler's (1962) research was the first to employ strategy as a *descriptive* concept. From his study of four companies that pioneered in diversification, Chandler concluded that strategy was the key mechanism used for charting a new direction, and its impact on organization structure and performance was substantial. In Chandler's view, strategy is "the determination of the basic long-term goals and objectives of the enterprise and the adoption of courses of action and the allocation of resources necessary for carrying out these goals" (1962, p. 13). Clearly, this definition of strategy includes elements of both ends (objectives and goals) and means (courses of action and allocation of resources). In a manner consistent with this early definition, strategic planning today is typically defined as a process of deciding which businesses a company should be in and how to allocate resources among these businesses in order to achieve long-term objectives (Pitts and Snow, 1986). Similarly, strategic decision making can be viewed as a series of "means-ends" decisions whereby long-term, global objectives are broken down into shorter-term goals and plans (Hrebiniak and Joyce, 1984).

The study of strategy has tended to occur at two levels of analysis: *corporate* and *business* (Ansoff, 1965; Vancil and Lorange, 1975; Hofer and Schendel, 1978). Corporate strategy defines the nature and range of businesses a firm intends to operate and often is characterized by the question, "What businesses should we be in?" Thus, corporate strategies are essentially diversification strategies, and approaches have been developed for designing and managing a corporation as a "portfolio" of diversified businesses (Wind and Mahajan, 1981; Haspeslagh, 1982). An early effort to describe the different forms diversification can take was that of Wrigley (1970), who described how a "single-business" corporation may diversify into areas that are "related" or "unrelated" to the firm's original business. Rumelt (1974) extended this framework to include ten types of corporate diversification, and others have described the process by which diversification occurs and the structural characteristics associated with different corporate strategies (e.g., Berg, 1965, 1973; Leontiades, 1980; Pitts, 1980; Miles, 1982). There have been only a few attempts to assess the performance of corporate strategies (e.g., Rumelt, 1974, 1982; Salter and Weinhold, 1979), but it is generally agreed that corporations that diversify into related businesses perform better than those which diversify into unrelated areas (Peters and Waterman, 1982). Recently, it has been claimed that in general corporate strategies have failed miserably, that leading corporations often divest more businesses than they acquire and thereby dilute shareholder value (Porter, 1987).

At the business level, the key strategic question is, "How should we compete in this business?" Competitive strategy has a long research tradition, and the literature generally takes firm competition within an industry as its central unit of analysis. A substantial portion of this literature is based on the *economics of industrial organization*, derived largely from the original structure-conduct-performance paradigm of Mason (1939) and Bain (1956, 1968). Over the years, the main contribution of industrial economics has been in the areas of oligopoly theory (Fellner, 1965) and game theory (von Neumann and Morgenstern, 1944), both of which helped to describe and explain the competitive behavior of firms in industry. Until recently, the concept of strategy did not play much of a role in industrial organization economics even though the original framework implicitly included it as part of "firm conduct." There are many reasons why industrial economic analysis has treated strategy in this manner, including: (a) a stronger concern for consumer welfare and public policy than individual firm performance, (b) a traditional belief that industry structure is a more powerful determinant of performance than firm conduct, and (c) an emphasis on formal quantitative modeling of firm conduct that requires simplification of managerial attributes and behaviors (Teece, 1984).

Industrial organization economics now embraces the strategy concept much more willingly and effectively, and the view of firms (and their business units) as purposeful entities embedded in dynamic environments is well accepted (Baumol, Panzar, and Willig, 1982; Nelson and Winter, 1982). Porter (1981) catalogued the most recent contributions of industrial economics to the strategy literature, and these included: (a) specification of key industry forces that drive competitive strategy (Porter, 1979a, 1980); (b) introduction of the concept of strategic groups (clusters of similar competitive strategies) to differentiate firm behavior within an industry (Hunt, 1972); (c) introduction of the concept of mobility barriers (deterrents to shifts in strategic position among firms within an industry) (Caves and Porter, 1977); (d) extension of the firm's industrial environment to include international trade and competition (Porter, 1986); and (e) development of more comprehensive models that include corporate as well as business strategies (e.g., Williamson, 1975). Some useful cross-fertilization between the literatures of industrial economics and strategic management has begun to occur in the 1980s (e.g., Harrigan, 1980, 1983, 1985).

Another important contribution to the business strategy literature originally came from management practice. This is the *PIMS* Project— Profit Impact of Market Strategy (Buzzell, Gale, and Sultan, 1975). The PIMS Program originated as an internal project at GE, where it was used for many years as a tool of corporate and business planning, and is now housed at the Strategic Planning Institute, a nonprofit business research organization. The PIMS database contains historical information on over

2,000 "businesses" operated by over 500 U.S. and European corporations representing a broad spectrum of industrial environments. The overall conclusion from the *PIMS* research is that business profitability is strongly correlated with market share, and many investigators have used the database to isolate various strategy-environment relationships that produce high profitability (Ramanujam and Venkatraman, 1984; Gale and Buzzell, 1987).

A third stream of research on business strategy has its genesis in *organization theory*. Building on the concepts of environmental uncertainty (Lawrence and Lorsch, 1967), enactment (Weick, 1977), and strategic choice (Child, 1972), Miles and Snow (1978) forged a link between business strategy and organization design. Their research identified competitive strategies commonly found in a variety of industries (Defenders, Prospectors, Analyzers, Reactors), as well as the structural and managerial features that accompany each strategy type. This research spawned a number of studies aimed at developing taxonomies of business strategies and organization structures suited to various environmental conditions (Miller, 1981, 1986, 1987; Hambrick, 1984; Zahra, 1987), and some of this research addressed aspects of performance associated with different strategy-structure approaches (e.g., Snow and Hrebiniak, 1980).

A final stream of research on business strategy comes from the literature on *organizational decision making* (Cyert and March, 1963). Strictly speaking, the decision-making literature ranges beyond business-level strategy. For example, it refers to specific decision processes such as those used between business units and corporate headquarters (e.g., Bower, 1970), or it examines more broadly strategic decision making wherever it may occur (e.g., Allison, 1971; Mintzberg, Raisinghani, and Theoret, 1976; Quinn, 1980). This research generally addresses the "process" rather than the "content" of strategy. Strategic decisions have been singled out because of their importance, novelty, complexity, and open-endedness (Mintzberg, et al., 1976), and intricate processes for managing strategy have been described (Quinn, 1980), but seldom does this literature directly relate the process of strategy to either the content of strategy or to the organization's performance (Mintzberg and Waters, 1985).

Structure

Structure refers to ways in which an organization divides its labor into distinct tasks and then achieves coordination among them (Mintzberg, 1979). In this sense, structure includes not only the basic design of the organization but also the management processes used to hold it together.

Types of Structure. Historically, developments in organization structure have been stimulated by changes in strategy, a phenomenon first discussed by Chandler (1962). Chandler's basic thesis was that strategic change resulted from certain managers' awareness of the opportunities and needs to employ existing or expanding resources more profitably. This usually meant that organizations wanted to diversify into larger and more diverse markets. A new strategy, in turn, required a new or at least refashioned structure if the enlarged organization was to be operated efficiently. Chandler described the evolutionary path from the *functional* structure, a form developed around the turn of the century to administer large-scale enterprise, to the *product* (or multidivisional) structure which flourished in the 1950s. The functional structure is especially well suited to stable strategies, and it is usually accompanied by centralized decision making and control, vertical communications and integration, and high degrees of technical specialization. The product structure works best in dynamic environments where maximum flexibility is needed, and this structure relies heavily on autonomous workgroups, project teams, or product divisions in which planning and control have been decentralized. Burns and Stalker (1961), conducting their research at approximately the same time as Chandler but in a very different context (Scottish and English electronics firms), suggested that the functional structure is often "mechanistic" and the product structure "organic."

In the 1950s, a few organizations, most notably in the aerospace industry, began to develop a structure that combined elements of both the functional and product structures. This new form was called the *matrix* (Galbraith, 1973; Davis and Lawrence, 1977). As a hybrid structure, the matrix was designed to be both efficient and effective—to be responsive to differing market or client needs while using resources economically. The matrix, which can assume several forms, allows organizations to pursue strategies that combine stable and innovative products, services, or programs.

In the 1970s and 1980s, yet another structure began to emerge and spread, and it has been called the *dynamic network* (Miles and Snow, 1986). The dynamic network organization is appropriate for competitive situations of extreme complexity and/or rapid change, and it is characterized by vertical disaggregation, extensive use of internal and external brokers, integration via real or simulated markets rather than administrative processes, and, in some instances, by the presence of full-disclosure information systems. A network organization can display the technical virtuosity of the functional structure, the market responsiveness of the product structure, and the balanced orientation of the matrix.

Strategy and Structure. There is widespread belief, supported by a limited amount of research, that in high-performing organizations structure needs to be properly fitted to strategy (e.g., Lawrence and Lorsch, 1967; Galbraith and Nathanson, 1978). The "stages of development" model, which described the structural adaptations that occur as a corporation diversifies and grows, illustrated the dynamics of Chandler's proposition that *structure follows strategy* (Thain, 1969; Salter, 1970; Scott, 1970). Further, by describing the various structural devices corporations use to engage in international business, Stopford and Wells (1972) extended the stages of development model to include the international dimension. Their work in multinational corporate structures has been refined and extended by other researchers (e.g., Daniels, Pitts, and Tretter, 1984, 1985; Doz, 1986).

The converse proposition, that *strategy follows structure,* has also received theoretical and empirical attention. The notion was implicitly raised by Fouraker and Stopford (1968), who found that organizations with functional structures had difficulty pursuing an international diversification strategy while organizations with product (divisionalized) structures were able to diversify much more easily. Hall and Saias (1980) noted that structure may constrain and even determine strategy in three major ways: (a) structure can determine the introduction and subsequent development of strategic planning in an organization, (b) structure affects managers' perceptions of both internal and external events, and (c) structure can affect the strength, speed, and character of strategic decisions. Their conclusion was that the strategy-structure relationship is complex, iterative, and symmetric.

Most recently, structure has been viewed as part of the *implementation* of strategy (Hrebiniak and Joyce, 1984). Thus, strategic decisions are actualized by first developing primary structures (functional, product, matrix, and so forth) and then supplementing these with operating structures, goals, incentives, and controls. This is the only framework developed thus far that integrates major planning and organizing decisions at multiple levels of strategy and structure. Earlier attempts at integration suggested that "everything depends on everything else," typified by approaches such as the McKinsey 7-S framework. The model developed by Hrebiniak and Joyce (1984) proposes a logical order among the elements considered in implementing strategy and provides a process and framework for determining the content of implementation activities. Important questions concerning the relative desirability of altering strategy, structure, or reward and control systems (or some combination of these) are addressed based on the nature of the strategic problems encountered and the time available for implementation.

Performance

Performance, the last component of the theoretical framework shown in Figure 1, refers to the economic and social outcomes associated with organizational actions. As a variable, performance often is difficult to define and measure, and its relation to environment, strategy, and structure is not well understood. Four major factors contribute to the problem of predicting and explaining organizational performance: (a) level of analysis, (b) referents and perspectives, (c) measures, and (d) time frames (e.g., Steers, 1977; Hrebiniak, 1978; Cameron, 1986; Chakravarthy, 1986; Venkatraman and Ramanujam, 1986; Jemison, 1987).

Performance has not been consistently defined by researchers using the strategy-structure-performance framework. The most glaring discrepancy occurs between the definitions of economists and those of strategy analysts. Traditionally, industrial economists have examined performance at the level of the total *economy*. At this level, the most important aspects of performance include production and allocative efficiency, technical efficiency and progress, full employment, and an equitable distribution of income (Scherer, 1980). Strategists, on the other hand, usually are concerned with performance at the *firm* or *business unit* level. Performance at this level often is defined as growth, profitability, leadership, and so forth. Therefore, one must be careful to specify the level at which performance is being analyzed before attempting to link it to environment, strategy, and structure.

Performance *referents* vary according to the different perspectives of an organization's stakeholders (Freeman, 1984). For example, stockholders might equate high performance with the creation of shareholder value (Rappaport, 1986), managers and employees might see performance as growth or job security, customers may regard quality and service as key performance indicators, and so forth. Because the typical organization has many stakeholders—and in many industries the number of stakeholder groups has increased substantially in recent years—researchers must define (or control for) performance in a way that accounts for these important referents. This is especially crucial to the generalizability of performance findings.

Once defined, performance must be assessed. *Measures* of performance must be identified that are both *accurate* and *consistent* over time. Performance measures frequently used by economists, such as return on equity, stock price-earnings ratio, and price-cost margins, tend to be relatively accurate and consistent (controlling for accounting differences across firms or industries), especially when compared to softer measures such as a firm's ability to innovate, be socially responsible, and so forth.

Finally, the literature is unclear about the appropriate *time frames* to use when defining and measuring performance. There is virtually no systematic evidence, for example, on how performance "lags" strategy. This makes it difficult to relate a performance measure to a strategy measure. Does a strategic decision made now impact performance one year later. Two years? On the other hand, studies of turnaround strategies (e.g., Schendel, Patton, and Riggs, 1976; Slatter, 1984) and bankruptcies (e.g., Altman, 1968) have provided insights into when and how performance "leads" strategy—that is, how long it takes before poor performance stimulates consideration of strategic change and how organizations respond to crisis situations.

Despite these problems of definition and measurement, however, it is widely believed that performance should be an integral part of studies of strategy and structure. This is an applied literature, with the ultimate goal of prediction and control, so performance should always be at the forefront of research in this area.

REVIEW OF EMPIRICAL STUDIES

In this section, we summarize the major empirical studies of strategy, structure, and performance (in addition to those discussed in previous sections). Our goal is not to identify and summarize every study conducted on this topic but rather to determine salient variables and relationships and to make a general assessment of the evidence on which knowledge in this area has been based. The 56 studies shown in Table 1 were drawn from major journals for the period 1975-1986. The guiding criterion for inclusion in Table 1 was that the study examined relationships across two or more of the major variable classes of environment, strategy, structure, and performance.

A close reading of these studies suggests the following conclusions:

1. The most systematic *sample* of organizations has come from the PIMS database. The entire organizational sample is heavily dominated by large, publicly-held manufacturing firms. Except for some businesses in the PIMS database, there are few international and service organizations.
2. Research *methodology* was broadly distributed, including computer analyses of ongoing databases (e.g., PIMS and Compustat), analysis of secondary data (e.g., content analysis of cases and use of census data on firms), interviews, and questionnaires. In general, studies based on primary data are narrow in scope. Interview studies have an average of 33 firms, minimal international and service representation, but a good mix of small and large organizations. Questionnaire studies have an average of 88 firms, minimal international and service representation, and contain mostly medium and large organizations.
3. Although some of the studies were difficult to classify accurately, an attempt was made to see which of the *bivariate* and *multivariate*

relationships associated with the theoretical framework shown in Figure 1 have been examined. The bivariate results were: strategy-performance ($n = 19$), strategy-structure (6), structure-performance (6), environment-strategy (4), and environment-performance (1). There were 19 multivariate studies, all but two of which were published in the 1980s. Thus, it appears that investigators have recently begun to conduct sophisticated studies that examine a more extensive set of strategy-structure-performance relationships.

4. None of the studies investigated the *process* of strategy formulation or implementation, probably because such studies seldom relate the strategy process to the organization's environment, structure, or performance (and hence did not meet the criterion for being included in Table 1). Therefore, it is not safe to derive explanations or make predictions about strategy-structure-performance relationships using process characteristics.

5. Only a handful of the studies were *longitudinal*. Therefore, because the bulk of the empirical evidence is cross-sectional, neither the stability nor the evolutionary pattern of strategy-structure-performance relationships is clear.

6. Understandably, the empirical evidence does not adequately address the *newer* ideas and practices in the strategy-structure-performance area. For example, the growing phenomenon of "strategic alliances" that cut across industry and national borders has not received systematic research attention (Astley and Brahm, 1989). Neither has the recently introduced concept of "industry synergy" been empirically examined (Miles and Snow, 1986). Less understandable, however, is the fact that several *well-established* concepts or beliefs have been allowed to persist without full empirical examination. For example, the idea of "competitive symbiosis"—that dissimilar organizations (or strategic groups) can coexist in the same general environment—is important and firmly established, but it is also in need of much stronger empirical support.

In sum, the empirical literature on strategy, structure, and performance is (a) small but growing in size and sophistication; (b) focused mostly on medium to large publicly-held U.S. manufacturing firms; and (c) incomplete in its testing of both established and new theoretical constructs. In the next section, we discuss ways in which the literature might be developed to make it more comprehensive, cumulative, and integrated.

(Text continues on page 41)

Table 1.　Empirical Studies of Strategy, Structure, and Performance

Study	Basic Research Problem	Data and Sample	Variables and Measures	Overall Findings
Anderson and Zeithaml (1984)	Tested the relationship between business strategy and performance at different stages of the product life cycle	1,234 industrial products manufacturing businesses drawn from the PIMS data base	Performance (return on investment, relative average market share) Product life cycle (growth, maturity, decline) Strategy (frequency of product change, product and process R&D, and so forth)	A different mix of strategy characteristics was related to performance at each stage of the product life cycle
Armour and Teece (1978)	Examined the M-form hypothesis (impact of multidivisional vs. functional structure on the performance of large companies)	Questionnaire data on 28 of the 32 Fortune 500 firms in the petroleum industry	Performance (return on equity) Structure (functional, functional with subsidiaries, divisionalized, holding company, transitional, multidivisional) Other (size, risk, capacity utilization, growth)	In the 1955-1968 period, M-form firms (multidivisional structure) outperformed functionally-structured firms
Beard and Dess (1981)	Examined the relative impact of corporate-level strategy and business-level strategy on firm performance	Compustat data on 40 single-industry manufacturing firms randomly selected from Standard and Poor	Performance (return on equity, return on investment) Corporate strategy (average industry profitability) Business strategy (debt-to-equity ratio, asset-to-sales ratio, the firm's sales divided by sales of all firms in the industry)	Both strategies significantly determined firm performance, but business-level strategy appeared to be more influential

Study	Purpose	Method/Sample	Variables	Findings
Bettis (1981)	Examined performance differences between related and unrelated diversified firms	Compustat data on 31 related-constrained firms, 24 related-linked firms, and 25 unrelated firms drawn from the Fortune 500	Performance (return on assets) Strategy (related-linked, related-constrained, unrelated diversification) Other (advertising, R&D plant investment, size, risk)	Related-diversified firms outperformed unrelated-diversified firms. Advertising, capital intensity, and R&D were different between related and unrelated firms
Bettis and Hall (1982)	Investigated the hypothesis that the superior performance of related-diversified firms is due largely to industry effects	Compustat data on 31 related-constrained firms, 24 related-linked firms, and 25 unrelated firms drawn from the Fortune 500	Performance (return on assets) Strategy (related-linked, related-constrained, unrelated diversification)	Related-diversified firms outperformed all other firms due largely to industry effects (e.g., related-constrained category included mostly pharmaceutical firms)
Bourgeois (1980)	Explored the relationship between decision-making consensus among top management teams and company performance	Interview data from top executives of 12 nondiversified public corporations headquartered in the Pacific Northwest	Performance (return on assets, growth in capital, earnings, and so forth) Consensus (degree of agreement on goals and means)	Whereas agreement on goals and means was positively associated with performance, agreement on means was more important
Bourgeois (1985)	Explored relationships among top management perceptions of environmental uncertainty, objectively measured environmental volatility, and corporate goal structures and their impact on company performance	Interview, questionnaire, and secondary data on 20 nondiversified public corporations headquartered in the Pacific Northwest	Performance (return on assets, growth in net earnings, growth in earnings per share, and so forth) Perceived environmental uncertainty (customer behavior, competitor predictability, and so forth) Environmental volatility (changes in sales, profits, and industry output) Strategic goals (goal diversity, number of goals)	The number and diversity of goals is less important to performance than accuracy of managerial perceptions. Successful firms in volatile environments accurately assessed uncertainty instead of reducing it.

Table 1. (continued)

Study	Basic Research Problem	Data and Sample	Variables and Measures	Overall Findings
Christensen and Montgomery (1981)	Investigated various market structure variables as moderators of the diversification-performance relationship	Secondary data on 128 Fortune 500 firms	Performance (sales growth, growth in earnings per share, return on invested capital, and so forth) Diversification strategy (single business, dominant-constrained, dominant-linked, related-constrained, related-linked, unrelated) Market structure (concentration ratio, market growth, industry return on assets, and so forth)	Performance differences existed across some types of diversification strategies. However, in general, there was no consistent diversification-performance relationship. Certain types of market structure variables were associated with distinctly high or low performance (e.g., firms in markets that constrain growth or profits were likely to diversify).
Daniels, Pitts, and Tretter (1984)	Examined organization structures of large U.S. multinational companies. Different structural groups were compared on various strategic dimensions.	Questionnaire data on 93 Fortune 500 multinational companies	Strategy (product diversity, foreign involvement, R&D intensity, marketing intensity, capital intensity) Control mechanism (ownership when investing abroad, acquisition method, international production integration) Organization structure (worldwide functional, worldwide product, international division, area, matrix)	Companies with low foreign sales handled foreign operations as an appendage to existing product or functional divisions. Increasing foreign sales and product diversity required international division structure.

Daniels, Pitts, and Tretter (1985)	Identified organization structures of firms that have both high foreign sales and high product diversity	Questionnaire data on 37 Fortune 500 firms (out of a population of 93 high foreign sales and high product diversity firms)	Strategy (foreign dependence, product diversity, research intensity) Structure (global product, international division, area or geographic, global functional, matrix)	The international division was the most popular structure for a multinational strategy (48% of all firms). The global product structure was also used extensively (30%). All conglomerates had global product structures. Use of area, functional, and matrix structures was minimal.
Dess and Davis (1984)	Examined the relationship between generic strategy and firm performance within a single industry	Questionnaire data on 22 firms in paints and allied products industry	Performance (sales growth rates, return on assets) Strategy (differentiation, low cost, focus)	Variations in intraindustry profitability and growth were related to strategic group membership. Firms with at least one generic strategy outperformed firms identified as "stuck in the middle."
Frederickson (1984)	Examined the relationship between the comprehensiveness of the strategic decision process and firm performance in a stable environment. Comprehensiveness is a measure of rationality and refers to the extent to which organizations are exhaustive or inclusive in making and integrating strategic decisions.	Questionnaire data on 45 firms in the paint and coatings industry	Performance (return on assets, percent change in gross sales) Comprehensiveness (43 Likert-type questions) Organization size	Comprehensiveness was consistently positively related to performance in a stable environment

Table 1. (continued)

Study	Basic Research Problem	Data and Sample	Variables and Measures	Overall Findings
Frederickson and Mitchell (1984)	Examined the relationship between the comprehensiveness of the strategic process and firm performance in an unstable environment	Questionnaire data on 34 firms in the forest products industry headquartered in the Pacific Northwest	Performance (return on assets, percent change in gross sales) Comprehensiveness (43 Likert-type questions) Organization size	Comprehensiveness was consistently negatively related to performance in an unstable environment
Galbraith and Schendel (1983)	Developed two typologies of business strategy (consumer goods and industrial products) and examined the relationship between strategy and performance	Cross-sectional and time-series data on 1,200 businesses in the PIMS data base	Performance (cash flow, return on investment, percent annual change in market share) Strategy (13 variables representing strategic posture and 13 representing strategic change)	Identified six consumer goods and four industrial products strategies. Different strategies were associated with different performance outcomes, with important tradeoffs existing between cashflow, return on investment, and changes in market share position. In general, however, businesses with large market share had higher performance.
Galbraith and Stiles (1983)	Investigated the relationship between a firm's performance and its power over suppliers, power over customers, and industry structure	Cross-sectional data on 1,200 businesses in the PIMS data base	Performance (return on sales) Purchase market conditions (percent of total purchases made from three largest suppliers, sales of the largest suppliers to the business as a percent of the suppliers' total revenues, availability of alternative sources of supply)	Firm profitability was determined not only by industry structure but also by the relative power of the firm over its suppliers and customers. This general finding was stronger in consumer goods businesses than in capital goods businesses.

				Sales market conditions (proportion of the total number of immediate customers accounting for 50% of the firm's total sales; the number of immediate customers; importance of installation, repair, and service provided to the user, and so forth) Industry structure (concentration, industry growth, product patents, and so forth) Other (firm's sales in the industry as a percent of the top four firms' annual sales)	
Grinyer, Yasai-Ardekani, and Al-Bazzaz (1980)	Examined relationships among strategy, structure, environment, and financial performance	Interview data on 48 large U.K. companies in 18 industries		Performance (standard deviation of return on investment, growth in return on investment, growth in sales, and so forth) Strategy (degree of diversification) Structure (degree of divisionalization, span of control, and so forth) Environment (market turbulence, need for new product innovation, rate of technological change, and so forth)	There was a strong relationship between strategy and structure. Organizations that properly matched structure to strategy perceived less environmental pressure. However, strategy-structure fit was not related to financial performance.

Table 1.   *(continued)*

Study	Basic Research Problem	Data and Sample	Variables and Measures	Overall Findings
Grinyer and Yasai-Ardekani (1981)	Examined various relationships among strategy, organization structure, and size	Interview data on 45 U.K. companies randomly selected from 502 electrical engineering companies	Strategy (degree of diversification) Structure (formalization, specialization, divisionalization, and so forth) Other (size, age of organization, technology, and so forth)	The relationship between strategy and structure was strong and largely independent of other organizational characteristics except size. It appeared that strategy and structure were related to each other because both were related to size, suggesting that size was the causal factor in the strategy-structure relationship.
Grinyer, Al-Bazzaz, and Yasai-Ardekani (1986)	Examined the relationship between various aspects of corporate planning, organizational characteristics, and environmental factors	Interview data on 48 large U.K. companies in 18 industries	Environmental variables (environmental change, market dominance, and so forth) Planning variables (number of planning staff, formality, scope, and so forth) Organizational variables (strategy, structure, size, and so forth)	Corporate planning process was contingent on company environment and organization. For example, controlling for size of organization: (a) companies that cannot change their technologies easily employed more planning specialists and more forecasting and evaluation techniques; (b) planners had greater status, involvement, and scope in companies facing turbulent environments; and (c) planning was more comprehensive and formal in diversified companies.

Gupta and Govindarajan (1983)	Examined relationships among managerial characteristics, strategic business unit (SBU) strategy, and SBU effectiveness	Questionnaire data on 58 SBUs in eight Fortune 500 diversified firms headquartered in the Northeast	Performance (self-report of general managers on 12 performance dimensions) SBU strategy (build, hold, harvest, divest) Managerial characteristics (SBU manager's experience in marketing/sales, willingness to take risks, tolerance for ambiguity)	Greater marketing/sales experience, greater willingness to take risks, and greater tolerance for ambiguity contributed to the effectiveness of "build" SBUs. In general, managerial characteristics should be fitted to business strategy to obtain high performance.
Hambrick (1983a)	Refined the Miles-Snow typology and examined its effectiveness in different environments	Data on 1,452 growing and mature businesses drawn from the PIMS data base	Performance (return on investment, cash flow on investment, market share change) Environment (product life cycle, new product innovation) Strategy (defender, prospector) Functional attributes (entrepreneurial attributes, engineering attributes, competitive devices) Market share (leader, follower)	In general, prospectors were more entrepreneurial and defenders more efficiency oriented. Each type differed in performance depending on the environment (new or mature industry) and on the type of performance sought (e.g., cash flow or market share gain).
Hambrick (1983b)	Examined successful strategies in two different types of mature industrial-products environments	PIMS data base ($n = 107$ for disciplined capital goods makers, $n = 57$ for aggressive makers of complex capital goods)	Performance (return on investment) Strategic position attributes (market share, capital intensity, number of customers, and so forth) Strategic choice attributes (value added, quality, product innovation, and so forth)	Within a mature industrial products industry, there were several successful strategies. However, each strategy capitalized on certain industry characteristics.

Table 1. *(continued)*

Study	Basic Research Problem	Data and Sample	Variables and Measures	Overall Findings
Hambrick and Lei (1985)	Examined various environmental contingency variables as moderators of the relationship between strategy and performance, and determined the relative importance of these contingency variables	Data on 636 businesses drawn from the PIMS data base	Performance (return on investment) Strategy (capacity utilization, new product development, relative market share, and so forth) Environmental contingency variables (user sector, product life cycle, purchase frequency, concentration, and so forth)	Ten environmental contingency variables moderated the relationship between strategy and performance. Among the ten, user sector and purchase frequency were the most significant. Product life cycle was a third but less important influence on the strategy-performance relationship.
Hambrick, MacMillan, and Day (1982)	Examined performance differences and strategic attributes of businesses using the Boston Consulting Group (BCG) matrix as a classification device	Data on 1,018 growing and mature businesses drawn from the PIMS data base	Performance (return on investment, cash flow on investment, return per risk, market share change) Strategic attributes (capacity utilization, customer fragmentation, relative prices, and so forth) BCG matrix (Stars, Cash Cows, Wildcats, Dogs)	There were significant differences in performance and strategic attributes of businesses in each of the four BCG categories
Hambrick and Schecter (1983)	Investigated the strategic moves associated with turnaround success in mature industrial markets	Secondary data on all mature industrial-products businesses in the PIMS data base (n = 770)	Performance (return on investment) Strategic moves (product/market initiatives, efficiency moves, asset levels and use)	Efficiency-oriented moves, but not entrepreneurial initiatives, were associated with successful turnarounds. Three successful turnaround strategies were identified.

Hatten, Schendel, and Cooper (1978)	Examined relationships among strategy, environment, and performance of firms in the brewing industry	Interview and secondary data on 13 firms in the brewing industry (1952-1971)	Performance (return on equity) Strategy (manufacturing, financial, market) Environment (8-firm concentration ratio, industry advertising intensity, strike days in industry)	Seven strategic groups were identified. The relative effects of particular strategic and environmental variables on performance differed from one group to another.
Hill and Pickering (1986)	Examined relationships among structure, operating procedures, and performance in divisionalized companies	Questionnaire data on 144 of the 500 largest U.K. companies	Performance (return on sales, return on employed capital) Organization structure (functional, holding company, geographical division, and so forth) Other (number of divisions, divisional product scope, divisional coordination, decentralization, and so forth)	The majority of firms used the multidivisional structure of which there were several different types. Divisionalization per se was not the key to successful financial performance; certain operating decisions must be decentralized to the divisions in order to achieve high performance.
Hitt, Ireland, and Palia (1982)	Examined the relationship between industrial firms' strategies and their top managers' perceptions of the relative strategic significance of different organizational functions. The moderating effects of technology and perceived environmental uncertainty were also examined.	Questionnaire data on 249 Fortune 1000 industrial firms	Strategy (stability, internal growth, acquisition, retrenchment) Functional importance (general administration, production/operations, engineering/R&D, marketing, and so forth) Perceived environmental uncertainty (25 Likert-type items) Technology (unit and small batch, mass production, continuous process)	The strategic importance of organizational functions varied by type of strategy. Technology and perceived environmental uncertainty showed weak moderating effects.

Table 1. (continued)

Study	Basic Research Problem	Data and Sample	Variables and Measures	Overall Findings
Hitt, Ireland, and Stadter (1982)	Investigated the relationship between the relative importance of different organizational functions and company performance as moderated by type of strategy and industry	Compustat and questionnaire data on 93 Fortune 1000 industrial firms	Performance (earnings per share, return on equity, and so forth) Strategy (stability, internal growth, acquisition, retrenchment) Functional importance (general administration, production/operations, and so forth) Industry type (consumer durable goods, consumer nondurable goods, capital goods, producer goods)	Both strategy and industry type significantly affected the relationship between functional importance and performance
Hitt and Ireland (1985)	Extended previous study of Hitt, Ireland, and Stadter (1982) using a different performance measure and larger sample	Questionnaire and secondary data on 185 Fortune 1000 industrial firms	Performance (market returns on the firm's securities) Strategy (stability, internal growth, acquisition, retrenchment) Distinctive competence (general administration, production, R&D, and so forth) Industry type (consumer durable goods, consumer nondurable goods, capital goods, producer goods)	Distinctive competencies associated with performance varied according to strategy and the firm's principal industry. Specific distinctive competencies were identified for each strategy and industry type.

Horovitz and Thietart (1982)	Examined firms both high and low in growth and profitability for patterns in strategic and organizational characteristics	Interview data on 52 companies in France, Great Britain, and Germany	Performance (sales growth, return on sales) Diversification strategy (an index composed of 2-digit SIC codes and evaluation of managers regarding product and market diversification) Management system (divisionalization, formalization, complexity of long-range planning, and so forth)	Patterns of fit among strategy, management system, and firm performance were found. In general, high growth and profit firms were distinguished by their strategies and organizational arrangements.
Hrebiniak and Snow (1982)	Examined the relationship between top-management agreement on an organization's strengths and weaknesses and its performance	Questionnaire data on 88 companies in four industries (two representing low environmental complexity and two high environmental complexity)	Performance (ratio of total operating income to total assets) Organizational strengths and weaknesses (respondents' ratings on ten organizational functions) Managerial agreement (mean standard deviation of respondents' ratings) Type of planning process (continuous, semiannual, and so forth)	Agreement among managers on organizational strengths and weaknesses was positively related to performance. Agreement was especially important to firm performance in industries characterized by high environmental complexity.

Table 1.   (*continued*)

Study	Basic Research Problem	Data and Sample	Variables and Measures	Overall Findings
Jauch, Osborn, and Glueck (1980)	Examined interrelationships of environmental and strategic variables with each other and with short-term performance	358 case studies taken from Fortune magazine between 1930 and 1974. Secondary data on performance obtained from Moody's Investors Services.	Performance (return on assets reported in Moody's for the year of case and Fortune ratings) Strategy (vertical integration, market penetration, production efficiency, and so forth) Environmental challenge (Socioeconomic, consumer, technological, and so forth) State of economy at the time of case (depression, prosperity, and so forth) used as a control variable	The most powerful predictor of firm performance was the state of the economy at the time. Also, a given environmental situation or challenge could be met with a variety of strategies.
Kerr (1985)	Examined the impact of diversification strategy (both type and process of development) on the managerial reward system	Interview data on 20 manufacturing firms located in the Midwest and Northeast	Diversification strategy (4x2 matrix of strategy constructed using two major dimensions: [1] single product, dominant product, related product, unrelated product; [2] steady-state strategy, evolutionary strategy) Reward system (quantitative versus qualitative performance criteria, subjective versus objective performance criteria, time frame of evaluation process, and so forth)	The design of the managerial reward system depended on the process by which diversification was achieved (evolutionary or steady state) rather than the cumulative amount of diversification at a given point in time

Study	Purpose	Data/Sample	Variables	Findings
Lecraw (1984)	Investigated relationships among industry structure, diversification strategy, organizational characteristics, and performance	Secondary data on 200 largest publicly-owned Canadian manufacturing firms	Performance (return on equity and return on equity weighted by industry average) Strategy (single business, vertically integrated business, related business, unrelated business) Industry structure (concentration, growth, profits, and so forth) Firm characteristics (market share, foreign ownership, and so forth)	A firm's diversification strategy depended on internal characteristics as well as industry structure. Firms in a given industry not following appropriate diversification strategies had low performance.
Lenz (1980)	Examined relationships among environment, strategy, structure, and performance	Interview and secondary data on 80 randomly selected savings and loan associations in a single state	Performance (return on average assets) Environment (goals pursued in a prescribed geographic area) Strategy (range of services offered, marketing tactics, and so forth) Organization structure (functional specialization, span of control, and so forth)	High-performing firms exhibited different combinations of environment, strategy, and organization structure than low-performing firms. Specifically, high-performing firms were in growing geographic areas, had fewer direct competitors, were strongly associated with a particular customer base, and had flatter, more efficient organization structures.

Table 1. (continued)

Study	Basic Research Problem	Data and Sample	Variables and Measures	Overall Findings
MacMillan, Hambrick, and Day (1982)	Examined the association between the strategic attributes and profitability of businesses using the Boston Consulting Group (BCG) matrix as a classification device	Data on 1,011 industrial products businesses drawn from the PIMS data base	Performance (return on investment, cash flow on investment) Strategic attributes (value added/revenue, product R&D/revenue, capacity utilization, and so forth)	Different strategic attributes were associated with profitability for particular types of businesses in the BCG matrix. However, the strategic attributes that contributed most to the explanation of profitability for all types of businesses were capital intensity, value added, and manufacturing cost.
McDougall and Round (1984)	Examined corporate motives for diversification and compared the performance of diversified and nondiversified firms	Questionnaire data on 108 Australian industrial firms	Performance (return on assets, return on equity) Diversification strategy (diversified versus nondiversified firms) Reasons for diversification (reduction in firm risk, poor growth prospects in traditional markets, and so forth) Other (level of debt financing, firm size, and so forth)	No significant differences in profitability or risk between diversified and nondiversified firms were found. However, within the diversified group, there was a positive relationship between profitability and extent of diversification.

Miller, Kets de Vries, and Toulouse (1982)	Examined relationships among top executives' personalities (i.e., locus of control), strategy-making behavior, organization structure, and organizational environments	Interview and questionnaire data on chief executives of 33 Canadian firms in 10 industries located in the Montreal region	Top executive personality (internal-external locus of control) Strategy-making behavior (innovation, risk taking, proaction, futurity) Environment (dynamism, heterogeneity) Structure (scanning, professionalization, differentiation)	The locus of control of the top executive had a direct and significant relationship to strategy-making behavior but an indirect relationship to environment and structure. More internal chief executives tended to pursue more product-market innovation, undertake greater risks, and lead rather than follow competitors.
Montgomery (1985)	Examined relationships among diversification, market structure, and firm performance	Secondary data on 128 Fortune 500 firms	Performance (return on invested capital) Diversification (continuous quantitative measure of level of diversification) Market structure (industry return on assets, industry return on equity, concentration, market growth) Market share	Market share, industry profitability, and industry growth were positively related to firm performance. Diversification did not explain firm performance.

Table 1. (continued)

Study	Basic Research Problem	Data and Sample	Variables and Measures	Overall Findings
Paine and Anderson (1977)	Explored the impact of perceived environmental uncertainty and need for internal change on firm strategy and organizational characteristics	62 longitudinal case studies taken from several graduate-level business policy textbooks	Performance (overall rater judgment on the extent to which the organization appeared to be attaining its objectives and goals) Perceived environmental uncertainty (amount of information required in policy formulation, reliability of information, amount of information available) Perceived internal change (competence, capabilities, resources) Strategic properties (innovation, risk taking, futurity, and so forth)	Different combinations of perceived environmental uncertainty and need for internal change required different emphasis on strategic properties (including risk taking, role performance of the key policymaker(s), degree of innovation, extent of futurity in planning) in order to achieve organizational success
Palepu (1985)	Examined the relationship between diversification strategy and firm performance	Compustat data on 30 firms randomly selected from the food products industry	Performance (return on sales) Diversification (related, unrelated)	At a given point in time, there was no relationship between amount of diversification (high/low) or type of diversification (related/unrelated). However, over time, the performance of related diversifiers was significantly greater than unrelated diversifiers.

Pearce (1983)	Explored the relationship between internal versus external orientations of top executives and their firms' financial performance	Questionnaire data on 137 managers in eight small public commercial banks	Performance (profit margins, return on assets, return on equity, net interest spread) Internal/external orientation (inside/outside board members, internal/external orientations of top managers, internal/external orientations of only dominant coalition members)	The primary finding was that high performance was associated with the internal orientation of dominant coalition members
Porter (1979b)	Examined structural determinants of profitability for firms differently situated within their industries	Secondary data on 38 consumer goods industries at the 3-digit SIC level	Performance (return on equity) Strategic group (industry leaders and followers based on size) Industry structure (concentration, minimum efficient scale, absolute capital requirements, and so forth)	Industry structure had different effects on profitability of firms in different strategic groups. Leaders on average were more profitable than followers, implying that mobility barriers and rivalry characteristics were generally more favorable for leaders. However, where economies of scale were negligible, and/or where the industry was highly fragmented thus allowing niche strategies, follower profitability was also high.

Table 1. (continued)

Study	Basic Research Problem	Data and Sample	Variables and Measures	Overall Findings
Prescott (1985)	Tested the hypothesis that (1) environments independently influence firm performance, or (2) environments modify the strength or form of the relationship between firm strategy and performance	Secondary data on 1,638 businesses in the PIMS data base	Performance (return on investment) Environment (fragmented, global, importing, mature, and so forth) Strategy (capacity utilization, employee productivity, relative market share, and so forth)	The findings indicated that environment modifies the strength but not the form of the relationship between strategy and performance. Therefore, the same strategy can be pursued in a different environment but may have different performance results.
Rumelt (1982)	Examined the relationship between diversification strategy and profitability after controlling for the effects of varying industry profitability	Compustat data on 273 corporations randomly selected from the Fortune 400 in 1949, 1959, 1969, and 1974	Performance (return on invested capital) Diversification strategy (single business, dominant vertical, constrained, and so forth) Profitability premium (firm profitability after controlling for average industry profitability)	Choice of industry had an impact on firm profitability as well as choice of diversification strategy. The previous finding of high profitability among related-constrained diversifiers was shown to be largely an industry effect.
Schoeffler (1977)	Summarizes the major findings of the early stages of the PIMS program (Profit Impact of Market Strategy)	PIMS data base (in 1974 approximately 600 businesses of about 50 major corporations)	Performance (return on investment, cash flow on investment) Key variables explaining return on investment and cash flow on investment (market share, product quality, investment intensity, and so forth)	The variables compiled in the PIMS data base accounted for about 80% of the variance in return on investment. Of these variables, market share was the strongest predictor of profitability.

Study	Purpose	Data	Variables	Findings
Smart and Vertinsky (1984)	Examined relationships between the type of perceived environment and the repertoire of strategic responses developed to cope with major environmental discontinuities	Questionnaire data on 94 role-playing executives in firms selected from the Fortune 500 and Canadian Business 400	Environment (turbulence, complexity, and predictability) Strategic responses (adaptive versus entrepreneurial, short versus long time horizon, and so forth)	An executive's propensity to adopt a particular strategic posture depended on his or her perceptions of how well the firm can control its environment and on the costs of introducing change into the organization
Snow and Hrebiniak (1980)	Examined relationships among strategy, distinctive competence, and organizational performance	Questionnaire data collected from 247 top managers of 88 companies in four industries (two low uncertainty and two high uncertainty)	Performance (ratio of total income to total assets) Strategy (defender, prospector, analyzer, reactor) Distinctive competence (managerial perceptions of strengths in general management, financial management, marketing/selling, and so forth)	Various strategies were feasible depending on the type of industry. For a given strategy to be successful, it had to be supported with appropriate organizational strengths or distinctive competencies.
Steer and Cable (1978)	Examined the joint impact on profitability of multinational structure and organization size	Secondary data on 82 large U.K. companies	Performance (rate of return on equity, rate of return on equity plus long-term debt, rate of return on assets) Organization structure (functional, mulidivisional, holding company, and so forth) Other (owner-controlled, size, growth, and so forth)	An organization's structure had to be optimally matched with its size in order for the firm to have high performance

Table 1. (continued)

Study	Basic Research Problem	Data and Sample	Variables and Measures	Overall Findings
Suzuki (1980)	Explored the strategic and structural developments of the 100 largest Japanese manufacturing firms (1950-1970)	Secondary data drawn from Stock Exchange Year Book and Companies Year Book	Strategy (single business, dominant business, related business, unrelated business) Structure (functional, multidivisional, holding company)	A positive relationship between diversification and multidivisionalization was found. The time gap between diversification was greater in Japan than in Britain or other European countries. In some instances, structure preceded strategy and in other cases followed strategy.
Teece (1981)	Examined the relationship between organization structure and performance (tested the M-form hypothesis)	Secondary data on 40 firms (20 matched pairs) in 20 industries drawn from Fortune 500 and Moody's Industrial Manual	Performance (return on equity, return on assets) Organization structure (functional, holding company, multidivisional, transitional multidivisional, and so forth)	Controlling for organization size, structure had a very large impact on performance
Thompson (1981)	A previous finding by Steer and Cable (1978) of a large performance differential between optimally and nonoptimally organized firms was reexamined using a different performance measure	Secondary data on 72 large U.K. firms (62 were the same as in the Steer-Cable study)	Performance (share price return) All other variables were the same as those used by Steer and Cable	Like the previous study, this replication found a highly significant performance differential between optimally and nonoptimally organized firms. However, much of this difference was attributable to an abnormal short-term decline in the performance of holding companies which were in crisis at the time.

Trostel and Nichols (1982)	Examined the impact of public or private ownership on a firm's business strategy and management process	Interview and questionnaire data on ten matched sets of privately-held and publicly-held firms	Strategy (growth in sales, consistency of sales, importance of short-term earnings, and so forth) Management processes (written policies, participativeness, formal education of managers, and so forth)	The results revealed several consistent differences in factors considered by management in making strategic decisions (e.g., privately-held firms placed more emphasis on sales growth) but no consistent differences in management processes
Woo (1983)	Examined factors which differentiate low performers from high performers in a group of market share leaders	Secondary data on 112 manufacturing businesses drawn from the PIMS data base (1972-1975)	Performance (market share, pretax return on investment, percent change in market share) Competitive strategy (relative price, relative quality, R&D intensity, and so forth) Market stability (life-cycle stage, real market growth, technological change, and so forth) Demand characteristics (auxiliary services, professional advisors, type of business) Organizational commitments (internal purchases, shared facilities, shared marketing, and so forth)	The findings showed that high market share did not always translate into high profitability. Some market leaders—e.g., those located in fragmented and regional markets where real growth was low and exit more prevalent than entry—had low returns on their investments.

Table 1. (continued)

Study	Basic Research Problem	Data and Sample	Variables and Measures	Overall Findings
Woo and Cooper (1981)	Examined the product-market choices and competitive strategies of successful low-market-share businesses, comparing them with two control groups: successful high-share and unsuccessful low-share businesses	Secondary data on 126 businesses in the PIMS data base (1972-1975)	Performance (return on investment, relative market share) Competitive strategy (relative price, relative quality, R&D intensity, and so forth) Product-market-industry characteristics (type of product, product life cycle, purchase frequency, and so forth)	The findings showed that some businesses can be profitable in spite of low market share. Effective low-share businesses tended to be located in stable environments characterized by slow growth and infrequent product changes. Compared to similar but ineffective businesses, these organizations relied on specific strengths such as intense marketing, high product value, and careful cost control.
Zeithaml and Fry (1984)	Examined the conditions under which a simultaneous increase in market share and profitability are found	Secondary data on 294 businesses in mature industrial products industries, selected from the PIMS data base.	Performance (relative market share, return on investment) Industry structure (long-term growth, concentration, buyer fragmentation, and so forth) Strategy (relative product quality, R&D intensity, relative direct cost, and so forth)	Simultaneous increases in market share and profitability were possible under certain market conditions and with the use of certain strategies. For example, some "superstar" businesses increased share and profitability by entering moderately growing markets with few competitors and by offering innovative, customized products of higher quality and price.

FUTURE RESEARCH DIRECTIONS

The review of the conceptual and empirical literature suggests several promising directions in which future research on strategy, structure, and performance might proceed. Some of these avenues are substantive in nature, and some are methodological. Both are discussed in the following sections.

Substantive Problems and Issues

Choice, Determinism, and Their Interaction. In summarizing our observations of the empirical literature, we noted that recently studies have begun to test for multivariate interactions among strategy, structure, and performance. Thus, it is paradoxical that the dominant paradigms guiding these inquiries have emphasized choice *or* determinism but rarely the interaction between them. Where choice predominates, one would expect significant main effects due to strategy and structure. Where determinism is largely present, environment should dominate in its effects. Interactions should be more important where there is an interplay of these conditions. Hrebiniak and Joyce (1985) argued, for example, that organizational adaptation and performance are affected by the relative strength of strategic choice and environmental determinism. Whether adaptation is "by design," "within constraints," "by choice," or totally ineffective ("selected out") depends on the relative importance of organizational and exogenous factors (Hrebiniak and Joyce, 1985).

The relative impact of main and interaction effects on firm performance is of both theoretical and practical interest. However, the limited number of multivariate studies listed in Table 1 does not permit useful conclusions to be drawn. Because it is impossible to test for interaction effects on criteria when only one predictor has been measured, many of the studies reporting only main effects may actually represent findings that are contingent on unmeasured aspects of environment, strategy, and structure. Detection of the existence of such effects, therefore, rests on the ability to recognize them in studies addressing similar questions but conducted in different settings and perhaps by different researchers. This is difficult, however, because there are few (if any) programmatic research efforts represented in Table 1. Whereas some researchers have used the same *database* for more than one study, such use does not necessarily constitute programmatic research. It is the continuity and development of *ideas* rather than data that is important. Without measurement of more than two key variables in a single study, one must rely on noticing differences in results as a function of differences in research settings. Because nonprogrammatic research precludes even a common frame of reference in this process, recognition of these moderating effects is not likely without extremely diligent reporting of research contexts.

The implications of these observations are straightforward. Assessment of the relative dominance of main and interaction effects among environment, strategy, structure, and performance requires researchers to do four things: (1) measure variables from at least three of the four conceptual categories (environment, strategy, structure, performance); (2) provide for as much "experimental" control as possible of important variables not being measured; (3) present a careful description of the study's context as well as of the sample selection providing these controls; and (4) conduct programmatic research. These actions are essential to the proper accumulation of research findings in the strategy-structure-performance area.

Causality and Comparative Evolution.   In our judgment, research in the near term should not be directed at the issue of causality in organizational strategy, structure, and performance. The web of relations among these variables is too complicated, and the state of theory development too primitive, to permit a concerted effort to identify causal relationships. Instead, the current bywords for strategy-structure-performance research should be *interaction, control, and comparison.* As already noted, studies that address main and interaction effects are on the rise, a positive development in the literature. As these studies increase in size and sophistication, it is important to simultaneously control for additional relevant variables in the strategy-structure-performance framework. It would be especially helpful if investigators began to control for the same variables across studies so that findings could be more accurately compared.

Both organizations *and* environments evolve. Organizational ecologists have developed rigorous means of tracking environmental evolution. However, they have tended to study relatively insignificant types of organizations and have made only broad distinctions among the strategies and structures of organizations in a given population. Conversely, strategy researchers, to the extent that they concern themselves with evolution at all, tend to focus on organizational evolution. Their rich descriptions of how strategy and structure develop often are accompanied by characterizations of the environment that are not generalizable.

Both groups need to focus their research on *comparative evolution.* The strategy-structure-performance literature needs well-developed models of how environments and organizations evolve so that comparisons between both sets of characteristics can be made. Initially, this can be accomplished by reconstructing events and actions that have already taken place (e.g., as in the traditional industry study). After appropriate models have been developed, longitudinal or panel data can be collected. By observing the same organizations in their environments over time, it is possible to address causal problems such as the performance of a particular strategy during good and bad times, the sequence of actions taken when performance declines, and so forth.

Environment, Strategic Processes, and Performance. As noted, there have been no large empirical studies that have attempted to examine strategic decision making processes under different environmental conditions and to relate these to organizational performance. This is unfortunate because an emerging perspective suggests that under certain conditions social actors, each pursuing parochial self-interests, make local decisions that taken cumulatively produce "choices" of strategy and structure (Pfeffer, 1981; Joyce and Hrebiniak, 1988). Moreover, these choices are frequently made outside of formal strategic planning systems because such systems are unable to deal with the complexity, uncertainty, or secrecy that characterize many strategic issues (Quinn, 1980).

Different types of strategic processes may have a significant impact on organizational performance. In addition to traditional synoptic planning processes, these include the "method of successive approximations" (Lindblom, 1959), "logical incrementalism" (Quinn, 1980), and "minimum intervention" (Hrebiniak and Joyce, 1984). In these newer views, the choice of a decision process is itself a strategic decision because the method chosen subsequently constrains strategy. For example, faced with an impasse on goals, strategic decision makers *may* be able to agree on a process for deciding these goals. This process may produce a goal structure considerably different than that preferred by individual participants in the process but one that nonetheless is politically acceptable. In this case, the process (given a set of initial conditions) determines the goals to be pursued, and decision making may then move to considerations of means rather than ends. Thus, the strategic decision context is simplified, allowing action to proceed in a more computational manner (Hrebiniak and Joyce, 1984).

Currently, the literature is not clear about the relative merits of alternative strategic-decision-making processes. Joyce (1986) called for research that identifies various types of incrementalism, the conditions under which incrementalism contributes to performance, and the interaction between incrementalism and comprehensive planning processes. This comment applies not only to incrementalism but to other strategic processes as well.

Effects of Performance. Another interesting substantive issue involves the effects of performance on strategy, structure, and organizational processes of decision making. Performance is not simply a dependent variable; it is an independent variable as well. Accordingly, it has been suggested that the amount and type of search or environmental surveillance undertaken by an organization depends on the performance-related problems or opportunities confronting it (March, 1981; Hrebiniak and Joyce, 1984). Structure may follow performance, as when the structural location and power of research and development relative to other units are altered as a result of past performance. Similarly, decision processes may be risk prone or averse and centralized or decentralized as a result of performance. Studies of the effects of performance will help researchers understand the adaptation process in organizations and how strategies and structures determine, and are determined by, organizational performance.

Methodological Issues

Measures and Data Bases. Strategy-structure-performance studies have utilized data from a variety of sources with many competing operationalizations of major variables. At the early stages of a field's development, ecumenicalism of both data and measurement is desirable. However, there are some disturbing trends in the literature that should be corrected as the field of Strategic Management continues to mature.

The first trend has to do with measurement methods. Research on strategy and structure occupies a unique position in organization science, lying squarely in the middle of the fields of Strategic Management and Organizational Behavior. Investigators who study relationships between strategy and environment (strategic contingency theory) have come mainly from the Strategic Management discipline. Researchers who study relationships between structure and environment (structural contingency theory) have come mainly from Organizational Behavior and Sociology (ecology theorists).

Each group has tended to rely upon the dominant methodologies of its field in conducting research. Researchers from Organizational Behavior have made heavy use of questionnaire measures of environment, structure, and performance. Strategic Management researchers have relied on the case-study method or have favored measures derived from archival data bases containing accounting and demographic information. To an unnecessary degree, each group has ignored the strengths of the other's methodologies.

Researchers in Strategic Management could benefit greatly from application of methods practiced in Organizational Behavior and vice versa. Certainly, research in structural contingency theory could benefit from more objective measures of industry characteristics and firm performance. The limitations of questionnaire measures are well known and require no elaboration here except to say that they are overused.

The Strategic Management field can be similarly admonished. Here objective measures have been emphasized with a disproportionate number of studies being based on quantitative data drawn from the PIMS and Compustat data bases. The seductive appeal of these data bases, due perhaps to their size and availability, may have encouraged researchers to avoid assessing the quality of variables and measures, a traditional concern in Organizational Behavior. The use of existing data bases does not relieve researchers of the responsibility of assessing the validity and reliability of variables and measures before reporting results based on them. Indeed, it heightens such responsibility because so many factors are outside of the investigator's control, requiring even more assurance of the adequacy of the data.

A particularly disturbing trend has been to rely on archival data drawn from publicly available sources to construct measures of strategy. While theoretical distinctions allowing such constructions have been made—for example, between "intended" and "realized" strategies (Mintzberg, 1978)— the skewing of strategy research in this measurement direction has tended to underrepresent the intentional and cognitive aspects of strategy. Strategic intentions cannot be measured objectively or derived from archival sources, although such information would be useful in evaluating the validity of a more appropriate measure (Snow and Hambrick, 1980). Strategy, in this intentional sense, is intrinsically psychological. It is thus best suited to methods aimed at preserving this quality, methods that have been refined in Organizational Behavior.

In sum, the strategy-structure-performance literature has been constructed from variables that are economic and behavioral, that encompass elements of choice and determinism, and that portray intended and unintended outcomes. Researchers who study this complicated web of relationships should be aware of the range of relevant variables and the methods best suited to measure them.

The Problem of Fit. Even if current problems of variable definition, measurement, and data were solved, there remains the difficult task of arranging variables into integrated theoretical frameworks—a challenge that can be referred to as the "problem of fit." The concept of fit has become an umbrella under which issues of interaction and contingency among environment, strategy, structure, and performance have been discussed (Miles and Snow, 1984). Unfortunately, use of the fit concept in the literature has been inconsistent and sometimes even incorrect (Schoonhoven, 1981). Because of its importance to theory development, it is worth clarifying the fit concept so that the designs of future empirical studies are methodologically sound.

Joyce, Slocum, and Von Glinow (1982) proposed a framework that clarifies alternative definitions of fit, distinguishes between interactive and noninteractive models, specifies operational forms of the models consistent with their conceptual forms, and avoids unnecessarily constraining statistical assumptions. The framework describes three identifiable but different concepts of fit used in the literature. The first is called *effect congruency,* and it is the type of fit that occurs when two variables are consistent in their main effects on a criterion. For example, if both a low-cost-producer strategy and a participative strategic-decision-making process independently resulted in improved firm performance, then this definition would indicate that there was a fit between these two strategy variables.

Theoretical congruency occurs when variables are judged to be consistent with one another on the basis of accepted theory but without reference to a specific outcome criterion. Thus, it is widely accepted that flexible organization structures should be matched with changing or uncertain environments, a Cash Cow strategy should be headed by a manager with expertise in cost control, and so forth.

Finally, *functional congruency* is a type of fit based on the effects of interactions among variables on relevant criteria. Fit is whatever configuration of predictor variables that results in effects on outcome variables of interest. In this case, there are as many "fits" as there are outcome criteria, and fit is empirically rather than theoretically determined. This third type of fit allows for the possibility that variables may substitute or compensate for one another—where, for example, raising the level of either independent variable produces improvement in outcomes but raising both does not result in more improvement than that obtained through manipulating either one alone. Such effects are similar to the type of nonsymmetrical and nonmonotonic relationships among predictors and criteria identified by Schoonhoven (1981) as needed for rigorous theory development.

Functional congruency is especially important to sophisticated models of relationships among environment, strategy, structure, and performance. For example, some studies have attempted to assess the relative dominance of either industry characteristics or strategy on firm performance. Because of the simplistic way in which these tests often have been constructed, the only possible finding is that one or the other of these variables must dominate. A more interesting possibility is that *either* a munificent environment *or* a good strategy may be sufficient to produce high levels of performance, but reliance on simpler notions of fit in tests of contingency hypotheses precludes examination of such a possibility. Thus, environment and strategy may be able to substitute for one another in their effects on firm performance in as yet undetermined ways.

These alternative notions of fit have become confounded in the contingency literature, leading to unnecessary confusion. All are important, and each concept of fit must be used appropriately. Effect congruency means that "more is better"; theoretical congruency says that "less can be better, if appropriate" (as when a pairing of low levels of two predictors produces the same criterion levels as a pairing of high levels of the same two variables); and functional congruency argues that "more can be too much" as in the substitute case where the combined effect of two predictors yields no more improvement in outcomes than what would be produced by high levels of either taken alone.

For the most part, research testing for contingent effects of environment, strategy, and structure on performance has not been very sophisticated in its utilization of the fit concept. Most tests have corresponded to what Joyce, et al. (1982) called effect or theoretical congruency models. The more powerful functional congruency form of fit remains to be explored both more rigorously and systematically. The concern for constructing appropriate tests of fit is of more than academic interest. Unclear thinking confuses not only theory but also practice.

CONCLUSIONS

The underlying thrust of this chapter has been that the strategy-structure-performance literature is an important one. The literature focuses on the basic ways organizations compete in their industries and on how they are designed and managed to pursue their competitive strategies. As scholars, practitioners, or consumers, all of us have a stake in making this literature as strong as possible.

The central conclusion that can be drawn from our review is mixed. On one hand, the concepts and theories that guide the literature tend to be practical and basic—there is relatively little diversion into areas that are faddish or esoteric. On the other hand, the literature is not very large or cumulative. Clearly, it would be desirable if the literature was composed of more programmatic, comprehensive, and large-scale empirical research.

We offered a number of recommendations for improving the strategy-structure-performance literature. None of these recommendations, however, implied a sense of urgency in developing the literature further. And yet it is clear that competition in many industries is intensifying and becoming more complex and far-reaching. Organizations that cannot keep pace with these developments will falter or fail. Contributors to the literature should bear this fact in mind and accelerate their efforts to study truly important issues.

ACKNOWLEDGMENT

The authors wish to express their appreciation to Se Joon Yoon for his help in conducting the review of the empirical literature.

REFERENCES

Allison, Graham T. (1971). *Essence of Decision: Explaining the Cuban Missile Crisis*. Boston: Little, Brown.

Altman, Edward I. (1968). "Financial Ratios, Discriminant Analysis, and the Prediction of Corporate Bankruptcy." *Journal of Finance* 23:589-609.

Anderson, Carl R., and Carl P. Zeithaml (1984). "Stage of the Product Life Cycle, Business Strategy, and Business Performance." *Academy of Management Journal* 27:5-24.

Ansoff, H. Igor (1965). *Corporate Strategy.* New York: McGraw-Hill.

Armour, Henry O., and David J. Teece (1978). "Organizational Structure and Economic Performance: A Test of the Multidivisional Hypothesis." *Bell Journal of Economics* 9:106-122.

Astley, W. Graham, and Richard A. Brahm (1989). "Organizational Designs for Post-Industrial Strategies: The role of Interorganizational Collaboration." In Charles C. Snow (ed.), *Strategy, Organization Design, and Human Resource Management.* Greenwich, CT: JAI Press (pp. 233-270).

Bain, Joseph S. (1956). *Barriers to New Competition.* Cambridge: Harvard University Press.

_____ (1968). *Industrial Organization.* New York: Wiley.

Baumol, William J., John C. Panzar, and Robert D. Willig (1982). *Contestable Markets and the Theory of Industry Structure.* New York: Harcourt Brace Jovanovich.

Barnard, Chester I. (1938). *The Functions of the Executive.* Cambridge: Harvard University Press.

Beard, Donald W., and Gregory G. Dess (1981). "Corporate-Level Strategy, Business-Level Strategy, and Firm Performance." *Academy of Management Journal* 24:663-668.

Berg, Norman A. (1965). "Strategic Planning in Conglomerate Companies." *Harvard Business Review* 42:79-92.

_____ (1973). "Corporate Role in Diversified Companies." In Bernard Taylor and K. MacMillan (eds.), *Business Policy: Teaching and Research.* New York: Halsted Press.

Bettis, Richard A. (1981). "Performance Differences in Related and Unrelated Firms." *Strategic Management Journal* 2:379-394.

Bettis, Richard A., and William K. Hall (1982). "Diversification Strategy, Accounting Determined Risk, and Accounting Determined Return." *Academy of Management Journal* 25:254-264.

Bourgeois, L. Jay (1980). "Performance and Consensus." *Strategic Management Journal* 3:227-248.

_____ (1985). "Strategic Goals, Perceived Uncertainty, and Economic Performance in Volatile Environments." *Academy of Management Journal* 28:548-573.

Bower, Joseph L. (1970). *Managing the Resource Allocation Process.* Homewood, IL: Irwin.

Brown, A. (1945). *Organization.* New York: Hibbert.

Burns, Tom, and G. M. Stalker (1961). *The Management of Innovation.* London: Tavistock.

Buzzell, Robert D., Bradley T. Gale, and Ralph G. M. Sultan (1975). "Market Share—A Key to Profitability." *Harvard Business Review* 53:97-106.

Cameron, Kim S. (1986). "Effectiveness as Paradox: Consensus and Conflict in Conceptions of Organizational Effectiveness." *Management Science* 32:539-553.

Carroll, Glenn R. (1984). "Organizational Ecology." *Annual Review of Sociology* 10:71-93.

Caves, Richard E. (1980). "Industrial Organization, Corporate Strategy, and Structure." *Journal of Economic Literature* 18:64-92.

Caves, Richard E., and Michael E. Porter (1977). "From Entry Barriers to Mobility Barriers." *Quarterly Journal of Economics* 91:241-262.

Chakravarthy, Bala S. (1986). "Measuring Strategic Performance." *Strategic Management Journal* 7:437-458.

Chandler, Alfred D., Jr. (1962). *Strategy and Structure.* Garden City, NY: Doubleday.

Child, John (1972). "Organizational Structure, Environment, and Performance—The Role of Strategic Choice." *Sociology* 6:1-22.

Christensen, H. Kurt, and Cynthia A. Montgomery (1981). "Corporate Economic Performance: Diversification Strategy Versus Market Structure." *Strategic Management Journal* 2:327-343.

Coase, Ronald H. (1937). "The Nature of the Firm." *Economica* 4:386-405.

Cyert, Richard M., and James G. March (1963). *A Behavioral Theory of the Firm.* Englewood Cliffs, NJ: Prentice-Hall.

Daniels, John D., Robert A. Pitts, and Marietta J. Tretter (1984). "Strategy and Structure of U.S. Multinationals: An Exploratory Study." *Academy of Management Journal* 27:292-307.

————— (1985). "Organizing for Dual Strategies of Product Diversity and International Expansion." *Strategic Management Journal* 3:223-237.

Davis, Stanley M., and Paul R. Lawrence (1977). *Matrix.* Reading, MA: Addison-Wesley.

Dess, Gregory G., and Peter S. Davis (1984). "Porter's (1980) Generic Strategies as Determinants of Strategic Group Membership and Organizational Performance." *Academy of Management Journal* 27:467-488.

Dill, William R. (1958). "Environment as an Influence on Managerial Autonomy." *Administrative Science Quarterly* 2:404-443.

Doz, Yves (1986). *Strategic Management in Multinational Companies.* Oxford: Pergamon Press.

Fayol, Henri (1949). *General and Industrial Management,* translated by Constance Stours. London: Pitman.

Fellner, William J. (1965). *Competition Among the Few.* New York: Augustus M. Kelly.

Fouraker, Lawrence E., and John M. Stopford (1968). "Organization Structure and the Multinational Strategy." *Administrative Science Quarterly* 13:47-64.

Frederickson, James W. (1984). "The Comprehensiveness of Strategic Decision Processes: Extension, Observations, Future Directions." *Academy of Management Journal* 27:445-466.

Frederickson, James W., and Terence R. Mitchell (1984). "Strategic Decision Processes: Comprehensiveness and Performance in an Industry with an Unstable Environment." *Academy of Management Journal* 17:399-423.

Freeman, R. Edward (1984). *Strategic Management: A Stakeholder Approach.* Boston: Pitman.

Galbraith, Craig S., and Dan E. Schendel (1983). "An Empirical Analysis of Strategy Types." *Strategic Management Journal* 4:153-173.

Galbraith, Craig S., and Curt H. Stiles (1983). "Firm Profitability and Relative Firm Power." *Strategic Management Journal* 4:237-249.

Galbraith, Jay R. (1973). *Designing Complex Organizations.* Reading, MA: Addison-Wesley.

Galbraith, Jay R., and Daniel A. Nathanson (1978). *Strategy Implementation: The Role of Structure and Process.* St. Paul: West.

Gale, Bradley T., and Robert D. Buzzell (1987). *Market Position and Competitive Strategy.* Cambridge, MA: The Strategic Planning Institute.

Grinyer, Peter H., Masoud Yasai-Ardekani, and Shawki Al-Bazzaz (1980). "Strategy, Structure, the Environment and Financial Performance in 48 United Kingdom Companies." *Academy of Management Journal* 23:193-220.

Grinyer, Peter H., and Masoud Yasai-Ardekani (1981). "Strategy, Structure, Size and Bureaucracy." *Academy of Management Journal* 24:471-486.

Grinyer, Peter H., Shawki Al-Bazzaz, and Masoud Yasai-Ardekani (1986). "Towards a Contingency Theory of Corporate Planning: Findings in 48 U.K. Companies." *Strategic Management Journal* 7:3-28.

Gulick, Luther, and Lyndall F. Urwick (eds.) (1937). *Papers on the Science of Administration.* New York: Institute of Public Administration, Columbia University.

Gupta, Anil K., and V. Govindarajan (1983). "Business Unit Strategy, Managerial Characteristics, and Business Unit Effectiveness at Strategy Implementation." *Academy of Management Journal* 27:25-41.

Hall, David J., and Maurice A. Saias (1980). "Strategy Follows Structure!" *Strategic Management Journal* 1:149-163.

Hambrick, Donald C. (1983a). "Some Tests of the Effectiveness and Functional Attributes of Miles and Snow's Strategic Types." *Academy of Management Journal* 26:5-26.

———— (1983b). "High Profit Strategies in Mature Capital Goods Industries: A Contingency Approach." *Academy of Management Journal* 26:687-707.

———— (1984). "Taxonomic Approaches of Studying Strategy: Some Conceptual and Methodological Issues." *Journal of Management* 10:27-41.

Hambrick, Donald C., Ian C. MacMillan, and Diana L. Day (1982). "Strategic Attributes and Performance in the BCG Matrix: A PIMS-Based Analysis of Industrial Products Businesses." *Academy of Management Journal* 25:510-531.

Hambrick, Donald C., and Steven M. Schecter (1983). "Turnaround Strategies for Mature Industrial-Product Business Units." *Academy of Management Journal* 26:231-248.

Hambrick, Donald C., and David Lei (1985). "Toward an Empirical Prioritization of Contingency Variables for Business Strategy." *Academy of Management Journal* 28:763-788.

Hannan, Michael T., and John H. Freeman (1977). "The Population Ecology of Organizations." *American Journal of Sociology* 82:929-964.

———— (1984). "Structural Inertia and Organizational Change." *American Sociological Review* 89:149-164.

Harrigan, Kathryn R. (1980). *Strategies for Declining Businesses.* Lexington, MA: D.C. Heath.

———— (1983). *Strategies for Vertical Integration.* Lexington, MA: D.C. Heath.

———— (1985).*Strategies for Joint Ventures.* Lexington, MA: D.C. Heath.

Haspeslagh, Philippe (1982). "Portfolio Planning: Uses and Limits." *Harvard Business Review* 60:58-73.

Hatten, Kenneth J., Dan E. Schendel, and Arnold C. Cooper (1978). "A Strategic Model of the U.S. Brewing Industry: 1952-1971." *Academy of Management Journal* 21:592-610.

Hill, C.W.L., and J.F. Pickering (1986). "Divisionalization, Decentralization, and Performance of Large United Kingdom Companies." *Journal of Management Studies* 1:26-50.

Hitt, Michael A., and R. Duane Ireland (1985). "Corporate Distinctive Competence, Strategy, Industry and Performance." *Strategic Management Journal* 6:273-293.

Hitt, Michael A., R. Duane Ireland, and K.A. Palia (1982). "Industrial Firms' Grand Strategy and Functional Importance: Moderating Effects of Technology and Uncertainty." *Academy of Management Journal* 25:265-298.

Hitt, Michael A., R. Duane Ireland, and Gregory Stadter (1982). "Functional Importance and Company Performance: Moderating Effects of Grand Strategy and Industrial Type." *Strategic Management Journal* 3:315-330.

Hofer, Charles W., and Dan E. Schendel (1978). *Strategy Formulation: Analytical Concepts.* St. Paul: West.

Horovitz, Jacques H., and R.A. Thietart (1982). "Strategy, Management Design, and Firm Performance." *Strategic Management Journal* 3:67-76.

Hrebiniak, Lawrence G. (1978). *Complex Organizations.* St. Paul: West.

Hrebiniak, Lawrence G., and Charles C. Snow (1982). "Top Management Agreement and Organizational Performance." *Human Relations* 35:1139-1158.

Hrebiniak, Lawrence G., and William F. Joyce (1984). *Implementing Strategy.* New York: MacMillan.

———— (1985). "Organizational Adaptation: Strategic Choice and Environmental Determinism." *Administrative Science Quarterly* 30:336-349.

Hunt, Michael S. (1972). "Competition in the Major Home Appliance Industry, 1960-1970." Ph.D. Dissertation, Harvard University.

Jauch, Lawrence R., Richard N. Osborn, and William F. Glueck (1980). "Short Term Financial Success in Large Business Organizations: The Environmental Connection." *Strategic Management Journal* 1:49-63.

Jemison, David B. (1987). "Risk and the Relationship Among Strategy, Organizational Processes, and Performance." *Management Science* 33: 1087-1101.

Joyce, William F. (1986). "Towards a Theory of Incrementalism." In Robert Lamb and Paul Shrivastava (eds.), *Advances in Strategic Management*, vol. 4. Greenwich, CT: JAI Press (pp. 43-58).

Joyce, William F., and Lawrence G. Hrebiniak (1988). "Power, Politics, and Organization Design." In Max Bazerman, Roy Lewicki, and Blair Shepard (eds.), *Research in Negotiation*, vol. 2. Greenwich, CT: JAI Press.

Joyce, William F., John W. Slocum, and Mary Ann Von Glinow (1982). "Person-Situation Interaction: A Test of Competing Models of Fit." *Journal of Occupational Behavior* 3:265-280.

Kerr, Jeffrey L. (1985). "Diversification Strategies and Managerial Rewards: An Empirical Study." *Academy of Management Journal* 28:155-179.

Lawrence, Paul R., and Jay W. Lorsch (1967). *Organization and Environment*. Boston: Harvard Graduate School of Business Administration.

Learned, Edmund P., C. Roland Christensen, Kenneth R. Andrews, and William D. Guth (1965). *Business Policy: Text and Cases*. Homewood, IL: Irwin.

Lecraw, Donald J. (1984). "Diversification Strategy and Performance." *The Journal of Industrial Economics* 33:179-198.

Lenz, R. Thomas (1980). "Environment, Strategy, Organization Structure, and Performance: Patterns in One Industry." *Strategic Management Journal* 1:209-226.

Leontiades, Milton (1980). *Strategies for Diversification and Change*. Boston: Little, Brown.

Lindblom, Charles E. (1959). "The Science of 'Muddling Through.'" *Public Administration Review* 19:79-88.

MacMillan, Ian C., Donald C. Hambrick, and Diana L. Day (1982). "The Product Portfolio and Profitability: A PIMS-Based Analysis of Industrial Product Businesses." *Academy of Management Journal* 25:733-755.

McDougall, Fred M., and David K. Round (1984). "A Comparison of Diversifying and Nondiversifying Australian Industrial Firms." *Academy of Management Journal* 27:384-398.

March, James G. (1981). "Decisions in Organizations and Theories of Choice." In Andrew H. Van de Ven and William F. Joyce (eds.), *Perspectives on Organization Design and Behavior*. New York: Wiley (pp. 205-244).

Mason, Edward S. (1939). "Price and Production Policies of Large-Scale Enterprises." *American Economic Review* 29:61-74.

Miles, Raymond E., and Charles C. Snow (1978). *Organizational Strategy, Structure, and Process*. New York: McGraw-Hill.

─────── (1984). "Fit, Failure, and the Hall of Fame." *California Management Review* 26:10-28.

─────── (1986). "Organizations: New Concepts for New Forms." *California Management Review* 28:62-73.

Miles, Robert H. (1982). *Coffin Nails and Corporate Strategies*. Englewood Cliffs, NJ: Prentice-Hall.

Miller, Danny (1981). "Toward a New Contingency Approach: The Search for Organizational Gestalts." *Journal of Management Studies* 18:1-26.

─────── (1986). "Configurations of Strategy and Structure: Towards a Synthesis." *Strategic Management Journal* 7:233-250.

─────── (1987). "The Genesis of Configuration." *Academy of Management Review* 12:686-701.

Miller, Danny, Manfred F.R. Kets De Vries, and Jean-Marie Toulouse (1982). "Top Executive Locus of Control and its Relationship to Strategy-Making, Structure and Environment." *Academy of Management Journal* 25:237-353.

Mintzberg, Henry (1978). "Patterns in Strategy Formulation." *Management Science* 24:934-948.

————— (1979). *The Structure of Organizations*. Englewood Cliffs, NJ: Prentice-Hall.

Mintzberg, Henry, and James A. Waters (1985). "Of Strategies, Deliberate and Emergent." *Strategic Management Journal* 6:257-272.

Mintzberg, Henry, Duru Raisinghani, and Andrew Theoret (1976). "The Structure of 'Unstructured' Decision Processes." *Administrative Science Quarterly* 21:246-274.

Montgomery, Cynthia A. (1985). "Product-Market Diversification and Market Power." *Academy of Management Journal* 28:789-798.

Mooney, James (1947). *Principles of Organization*. New York: Harper.

Nelson, Richard R., and Sidney G. Winter (1982). *An Evolutionary Theory of Economic Change*. Cambridge: Harvard University Press.

Paine, Frank T., and Carl R. Anderson (1977). "Contingencies Affecting Strategy Formulation and Effectiveness: An Empirical Study." *Journal of Management Studies* 14:147-158.

Palepu, Krishna (1985). "Diversification Strategy, Profit Performance, and the Entropy Measure." *Strategic Management Journal* 6:239-255.

Pearce, John A. II (1983). "The Relationship of Internal-External Orientations to Financial Measures of Strategic Performance." *Strategic Management Journal* 4:297-306.

Peters, Thomas J., and Robert H. Waterman, Jr. (1982). *In Search of Excellence*. New York: Harper & Row.

Pfeffer, Jeffrey (1981). *Power in Organizations*. Marshfield, MA: Pitman.

Pitts, Robert A. (1980). "Toward a Contingency Theory of Multibusiness Organization Design." *Academy of Management Review* 5:203-210.

Pitts, Robert A., and Charles C. Snow (1986). *Strategies for Competitive Success*. New York: Wiley.

Porter, Michael E. (1979a). "How Competitive Forces Shape Strategy." *Harvard Business Review* 57:137-145.

————— (1979b). "The Structure Within Industries and Companies' Performance." *Review of Economics and Statistics* 2:214-217.

————— (1980). *Competitive Strategy*. New York: Free Press.

————— (1981). "The Contributions of Industrial Organization to Strategic Management." *Academy of Management Review* 6:609-620.

————— (1986). *Competition in Global Industries*. Boston: Harvard Business School Press.

————— (1987). "From Competitive Advantage to Corporate Strategy." *Harvard Business Review* 65:43-59.

Prescott, John E. (1985). "Environments as Moderators of the Relationship between Strategy and Performance." *Academy of Management Journal* 29:329-346.

Quinn, James Brian (1980). *Strategies for Change: Logical Incrementalism*. Homewood, IL: Irwin.

Ramanujam, V., and N. Venkatraman (1984). "An Inventory and Critique of Strategy Research Using the PIMS Database." *Academy of Management Review* 9:138-151.

Rappaport, Alfred (1986). *Creating Shareholder Value*. New York: Free Press.

Rumelt, Richard P. (1974). *Strategy, Structure and Economic Performance*. Cambridge: Harvard University Press.

————— (1982). "Diversification Strategy and Profitability." *Strategic Management Journal* 3:359-369.

Salter, Malcolm S. (1970). "Stages of Corporate Development." *Journal of Business Policy* 1:23-37.

Salter, Malcolm S., and Wolf Weinhold (1979). *Diversification Through Acquisition.* New York: Free Press.

Schendel, Dan E., G.R. Patton, and James Riggs (1976). "Corporate Turnaround Strategies: A Study of Profit Decline and Recovery." *Journal of General Management* 3:3-11.

Scherer, Frederick M. (1980). *Industrial Market Structure and Economic Performance.* Chicago: Rand McNally.

Schoeffler, Sidney (1977). "Cross-Sectional Study of Strategy, Structure, and Performance: Aspects of the PIMS Program." In Hans B. Thorelli (ed.), *Strategy + Structure = Performance.* Bloomington, IN: Indiana University Press (pp. 108-121).

Schoonhoven, Claudia Bird (1981). "Problems with Contingency Theory: Testing Assumptions Hidden within the Language of Contingency 'Theory.'" *Administrative Science Quarterly* 26:349-377.

Scott, Bruce E. (1970). "Stages of Corporate Development—Parts I and II." Working Paper, Harvard Graduate School of Business Administration.

Slatter, Stuart (1984). *Corporate Recovery: Successful Turnaround Strategies and Their Implementation.* New York: Penguin Books.

Smart, Carolyne, and Ilan Vertinsky (1984). "Strategy and the Environment: A Study of Corporate Responses to Crises." *Strategic Management Journal* 5:199-213.

Smircich, Linda, and Charles Stubbart (1985). "Strategic Management in an Enacted World." *Academy of Management Review* 10:724-736.

Snow, Charles C., and Donald C. Hambrick (1980). "Measuring Organizational Strategies: Some Theoretical and Methodological Problems." *Academy of Management Review* 5:527-538.

Snow, Charles C., and Lawrence G. Hrebiniak (1980). "Strategy, Distinctive Competence, and Organizational Performance." *Administrative Science Quarterly* 25:317-336.

Steer, Peter, and John Cable (1978). "Internal Organization and Profit: An Empirical Analysis of Large U.K. Companies." *The Journal of Industrial Economics* 27:13-30.

Steers, Richard M. (1977). *Organizational Effectiveness: A Behavioral View.* Santa Monica, CA: Goodyear.

Stopford, John M., and Louis T. Wells, Jr. (1972). *Managing the Multinational Enterprise.* New York: Basic Books.

Suzuki, Y. (1980). "The Strategy and Structure of Top 100 Japanese Industrial Enterprises, 1950-1970." *Strategic Management Journal* 1:265-291.

Taylor, Frederick W. (1911). *The Principles of Scientific Management.* New York: Harper & Row.

Teece, David J. (1981). "Internal Organization and Economic Performance: An Empirical Analysis of the Profitability of Principal Firms." *The Journal of Industrial Economics* 30:173-199.

———(1984). "Economic Analysis and Business Strategy." *California Management Review* 26:87-110.

Thain, Donald H. (1969). "Stages of Corporate Development." *Business Quarterly* 34:33-45.

Thompson, James D. (1967). *Organizations in Action.* New York: McGraw-Hill.

Thompson, R.S. (1981). "Internal Organization and Profit: A Note." *The Journal of Industrial Economics* 30:201-211.

Trostel, Albert O., and Mary L. Nichols (1982). "Privately-Held and Publicly-Held Companies: A Comparison of Strategic Choices and Management Processes." *Academy of Management Journal* 25:47-67.

Vancil, Richard F., and Peter Lorange (1975). "Strategic Planning in Diversified Companies." *Harvard Business Review* 53:81-90.

Venkatraman, N., and Vasudevan Ramanujam (1986). "Measurement of Business Performance in Strategy Research: A Comparison of Approaches." *Academy of Management Review* 11:801-814.

von Bertalanffy, Ludwig (1950). "The Theory of Open Systems in Physics and Biology." *Science* 111:23-28.

———— (1956). "General Systems Theory." *General Systems*, Yearbook of the Society for General Systems Theory. Ann Arbor, MI.

von Neumann, John, and Oscar Morgenstern (1944). *Theory of Games and Economic Behavior*. Princeton, NJ: Princeton University Press.

Weber, Max (1947). *The Theory of Social and Economic Organization*. Translated by A.M. Henderson and Talcott Parsons. New York: Free Press.

Weick, Karl E. (1977). "Enactment Processes in Organizations." In Barry M. Staw and Gerald R. Salancik (eds.), *New Directions in Organizational Behavior*. Chicago: St. Clair (pp. 267-300).

Wholey, Douglas R., and Jack W. Brittain (1986). "Organizational Ecology: Findings and Implications." *Academy of Management Review* 11:513-533.

Williamson, Oliver E. (1975). *Markets and Hierarchies*. New York: Free Press.

Wind, Yoram, and Vijay Mahajan (1981). "Designing Product and Business Portfolios." *Harvard Business Review* 59:155-165.

Woo, Carolyn Y. (1983). "Evaluation of the Strategies and Performance of Low ROI Market Share Leaders." *Strategic Management Journal* 4:123-135.

Woo, Carolyn Y., and Arnold C. Cooper (1981). "Strategies of Effective Low Share Businesses." *Strategic Management Journal* 2:301-318.

Woodward, Joan (1958). *Management and Technology*. London: Her Majesty's Stationery Office.

Wrigley, Leonard (1970). "Divisional Autonomy and Diversification." Ph.D. Dissertation, Harvard University.

Zahra, Shaker A. (1987). "Research on the Miles-Snow (1978) Typology of Strategic Orientation: Review, Critique, and Future Directions." Paper presented at the Academy of Management Meeting, New Orleans.

Zeithaml, Carl P., and Louis W. Fry (1984). "Contextual and Strategic Differences Among Mature Businesses in Four Dynamic Performance Situations." *Academy of Management Journal* 27:841-860.

GLOBAL COMPETITIVE STRATEGIES

Vijay K. Jolly

Global competitive strategies are today half reality, half fiction. We know more or less what they ought to be based on: notions of a homogeneous world market and the complete integration of all the elements of a business system across national boundaries. But we hesitate to be normative because the required conditions do not obtain for now. New York, after all, remains only slightly less different from Rangoon than it was a century ago; a strategy encompassing the latter can hardly be compared to one, for example, linking New York with London.

Despite the abstract connotations of the term "global," more features of international business transcend national differences today than at any time in the past. Competitive strategies designed for such an environment are, as a consequence, both cognitively and substantively different from their earlier multidomestic counterparts, even if only in degree. The aim of this chapter is to explore what changes this new geographic business scope has brought about and how they influence the formulation and implementation of international strategies. In order to set the stage, the first section summarizes the trends driving this "globalization phenomenon"—the summary term used today to describe both the substance and the impact of what is occurring. The second section reviews how firms internationalized and what enabled them to do so. Major types of global strategies are described in section three, which is the core of the chapter. Sections four and five draw the implications of these strategies for organization structure and management process, respectively. Finally, some suggestions for future research are offered along with ideas about how to conduct this research.

THE GLOBALIZATION PHENOMENON

If business is becoming more global today, in terms of transcending national boundaries, it is for a combination of reasons, many of which are mutually reinforcing. One of these is the convergence of consumer demand patterns all over the world. As Frederick Gluck vividly puts it:

> Kids everywhere are playing Pac-Man and bounding along the streets to the sound of a Sony Walkman. The videotape recorder (VTR) market took off simultaneously in Japan, Europe and the United States, but the most extensive use of VTRs today is probably in places like Riyadh and Caracas. Shopping centers from Dusseldorf to Rio sell Gucci shoes, Yves St. Laurent suits and Gloria Vanderbilt jeans. Siemens and ITT telephones can be found almost everywhere in the world. Mercedes-Benz and Toyota Corolla are as much objects of passion in Manila as in California (1982, p. 9).

This homogenization of the demand for certain products is no more than a vindication of the long-held belief in the universality of human nature. Advances in transportation, telecommunications, and media expertise have stoked demands that were latent, but they have also successfully created needs that had no sociocultural precedents. "Try it, you'll like it" is increasingly replacing "Tell me what you like" as a marketing slogan because people everywhere can apparently be manipulated in much the same way.

This has not, of course, happened suddenly. The universality of tastes in certain products was recognized by Phoenician traders in pewter wares four millenia ago, and the tobacco-spice-textile trade of the seventeenth century was similarly motivated. What is, perhaps, unprecedented is the range of products falling into this category today—as well as the capacity to market them.

This capacity to market, to use the vocabulary of economists, is related to the liberalization of product and factor markets worldwide. World trade, which is now on the order of $2 trillion a year, has doubled in volume since 1965, outpacing the growth in world output. From 1962 to 1984, the world's exports rose from 12% to 22% of total output. Even in the United States, which has not traditionally been heavily dependent on international trade, exports rose from 6% of GNP in 1962 to 13% in 1981, before retreating to 9% in 1985 on account of the overvalued dollar and international competition. Import tariffs, which were around 50% of dutiable imports in the United States after the passage of the Smoot-Hawley Act in 1930, are today no more than 5 to 7% (on a weighted average basis) for all industrial countries.

Liberalization in factor markets has been equally significant. The world's stock of foreign direct investment, which was approximately $580 billion in 1981, is now growing at the rate of $30 billion a year (OECD, 1986, p. 29), and countries can freely borrow larger sums on top of this up to the limits of their credit worthiness. Although harder to quantify, a complementary factor—technology—is no less mobile, with royalty payments and fees growing somewhat faster than trade. Royalties received by the 15 major Organization for Economic Cooperation and Development (OECD) countries, for example, grew from about $3 billion in 1970 to over $12 billion in 1983—a fourfold increase (OECD, 1986, p. 96). The fact that labor migration has followed the opposite trend since the turn of the century is of little consequence because it is now easier to take work to the workers. Previously, the reverse was required.

This liberalization of product and factor markets is manifest in the growing integration of national economies, particularly those in the OECD group. The European Economic Community (EEC) and European Free Trade Association (EFTA) countries practically form a single market for most products and services, and their relationship to the United States, Japan, and Canada is freer of trade and capital flow restrictions than at any time in history. Together, this multination market of 732 million consumers, with an average per capita income of around $10,000 in 1985, forms the core of today's global market.

Finally, the relationship between product and factor markets at an international level has also undergone change. Whereas, until relatively recently, one nation's factors were employed to produce products only in that nation, the integration of products and their factors no longer needs to be on a country by country basis. Cross-border integration, which was traditionally based on product specialization and sourcing, can now more feasibly be extended to include process specialization. As political, cultural, and communication barriers have diminished, it is now quite possible for two units to collaborate on a particular R&D problem, jointly develop a new piece of software, or come up with an advertising program together. The commercialization of these ventures may very well be in a third country, telecommunicated there via satellite.

These trends concerning tastes, products, and factors, as well as their integration across rather than just within countries, have evolved gradually and are still far from complete. The extent to which they have evoked a strategic response different from what characterized international business, say, in the 1950s and 1960s, is therefore mostly a matter of degree. Yet, this degree in itself is important because it poses an element of choice. Some companies have become more global in certain attributes because internationalization is another, newly available, dimension to compete on. Others, essentially facing the same set of circumstances, focus their strategies on individual countries, no longer out of necessity but because it differentiates them from global players.

THE PRELUDE TO GLOBAL STRATEGIES

Business expansion abroad has traditionally been a decision concerning diversification and an alternative to doing more or other things in a firm's home market. The economic reasons why firms chose to internationalize, instead of diversifying domestically, were similar to those invoked for deciding what to diversify into: (1) the nature of opportunities and their associated risks, (2) the firm's existing competence, and (3) future opportunities arising from the contemplated move. Thus, if a firm's competence is related to a narrow set of products and technologies, these could probably be better applied abroad in similar activities rather than to an unrelated field at home.

The fact that international markets also offered different factor costs and raw material access constitute additional variables to contend with. While investing in new process technologies could reduce costs at home, these cost reductions needed to be compared with an often substantial difference in wage rates and capital costs available abroad, due to natural endowments and subsidies. In other words, cost reduction or access to country-specific factors of production were as important reasons to expand abroad as market access.

As to which form international business took, a number of additional variables came into play: scale economies, transportation costs, trade barriers, national regulations, and so on. Whereas exporting was the most cost-effective means to gain market access, under nondiminishing returns to scale, this was not always feasible for the other reasons listed. Moreover, certain of the firm's assets often needed to be deployed in foreign markets to support international business, either alone or in partnership with others.

The Internationalization of Assets

Table 1a lists the major categories of assets available to a typical manufacturing company for deployment abroad. Though qualitatively different, service companies possess a similar range of assets. For ease of exposition later in the chapter, two broad groups of assets have been circumscribed: (1) product development and manufacture (assets 1 to 6), and (2) marketing (assets 7 and 8).

Table 1.   A Suggestive List of Assets and International Business
Participation Modes of a Manufacturing Company

a.   Assets

    1.   Financial
    2.   Managerial and Technical Personnel
    3.   Privileged Access to Raw Materials and Components
    4.   Product Technical Know-how

       a.   Patented
       b.   Secret
       c.   Public domain

    5.   Equipment, Tools, and Process Know-how

       a.   Patented
       b.   Secret, specially designed
       c.   Commercially available

    6.   Manufacturing Capacity for Intermediary Products,
       Subassemblies, and Final Products

       a.   Unique, not commercially available
       b.   Commercially available

    7.   Acquired Market Access

       a.   Brand recognition and customer loyalty
       b.   Privileged access to or control over distribution
          channels, transportation, and warehousing
       c.   Servicing facilities and expertise
       d.   Knowledge of and established relationships with
          market constituents and relevant institutions

    8.   Product/Market Concept

       a.   Product features
       b.   Function/segment relation
       c.   Optimum marketing mix

b.   Participation Modes (and Assets Deployed Abroad)

    1.   Portfolio Investment (1)
    2.   Exports (7 and 8)
    3.   Wholly-Owned, Full Capability Subsidiary (1-8)
    4.   Joint-Venture (parts of 1-8 depending on mission and partner's contribution)
    5.   Franchising (8 plus elements of 3, 4, 5, and 7)
    6.   Licensing (4 and 5)
    7.   Technical Assistance and Management Contracts (2, 4c, and 5c)
    8.   Turnkey Project for Third Party (2, 4, 5, and 8 time-bound deployment)

c.   Competitor Types (and Assets Deployed Abroad)

    1.   Full-Spectrum Manufacturers and Sellers (1-8)
    2.   Financial Conglomerates (1 and 2)
    3.   Managing Agents or Management Contractors (2)
    4.   Consulting Engineers (4c and 5c)
    5.   Marketing Companies (8)
    6.   Private Inventors and Research Institutes (4 and/or 5)
    7.   Contract Manufacturers (6)
    8.   Trading Companies (7b, c, d)

Traditionally, most companies have started by building a full complement of assets in their home market. This functional integration has usually been motivated by the need to control essential transactions, assure quality, and preserve the distinctive character and confidentiality of certain assets. A major consequence of domestic integration, however, is that a company's available capacity at any point in time is a function of the asset that is most scarce.

Certain intangible assets, such as know-how or a brand, have the character of public goods and are in themselves not subject to the same capacity constraints generally associated with assets such as finance or manufacturing facilities. Such intangibles, once developed and applied in one location, can be put to work elsewhere at little extra cost and without reducing the amount of the asset available at the original site (Johnson, 1970). However, if they are used exclusively in-house, their utilization is determined by the other assets available.

In international operations, all or some of these tangible and intangible assets can be deployed abroad, based on that combination which maximizes the long-term net present value of the assets available. In some situations, simply licensing (or renting) the use of a particular asset would meet this criterion. In others, a wholly owned subsidiary involving the joint deployment of a firm's assets could be the preferred choice. Table 1b lists the alternative modes of participation available, and Table 1c illustrates the potential competitors which may theoretically compete against one or more of a firm's assets.

Theories of Asset Selection and Deployment

A number of theoretical and empirical studies over the past couple of decades have tried to examine how and in what sequence firms actually deploy their assets abroad. The starting point of the analysis concerns the efficiency of the market for individual assets. As Coase (1937) recognized as early as the 1930s, assets (or activities) for which there is either no external market, or only an inefficient and costly one, will be organized within a firm's administrative boundaries rather than traded individually. The benefits of such "internalization" arise particularly when there is:

1. *information impactedness,* that is, exchange parties are not equally well informed about the outcomes to be expected from a particular transaction, or both parties have inadequate information;
2. *a small number of bargainers,* which compounds the problem of impactedness because those with more information can exploit others, making market transactions costly as a result of this opportunistic behavior;

3. *uncertainty and complexity of transactions* thereby requiring elaborate contingency contracts; and
4. *bounded rationality of individuals* that makes them incapable of handling all uncertainty and complexity, otherwise they would be able to write complete "contingency claims contracts" for those exchange relations that involve long-term obligations (Williamson, 1975).

In most industries, the market for finished products and services supplied to a broad base of consumers is usually more efficient than the inputs required to produce them. Of the input market, furthermore, the market for tangible inputs such as raw materials and certain types of components and hardware is better developed than that for intangibles such as a company brand, managerial expertise, or technological know-how. Internalizing these intangible assets and exploiting them in the production of goods and services within the firm is, therefore, often more profitable.

The role of intangible assets has actually been an ironical one. Because they have the characteristic of public goods, and are hence not subject to capacity constraints, they could have been exploited more widely. Yet, in the absence of proper markets for them individually, their value has been best achieved by internal utilization. Suffering from all of the "market failures" listed above, intangible assets have not only been difficult to price but also difficult to transact in the open market. Although counterfeiting still abounds, intellectual property rights (e.g., patents and trademarks) have alleviated some of the transaction problems (e.g., guarding the integrity of the asset), but they have not solved the other sources of market failure.

The technology asset is actually one of the few intangibles for which the choice between in-house usage and licensing to others is sometimes available. This is especially true when patents and trade secret protection allow it to be disclosed to potential buyers without compromising its value. Even so, licensing technology is seldom a best first choice, not least because of the problems associated with determining an appropriate price for it. Because it is usually dedicated to a narrow set of uses, there are relatively few buyers. Potential buyers deem it a risky purchase because they do not have adequate information about it and tend to consequently undervalue its worth compared to the seller. On the other hand, the more details the seller provides, the less the buyer is willing to pay, having already acquired the technology through disclosure. A patent might deter a buyer but is in itself unrepresentative of the worth of the technology.

The above assymetry in judgment is not, however, unique to intangible assets. It also applies to certain pieces of hardware and intermediate materials and components. Their use is linked to a specific activity only and, in the case of components, requires on-time supply and quality checks that may be better provided within the confines of a single organization.

In theory, the choice of which assets (or their combination) are to be deployed abroad therefore turns on the relative efficiency properties of markets for them versus their use within the organization. There are, however, a number of constraints, both internal and external to the firm, that also influence the choice. Thus, if technology is the most valuable asset a firm possesses, and the firm is wanting in the various complementary assets such as finance and human resources, a strategy of foreign licensing may be the only feasible choice whether or not it is optimal. Similarly, if managerial skills, technology, brand name, and financial assets are all equally available, and for efficiency reasons best applied jointly in a foreign venture, the host country may insist on a different and less ideal combination. Further, as with domestic business, the cost of internal organization increases with the spatial distribution and complexity of the required transactions, placing natural limits on what can be internalized for international business purposes.

Even so, the mere fact that firms *can* internalize their assets, to a greater or lesser degree depending on the external constraints they face, explains much of why firms sought international business opportunities and what enabled them to realize their goals. By extending the use of their assets abroad, and keeping certain transactions within their organizational boundaries, they were able to compensate for the inherent advantages possessed by firms indigenous to the country they entered: shorter communication channels, fewer cultural differences, and greater knowledge of consumer tastes, local laws, and the administrative context of business (Hymer, 1960; Kindleberger, 1969; Caves, 1971; Buckley and Casson, 1976).

These arguments concerning asset selection and their deployment abroad have been pulled together by Dunning (1985, pp. 6-9) into what he calls an "eclectic" theory explaining the nonexport international involvement of firms. According to this theory, international production is more likely to take place when:

1. A firm possesses certain strong, though not necessarily unique, advantages such as exclusive or privileged possession of a new product, production technology, market skills, or managerial skills. These *ownership* advantages, furthermore, need to be complemented by a firm's ability to coordinate the activity in which they are used better than other firms or other economic forms (e.g., the open market).
2. It is more profitable for the firm to use ownership advantages itself rather than leasing them to unaffiliated firms abroad. This advantage of *internalization* is determined by the comparative transaction costs of organizations vis-à-vis those of the market.
3. When it is profitable to combine the use of internalized ownership advantages (which are generally but not always mobile between

countries) with immobile resources in a foreign country rather than in the country which generates the ownership advantage. The more the *location specific* advantages favor a foreign country, then, other things being equal, the more likely it is that international production will take place.

The Location, Timing, and Sequence of Internationalization

The question as to when and where firms move abroad has been addressed using a combination of concepts based on managerial behavior, observed patterns of product and factor market differences among countries, and technological change. The dominant theory has been that of the International Investment and Trade Life Cycle (IITLC) developed by Vernon (1966). In addition to national factor endowment differences, this theory draws upon concepts such as the product life cycle, the manufacturing or process life cycle, communication requirements, cognitive limitations of managers, and national industrial and commercial policies.

The starting point of the IITLC is the often observed pattern of new product introduction. Many studies have suggested that new products are introduced in disproportionate numbers by companies and units located in or near affluent markets with strong science-based universities (or other research institutions) and entrepreneurially oriented financial institutions. Also, the competitive advantage of such new products over their predecessors tends to rest more on superior functional performance than on lower initial price (Abernathy and Utterback, 1978).

Because the initial basis of competition is not strongly related to cost, the locus of innovation has traditionally been in industrialized nations, notably the United States, where technological resources are relatively more abundant and where there is greater demand for new products. Physical proximity to consumers, furthermore, is important to obtain rapid feedback during the early stages of product development. It is only when the product becomes more stable in its characteristics, and the firm gains experience with its commercialization, that distant markets are considered and factor cost differences explicitly taken into account.

Figure 1 summarizes the main features of the internationalization pattern that emerges as a product moves through the various stages of its life cycle and as managers look further afield. Taking the example of an innovating firm in Switzerland, the essence of the model can be explained by looking at the three stages of the product life cycle (Figures 1a and 1b). The first stage is characterized by a demand pattern that is irregular, experimental, and generally price inelastic depending on the novelty of the product. The manufacturing system appropriate at this stage of the product's life cycle

Figure 1. The Location, Timing, and Sequence
of Internationalization as Derived from a
Product's Demand and Manufacturing Characteristics

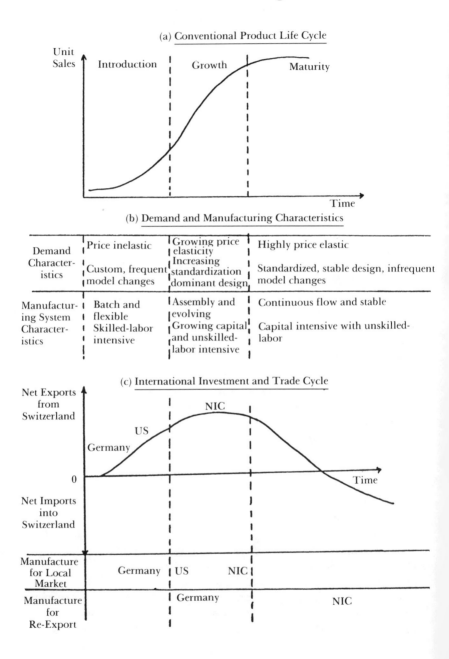

is one that is flexible, batch oriented, and with little automation (except perhaps during the design phase). It tends to be, therefore, labor intensive often using highly skilled labor. The fact that such labor is relatively expensive in Switzerland is not a significant drawback at this stage because price is not the main competitive variable.

As the product evolves along its life cycle through the stages of growth and maturity, both the demand and the manufacturing pattern change. Demand becomes progressively standardized, more price sensitive, and broader based, giving the firm an opportunity to exploit a larger market. The manufacturing system, in turn, begins to emphasize larger batches and eventually, depending on the nature of the product, continuous flow production. This phase of the manufacturing system is typically characterized by widespread automation, focused lines (and even factories), and significant economies and learning effects.

The internationalization pattern followed by the hypothetical Swiss firm that emerges from such an evolution in demand and manufacturing is illustrated in Figure 1c. For sake of simplicity, only three types of countries are included in the diagram: (1) a neighboring country with similar product and factor markets (e.g., Germany), (2) a large but distant market also with similar characteristics (e.g., United States), and (3) a newly industrialized country (NIC) with a less developed and affluent product market but significantly lower labor costs.

In keeping with the changes taking place over time in demand and manufacturing, the natural inclination of the Swiss firm would be to first sell within the Swiss market, benefitting from being close to customers and the feedback they provide. As communication and feedback become less important, and the product more standardized, exports to the German and U.S. markets follow, with the NIC coming last.

The location of foreign manufacturing to serve domestic markets would, theoretically, follow the same sequence as exports provided it mainly depends on the volume of sales generated in those countries. When the product becomes mature, however, manufacturing costs assume greater importance, and foreign sourcing not only becomes desirable but feasible as well.

The actual form the IITLC takes is a function of a number of variables (the nature of the product, the size and multinational spread of the firm commercializing it, distortions introduced by commercial and industrial policies abroad, and so forth). Products with extremely high income elasticity of demand, such as a Rolls Royce automobile, continue to be manufactured in "pockets" of specialized production, either in a single country or near affluent consumers. Others, such as U.S. refrigerators, become subject to intra-industry trade, with high-priced luxury models exported from the originating country coupled with the import of low-priced versions (Wells, 1972, pp. 16-17). Import tariffs, in turn, accelerate the local manufacture of products in the countries imposing such tariffs; if export subsidies are also provided, the product becomes exported sooner than it would otherwise be (Jolly, 1979). Finally, the more of a multinational infrastructure an innovating firm possesses, the greater the likelihood of its exploiting market and factor cost differences aggressively compared to a firm with limited access to information and less experience in coping with the risks inherent to foreign manufacture.

The fact that the IITLC varies widely in practice does not mean that the model itself is irrelevant. Its explanatory power rests on how these variations are taken into account. Industries such as automobiles, consumer appliances, and semiconductors, to name some conspicuous examples, have all more or less followed the pattern suggested by the IITLC. Where there have been major departures, these can be at least partially explained by the factors previously mentioned. The pattern of foreign investment followed by Japanese firms can also be explained by the model if one bears in mind their starting position and their special cognitive and other limitations. Japanese firms initially kept production at home because of their factor cost advantage and not, as some have argued, because they were more insightful in betting on the role of technology and scale economies compared to U.S. and European firms. Similarly, their first manufacturing was in the neighboring countries of Southeast Asia, rather than in the United States or Europe, because of the stage of evolution of their products, the relative ease of overcoming cultural and other barriers, and the import substitution policies adopted by these countries. The fact that they are today setting up manufacturing in the United States, late in the life cycle of the products concerned, is related to their history and the protectionism in the United States more than to an alternative strategy as such (Jolly, 1984).

The Traditional Nature of Competition

With the main objective being to exploit assets developed at home over a wider geographic base, the traditional emphasis of international strategies was on business development. It was mostly the larger firms that ventured abroad, and the superiority of some of their assets meant that it was easy to ward off competition from indigenous firms in the markets they entered. This, coupled with the leisurely pace and ordered sequence of internationalization, allowed firms to deploy and build up whatever complement of assets was required in a particular market to maximize value added and develop an unassailable position. To the extent there was competition, it was usually vis-à-vis peers in the home country which constituted the main arena for competitive struggles and product or asset dominance. This was apparently true of U.S. companies (Knickerbocker,

1973) and probably, though to a lesser extent, of European companies on a regional basis. Both looked at markets abroad solely as generators of additional revenue.

This nature of competition, combined with the protectionist policies most countries had until recently, meant that assets deployed abroad were mainly exploited on a multidomestic basis. This also meant that the search for new opportunities, the subsequent commitment of assets, and the way in which performance was evaluated, were all based on host-country circumstances.

That this emphasis on building existing operations lasted a long time can be seen from the fact that much of the increase in the stock of total foreign direct investment came from earnings reinvested in countries where multinationals were already well established even during the relatively recent period 1972-1981. During this 10-year period, 58% of the new foreign investment made by U.K. companies, for example, came from earnings ploughed back into local operations. The figure for U.S. companies in the same period was 67% (*The Economist*, 1983, p. 84).

Attempts at some integration among subsidiaries did, however, start quite early. As local competition grew and trade barriers became less prohibitive, especially during the 1960s, more and more firms started specializing their operations and cross-shipping between subsidiaries in search of scale economies. This *trans-domestic* orientation of the manufacturing function was later amplified as firms searched for ever cheaper locations, combining the advantages of scale and focus with that of factor costs.

With better communication and liberalization in factor markets, other assets also gradually became dispersed, with each unit specializing in a particular activity but linked to and feeding the rest of the organization. Capital started to be sourced where it was cheapest and the returns on it transferred, often through transfer pricing of products and services, to where it encountered the lowest tax rate.

The integration of assets was, however, mainly intended to reduce the cost of supplying individual markets. It did not fundamentally change the orientation of managers, which remained multidomestic, nor the form and sequence of internationalization. Each country was an independent arena of competition, separated in time from others and treated mainly as a source of revenue for assets originating in the firm's home country.

The New Imperatives Forcing a Global View

When we speak of an environment for international business that is different from the one traditionally known, we refer to a number of attributes. Some of these, such as growing international competition and the possibilities for firms to combine competitive advantage with sources of comparative advantage on a worldwide basis, were already taken into account by trans-domestic integration. There are others, however, which call for a radically different strategic approach.

One such trend is the well-recognized phenomenon of shortening product life cycles. For example, for household appliances in the United States, the mean duration of the introductory stage of the cycle decreased from 12.5 years for products introduced between 1922 and 1942 to 7.0 years for those introduced between 1945 and 1964 and to 2.0 years for products introduced between 1965 and 1979. The corresponding decrease in the growth stage of the cycle was from 33.8 years (1922-1942), to 19.5 years (1945-1964), and to 6.8 years for the period 1965 to 1979 (Qualls, Olshavsky, and Michaels, 1981). Whereas products previously went through a naturally determined cycle based on endogenous rates of diffusion and technological change, there is now a question whether the product life cycle is actually a "dependent" variable, meaning that the actions of firms in shortening it are probably as important as basic changes in the economy.

At the international level, this phenomenon of short product life cycles is manifested by a more rapid diffusion of innovations across countries, helped no doubt by the ease of communication and transportation, a convergence in income levels, and the extensive network of subsidiaries that has already been established (Vernon, 1979).

A second trend concerns some enabling features of new manufacturing technologies such as computer aided design, computer aided manufacture (which includes numerical control and direct numerical control), and flexible manufacturing systems (Dean and Susman, 1989). In addition to raising labor productivity, these technologies permit cost reductions at each stage of the product life cycle by combining the economies of high-volume automation with the flexibility of batch or job-shop production (Ayres and Miller, 1982). As such, they allow companies to compete either from one location or, by breaking the link between labor cost and the choice of manufacturing system, allow greater freedom and simultaneity in the spread of business worldwide. Companies can also deliberately skip certain of the intervening stages of manufacturing and *start* a product's life with automated, continuous flow production in the home market, as Apple Computers, Inc. did with its Macintosh personal computer (Swanger, 1984).

Taken together, these trends point to a diminished validity of the sequence of internationalization contained in the IITLC. To the extent differences in income and factor costs remain, they offer a narrower time frame for the planning of entry into individual markets. With the liberalization in product and factor markets mentioned earlier, the link between serving particular markets and manufacturing in them has also become more tenuous—more so as new manufacturing technologies have eroded the traditional sources of comparative advantage. The premium is on simultaneity of market entry and, consequently, a more global view of how each market has to be developed and served in relation to others.

Simultaneous market entry and the diminished role for comparative advantage based on natural endowments are part of the reason for a more crowded international business scene and one based increasingly on competitive advantage rather than country specificity. Adding to competitive pressures is the fact that more companies of different sizes and from different regions of the world also now have international ambitions and the means to realize them.

The participation by small companies is related to the growing possibility of trading in individual assets. Although most of the arguments for internalizing technological and managerial know-how outlined above are still valid, there are more frequent examples of firms exploiting just one or two sources of competence widely rather than, as in the past, using them as a means of developing the complementary assets at home and in chosen locations abroad. This has come about in part due to a strengthening of intellectual property rights in a number of countries, but a more diverse and competitive business environment abroad has also played a role. More activities can now be organized outside a firm's own managerial and resource boundaries, even if these activities are dispersed geographically, as evidenced by the enormous growth in subcontracting, licensing, and franchising in recent years.

Until relatively recently, most competitors a multinational firm had to contend with were firms either based in its own home market, whose strategies and management methods it understood well, or from a handful of other industrialized countries whose behavior too was somewhat predictable. Taking a U.S. perspective, these "other" multinationals were, at first, mostly European, sharing a similar set of values, cultural predispositions, and notions of business conduct. To these were added the Japanese whose unique character too was slowly unraveled. Today, however, there are at least another 20 countries hosting indigenous firms of respectable sizes that not only pose major competitive threats in their own markets but have multinational ambitions of their own.

Whereas their reasons for internationalization and their strategies have been different from firms originating in North America, Western Europe, and Japan, multinationals in newly industrialized countries today are increasingly stressing the same assets. Thus, while they previously concentrated on small-scale, labor-intensive processes and products, which were compatible with the requirements of other newly industrialized countries that were typically their host markets, they are becoming more technology driven. Many have found it easier, in fact, to adopt products early in their life cycle and export them based on product differentiation and quality, rather than wait for them to mature and compete on the basis of price (Jolly, 1979; Ayal, 1981).

Part of the reason for this convergence in strategies between firms based in differently endowed regions is the nature of some of the technologies. Not only do they preempt a role for developing countries, which they would have had under the international scheme represented by the IITLC, but they promise much greater flexibility and precision which labor-intensive systems cannot match. Fortunately for them also, most of these new manufacturing technologies are not of a proprietary nature. Flexible automation tends to be based on a number of standard, off-the-shelf, general purpose, programmable machine tools loaded, operated, and unloaded by robots which, in themselves, are freely available.

Today the most aggressive companies in newly industrialized countries are those from Korea and Latin America. The traditional internationalization pattern of Korean firms, for example, emphasized investment in resource-rich countries to acquire a sure source of raw materials or in developing countries to serve the market locally (Jo, 1981, p. 71). Gradually, some of the largest firms began investing in technology-intensive firms in industrialized countries in order to gain access to new technologies. Today, firms like Hyundai and Lucky-Goldstar are investing in Western Europe and North America in their own local assembly plants, in almost the same manner and for the same reasons as American firms did in Europe and European firms did in the United States a couple of decades back.

GLOBAL COMPETITIVE STRATEGIES

The plurality of competition, and the need and ability of firms to look at all major markets simultaneously, set the stage for what is now referred to as "global competitive strategies." Conceptually, they differ from the earlier multi-domestic approaches of firms in that they (1) tend to be based on a product or service that has universal appeal from the beginning (which enables simultaneous market entry to be considered), (2) aim to exploit a firm's assets over the widest possible geographic area quickly, (3) consider assets deployed in one country as having meaning for strategies being implemented elsewhere, and (4) separate decisions concerning entering certain markets from the production system relevant to that market.

Global strategies, in other words, need to be defined along two dimensions: (1) searching for opportunities to exploit assets globally and (2) seeking ways to compete with other companies pursuing the same objective. These dimensions conform broadly to the typology of organizations postulated by Miles and Snow (1978) in that the first represents "prospecting" and "analyzing" orientations while the second those of "defending" and "reacting." The first dimension is an entrepreneurial one, seeking new markets and applications as well as accumulating assets abroad to supplement those available at home. The second lies more in the domain of reciprocal strategies, where the primary aim is to establish a competitive edge over others by serving existing opportunities better. The plurality of markets, factor costs, competitors, and participation modes inherent to international business means that both dimensions of global strategy are qualitatively different from their manifestation in a domestic setting.

Although trans-domestic strategies already coped with some aspects of international business, they did not adequately address all. Table 2 summarizes the main differences between global strategies and the earlier approaches to international business. Global strategies not only combine sources of comparative advantage (where they are still available) with those of competitive advantage (asset dominance) but attempt to gain maximum market access as well. Their emphasis is on dominating a particular asset worldwide, so as to obtain world leadership in some aspect of the business not just a strong position in particular markets.

Where such a global approach is appropriate depends partly on the nature of the product:

> Industries become global for different reasons. Convergence of income levels and standardization of tastes made universal products out of Gucci bags and designer jeans. Aircraft became global because of the massive R&D investments required and the manufacturer's need to amortize these investments over many markets. Consumer electronics became global because producers discovered that they could drive further and faster down the learning curve by going after fast-growing overseas markets (Gluck, 1982, p. 10).

Also, within each industry, there are various paths individual firms can follow in becoming global according to their size, country of origin, and the special assets they possess. Small firms approach globalization differently from large, resource-rich, multinational companies just as firms based in Korea, for example, look at global business differently from Japanese or European companies.

Yet, all of these firms have the same basic objective: gain access to as wide a consumer base as possible, quickly, and with the best product or service at lowest cost. As the director of Milano-based TV-5 recently put it, "We want the maximum number of spectators and to offer them the maximum quality in programming." The emphasis is on volume but not because of any minimum technological scale economies. Rather, it is the desire to maximize the use of any asset a firm might possess while the opportunity lasts.

Although the market opportunities offered by a global approach are immeasurably greater, they need to be looked at in a focused manner. Building the full complement of assets and achieving self-sufficiency through vertical integration or, for that matter, establishing all-purpose

Table 2.   What It Means to be Global in Strategic Scope

	Multi-Domestic	Trans-Domestic	Global
Nature of Foreign Involvement	Exports, licensing, and foreign manufacture in each country based on its own needs	Product specialization and sourcing but local marketing	Product sourcing, asset use, and marketing on global basis
Own Asset Commitment	Full spectrum in each country as required	Part spectrum as required but share with other units based on comparative cost	Based on competitive advantage of individual asset use worldwide
Asset Utilization	Maximize home-country asset utilization first	Maximize specific asset utilization in relevant countries	Maximize global asset utilization
Optimization Criteria	Net present value of investments in home country and in each country separately	Minimize supply cost worldwide	Maximize worldwide cash flow from investments in critical assets
Competitive Priority	Home country and then local market position	Market position in relevant countries	Global market position and critical asset dominance
Relevant Peer Group	Home country competitors and some local competitors	Traditional domestic and international competitors	All potential competitors by asset category

subsidiaries abroad, only slows down market penetration. As pointed out earlier, whereas some assets may suffer from capacity constraints, others, especially the knowledge-based and intangible ones, generally do not. As such, they would be needlessly penalized in the search for value-added through vertical integration. Compared to the cost minimization objective of trans-domestic strategies, global strategies are based on maximizing the cash flow potential of critical assets. In other words, if the critical asset is a well-known brand, realizing the maximum potential from that is what drives the strategy. Similarly, if technology is what matters, that becomes the optimization variable.

An important advantage of this asset approach to global strategies is that it is *not* based on minimizing national differences or ignoring political pressures exerted by sovereign nations as is the danger when viewing global strategies as mere extensions of generic product/market strategies. Whether firms like it or not, global competitive strategies have to be situated in the context of policies aimed at national competitiveness. One can fight these policies or exploit the opportunities they offer. An asset approach, particularly its asset accumulation dimension, favors the latter. Whether it is human resources, raw materials, capital, or government-funded technologies, these need to be seen as assets to be tapped wherever they might be available. They are not unique elements of a competitor's production function. To that extent, one of the things global strategies draw on is the advantage inherent to a global presence itself.

The asset approach results in a rich diversity of strategies. Returning to Table 1, firms have the choice of deploying either any one of the eight assets listed or a combination of them, depending on their size, industry, and their objectives vis-à-vis competition and future growth ambitions. The participation modes shown in Table 1b depend on the asset(s) chosen as well and, of course, the national policies and existing asset precommitments in the markets being entered. Further, some strategies can be more dependent on foreign asset accumulation than others, including the use of partner assets.

In practical terms, this range of strategies can be broadly classified into two categories: (a) *market-global* strategies, which emphasize a product/ market concept and usually, but not necessarily, acquired market access (assets 7 and 8); and (b) *asset-global* strategies, which focus in a *relative sense* on nonmarket assets (1-6), emphasizing management, technology, and manufacturing ability. Within these extremes are a range of possibilities. Also, whereas larger multinational companies may attempt to be both market- and asset-global because of their greater vertical integration and move extensive assets, smaller companies will typically emphasize one or the other dimension, probably no more than one or two assets at a time. The sections that follow examine what these categories mean in practice and what determines competitive advantage within them.

Market-Global Strategies

Market-global strategies are those that Levitt (1983) referred to in his widely cited article, "The Globalization of Markets," and which have created so much controversy (Thackray, 1985). What they consist of essentially is the creation of products with a universal appeal that can, with a minimum of adaptation, be marketed in at least all of the key countries of the world under a common core policy.

Products that lend themselves to this type of global strategy include Coca-Cola drinks, videotape recorders (especially the VHS format), and the Boeing 747. Steel, aluminum ingots, certain kinds of robots, and supercomputers (such as the Cray-1 and -2) also belong to this category. Franchised hotels, fast-food restaurant chains, and other services based on commercializing a product/market concept (asset 8) and related acquired market access are other examples. In fact, for industrialized countries at least, "high-touch" products, and products perceived as having no close substitutes and as being essential, all seem to have some "universal appeal" (Huszagh, Fox, and Day, 1986). Further, Levitt (1983) is probably right in his claim that more products are potentially market-global today than at any time in the past and that trade liberalization is helping companies realize this potential.

Consumer Tastes. Apart from industrial commodities, which have always been globally marketed, what makes market-global strategies possible is essentially a convergence in consumer tastes that has resulted from increased travel, communication possibilities, and exposure to and acceptance of some kind of universally desirable behavior on the part of individuals. This convergence has made "different cultural preferences, national tastes and standards, and business institutions vestiges of the past" (Levitt, 1983, p. 96). Water will quench a thirst in any part of the world but, as the advertisement slogan says, "Coke Is It." Who is the consumer to argue? A product becomes market-global not only because it is intrinsically so but because it is made to look so through all kinds of psychological associations between the product, its brand, the company which purveys it, and a lifestyle that is "in" the world over. Little wonder, then, that it is the large advertising companies which are the most ardent advocates of globalization in business today.

Markets and Technical Standards. Uniform technical standards and relatively open markets (in terms of trade and the criteria used by purchasing agents) are other preconditions for a global approach to marketing. When combined with a well-recognized brand, they permit scale economies either in the investment made for market access (asset 7 in Table 1) or, if necessary, the exploitation of joint scale economies in research and development.

Scale Economies. The manner in which firms approach global markets, in fact, depends on the scale economies they wish to realize. In the case of pharmaceuticals, for example, the economies involve the R&D investment made in the development of new drugs. As is well known, the cost of developing and introducing a new pharmaceutical product is now on the order of $150 million. Because it can take as long as 10 to 12 years to go through all the tests necessary for launching the drug, after the patent has been applied for (Bartling and Hadamik, 1982), it is almost obligatory for a firm to gain a strong position in a number of markets simultaneously to amortize the investment while the patent is still valid. Without a global brand, worldwide distribution channels, and marketing support, this would be virtually impossible.

Aircraft, digital exchanges in telecommunication, and large computer systems fall in the same category as pharmaceuticals. They involve a uniform technology applied to a common function, target a fairly universal set of needs, and involve a minimum of local adaptation. If, at the same time, they can be produced and sold in a manner so as to exploit whatever economies are possible—such as scale of facilities, quality assurance, delivery, maintenance, logistics, and marketing—their viability becomes more assured.

At the other extreme are companies for which the main investment is in marketing itself. It is irrelevant whether these firms use their own complementary assets (1-6 in Table 1) or subcontract those of another company. Rather than being *forced* to market globally because of investments in product development and manufacturing, they see global markets as a *means* to expansion and to *develop assets,* in this case market access (asset 7).

A good illustration of this emphasis on marketing assets, combined with only a selective use of others, is that of Coca-Cola. It invested heavily in marketing worldwide but engaged a number of independent bottlers to which it merely supplied its formulation and some technical support. The fact that it had a common trademark and bottle shape helped, but it was market-global long before it attempted to standardize its advertising message.

Other well-known examples of companies starting as market-global are in toys, shoes, and personal computers. Lewis Galoob Toys, Inc., for example, sold $58 million worth of its sword-wielding Golden Girls "action figures" and other toys in 1985, 10 times its turnover in 1981. With a mere 115 employees, its only investment is in marketing. Product ideas come from independent inventors and entertainment companies, while outside specialists do most of the design and engineering. Manufacturing and packaging is farmed out to a dozen or so contractors in Hong Kong which, in turn, pass on the most labor-intensive work to factories in China. To top it all, even local distribution and collection of accounts in the United States is subcontracted (*Business Week*, 1986, p. 60).

The approach of Nike, Inc. has been similar. Rather than invest in manufacturing, it used offshore contract manufacturers since it started in 1964, thinking of itself mainly as a research, development, and marketing corporation. Leading Edge Products, Inc. of Massachusetts has captured 6% of the U.S. market for personal computers by also sourcing finished products from Daewoo of South Korea. And these are by no means isolated examples. The enormous growth in the original equipment manufacturing (OEM) business during the past couple of decades is proof of how widespread the phenomenon is. A major proportion of the VCRs, photocopiers, cameras, and even IBM's early personal computers, are sourced from Japan and other countries in the Far East to be sold under a U.S. company's brand and based on its marketing investments.

Product/Market Concept. The potential for exploiting investments in global marketing is, in fact, now widely recognized. Not only do brands ensure continuing business for follow-on products and more effective control over marketing, they also favor mobile purchasing. Whether it is at airports around the world, or in downtown shopping centers, the affluent business and leisure traveler is already an important link in global markets. It is little wonder that practically all of the major Japanese companies that entered the U.S. market by supplying VCRs, cameras, and photocopiers on an OEM basis later introduced their own brands. More recent entrants in the global arena, like the Korean firms Hyundai and Samsung, have either skipped the OEM stage altogether or employed OEM relationships sparingly. Their advertising campaigns in the world press were done early and on a broad front, enabling a company like Hyundai to start selling cars in North America under its own brand from the beginning.

Market Access. In addition to a good product/market concept, investments in market access are, in fact, the key to market-global strategies. If products are to be developed for world markets from the start, the firm must already be present in those markets both to gain information and to be ready for commercialization. It is true that the most successful global marketers own or otherwise control their foreign sales and distribution companies. The more successful Japanese companies understood this early. Almost 60% of Japan's direct investment in the United States has been in disuribution. Also, Japanese firms were able to launch their VCRs almost simultaneously in Hamburg, Jeddah, and Sydney. In other words, it is more than just a standard product with universal appeal that makes for a market-global strategy. It is the ability to "sprinkle" it worldwide.

Summary. In sum, there are basically two broad categories of market-global approaches: (1) those driven by end-product marketing but based on maximizing revenue from investments in a particular *nonmarket* asset (such as R&D in the case of aircraft, drugs, and large computers) and (2) those based on maximizing revenue from investments in a product/market concept and acquired market access themselves (assets 7 and 8 in Table 1). The definition of a global strategy for both approaches depends first and foremost on whether it is market expansion around a novel product that is being aimed for or competition around an existing product. Generic competitive strategies such as cost leadership, focus, or differentiation (Porter, 1980) are more relevant to the latter. So is the implementation of these strategies by an optimal configuration and integration of the value chain, particularly for firms amortizing nonmarket investments.

Firms mainly emphasizing innovative products and investments in market access can be less uniform in their choice of strategy so long as they can achieve an optimal cost-quality relationship for *each* market. For them, vertical integration would only introduce rigidities and slow down market penetration without necessarily giving a cost-quality advantage over firms that are more flexible in their sourcing. Thus, if a product invented in Sweden is best manufactured in Taiwan to be test-marketed first in the United States, so be it. The important thing is to capitalize on market access. If some critical component is involved, such as Coca-Cola's base formulation, this can be supplied from a central source on an "as needed" basis to independent bottlers or assemblers. Maintaining flexibility for the rest of the business system not only permits speedier response to shifts in comparative advantage but also avoids the need to amortize asset precommitments.

Looking at market-global strategies as a spectrum of approaches also avoids the need to link global marketing with uniformity in the marketing mix. The difference from earlier multidomestic approaches lies more in the opportunities scanned than whether or not local adaptations are made. When local adaptations are undertaken, it is as much a means to tap a broader consumer base as it is a segmentation device or a means of creating barriers to entry against companies following a more homogeneous approach (Quelch and Hoff, 1986).

Asset-Global Strategies

Whereas the main thrust of market-global strategies is to obtain as many of the benefits of investments in product conceptualization and market access as possible, and to achieve some degree of product/market dominance on a world scale, asset-global strategies seek to obtain benefits from the other resources a firm possesses. This can be done by dominating and exploiting an individual asset, such as a new technology, or a combination of assets. If end-product dominance also results, so much the better. But unlike market-global strategies forced by a nonmarket investment discussed previously, that is neither the main objective nor a necessary by-product of the strategy.

In some instances, an asset-by-asset contest with competitors may be what drives this kind of strategy. The often cited battle between Michelin and Goodyear for each other's market, for example, had more to do with their respective asset base than the marketing of tires—which is hardly a global product to start with. As the story is told, in the early 1970s, Michelin, the French tire maker, used its strong European profit base to attack Goodyear's American home market. Goodyear could fight back in the United States by reducing prices, increasing advertising, or offering dealers better margins. Instead, it struck back in Europe, attempting to weaken Michelin's source of cash, making it more difficult for the latter to invest heavily in gaining a market position in the United States (Hamel and Prahalad, 1985, p. 140).

IBM's position in Japan is a similar example. Whether meant as an explicit strategy or not, the fact that it established a strong position in that country before its two key competitors, Fujitsu and Hitachi, could emerge had the effect of denying them vital cash and production experience in their own home market which they would otherwise have accumulated (Watson, 1982, p. 41).

Finance is but one asset involved in asset-global strategies. Firms in the supplier industry, for example, base their global strength on maximizing the use of manufacturing and engineering resources, deploying them abroad if necessary. Conceptually, they are the counterparts to market-global companies in OEM relationships. Thus, as automobile companies have gone about establishing assembly plants in more and more countries, their traditional suppliers have followed closely on their heels. In the United States, for example, as more Japanese companies have been assembling locally, their traditional suppliers have also set up manufacturing operations there. Tokyo Seat established a subsidiary in Lincoln, Nebraska and is participating in a joint venture with Honda and Sankei Giken Kokyo in Marysville, Ohio, to make seats, exhaust systems, and other parts for Honda. Isumi has set up in Yaphank, New York, to make steering wheels for Chrysler, Ford, and Nissan.

More generally, asset-global strategies are based on the exploitation of the most valuable asset a firm possesses rather than diluting and slowing down its impact in search of value-added and end-product market share. If the asset concerned has the character of a public good and is essentially inexhaustible, so much the better. For example, companies in the information business, like Reuters, take advantage of these asset characteristics. Once collected, financial information can be sold to a number of geographically dispersed buyers at insignificant marginal cost. The strength of Reuters lies in the quality and timeliness of its information, no doubt aided by its army of reporters and journalists. The infrastructure it uses to deliver information worldwide is of secondary importance as other firms can duplicate it quite easily.

Technology Licensing. The most traditional example of single asset deployment, of course, is in the field of technology licensing. When Pilkington Brothers PLC invented the float process for making flat glass in 1958, it decided to use the huge cost savings the process made possible as a basis for the worldwide licensing of the technology to competitors rather than try to gain market share from them in glass products (Quinn, 1977). Similarly, General Electric, by licensing its advanced gas turbine technology to foreign producers that were potential major competitors, created a captive market for its technology among such heavyweights as AEG (West Germany), Hitachi (Japan), Nuovo Pignone (Italy), and Alsthom Atlantique (France) in their respective countries, thus eliminating competition for the U.S. market from these sources (Watson, 1982, p. 41). ICI's strategy for commercializing its recently introduced FM-21 membrane cell technology (for chlorine/caustic soda production) represents focus within the technology asset itself. Rather than using the new membrane technology to advance its own chlorine business or, for that matter, use it as a unique feature of its overall chlorine technology in order to commercialize the latter, it chose instead to commercialize just the cell technology. The technology was offered for license to all chlorine manufacturers, both for new plants as well as for the retrofitting of old ones. When begun in 1981, an objective was set to capture 20% of the free world market capacity for chlorine/caustic soda production. In order to speed the diffusion of the technology, the cell's manufacture was subcontracted out, and two international engineering firms working with chlorine plant construction were engaged for marketing and installation (Jolly, 1982).

What these examples illustrate is that firms neither have to be big, nor in possession of a universally appealing and standard final product, to participate on a global basis. But they do need to have either a dominant or a highly differentiated asset and a strategy of effectively deploying it. This is also what enables multinational conglomerates which are not dominant players in any product line to compete globally; they hold their own by simple virtue of size, financial resources, and management abilities. Their portfolios, consisting of products, countries, and assets deployed, as well as access to a wide array of information, permit them to support a variety of strategic moves that are not available to single-product firms. To that extent they too are global competitors.

Factors Affecting Asset Deployment.   Just as with any other strategy, the actual deployment of assets is constrained by the nature of the environment, the industry concerned, and what competitors do. Among the environment-specific factors calling for an asset-global approach to international business is clearly national protectionism. Many of the asset-global strategies seen today would not, in fact, have come about had it not been for pressures from national governments to deploy assets locally for manufacturing and even for conducting local research and development. The more strategically important the industry and the greater its significance for income, employment, and trade policy, the greater these pressures have been. Also, once deployed, these assets have created their own need to be nationally responsive. The larger the assets already deployed, the greater the need and pressure to make follow-on investments in line with national priorities.

This is not to say that asset-global strategies are only relevant when market-global ones do not work. They are, in many instances, an alternative even in open markets. Frequently, it is the nature of the product and how it is commercialized which determines the strategic approach. Thus, while discrete transactions, such as a straightforward exchange of a product for cash, are amenable to a market-global approach, some deployment of assets becomes necessary when parties have to deal with each other regularly over a wide range of issues. Competitive advantage in such cases lies more in how good the deployed assets are than in the quality or cost-effectiveness of the product itself. In many such long-term relationships, after all, the issues themselves cannot be totally foreseen in advance, making it difficult to contractualize them.

Service support, either of a maintenance or upgrading nature, is one example of a situation calling for local asset deployment. In the past, it was industries such as automobiles, large home appliances, and factory equipment that required firms to set up their own service and repair facilities. As these industries matured and their service component became more standardized, direct contracts between buyers and sellers were no longer necessary. Local independent agents could both sell and service the products, often more cheaply, making the transaction for the supplying company a nearly discrete one. Today, other industries such as telecommunications, office equipment, large computers, and hospital management have taken their place. Local presence and service support is not only a source of competitive advantage but often a precondition for selling in these industries, not least because of the need to control warranties.

Retail banking has traditionally been another example where local asset deployment or exposure has been necessary. Because of restrictions on capital movements, banks had no choice but to set up local branches and subsidiaries in each country so as to collect deposits and lend to domestic clients. Apart from the initial equity, all of the bank intangible assets were transferred, particularly its name and method of doing business; in the case of branch establishments, the entire net worth of the parent was exposed to liability. Thus, while competition was locally defined, competitors were usually other foreign banks, also participating in an asset-global manner. Although certain banking transactions, such as foreign exchange, large capital market deals, and portfolio management, have today become inherently cross-national, having a significant local asset exposure is still important in this industry. Not only does this instill confidence, but it also fosters relationships between the bank and its customers over a wide range of transactions. A purely "transaction" orientation, based on price, is yet to become popular as the story of Continental Illinois showed. The bank grew rapidly at first, based on purchased money in the form of Eurodollar borrowings and certificates of deposit, but when the quality of its portfolio became questioned, large CD and foreign depositors removed their funds from the bank. Customers had no continuing relationship with the bank and had merely "parked" their money there because of price factors; for them there was no incentive to stay.

In telecommunications equipment, particularly large main exchange switchgear, an asset-global approach has also been the traditional method of doing international business. Because of the strategic or essential nature of the product, the predominance of government-owned postal, telegraph, and telephone (PTT) systems as customers with quasi-monopsony power and, in some cases, the presence of locally unique standards and type test criteria, the only way to serve individual country markets has been to set up a strong local manufacturing and service presence.

The company with the strongest presence was ITT with 80% of its sales in countries of manufacture, mainly France, Belgium, United States, and Spain (Bradbury, 1978, p. 110). Not only had ITT set up large, fairly autonomous subsidiaries in a number of countries, often with names that had no connection with the parent, it also decentralized R&D facilities, developing several types of exchanges each tailored to the needs of a major PTT rather than a single versatile system. During the early 1970s, a series of analog electronic switching systems, called Metaconta, were developed. Even when, in the late 1970s, work began on the digital switches under the broad "System 12" program, different versions were developed to suit different PTTs with much of the development taking place in laboratories in the United States, United Kingdom, Belgium, and West Germany (Doz, 1986).

LM Ericsson, in contrast, centralized most of its R&D in Sweden, cooperating closely with Sweden's PTT. Even it, however, traditionally relied heavily on contributions from its French, Italian, and Australian laboratories and made sure it was close to the markets it served. Although components and mechanical features were similar, each system was tailored to user needs and the software adapted in each location. Because growth came more from an increase in the volume of traffic rather than replacement (the average expected life of telecommunication exchanges being 40-60 years), the sales as well as technical work needed to be close to the client (Bradbury, 1978, p. 110).

The Asset Accumulation Dimension. The nature and extent of resources *deployed* abroad in pursuit of business opportunities is one dimension of competition among firms adopting asset-global strategies. Because it is asset dominance which ultimately counts, asset *accumulation* is equally important. Unlike firms following a strictly market-global approach, asset-global firms invariably deploy some of their assets abroad in order to harness other assets locally. With capital, technology, and natural and human resources spread over different countries, and the level of their quality and abundance converging among countries, this is also likely to be the relatively more important dimension in the future. Firms which are able to attract and draw upon these resources will not only command a larger asset base to exploit but a qualitatively richer one. As Bjorn Svedberg, LM Ericcson's President, put it recently:

> We have made large investments in recent years to build up close-to-the-customer research and development operations in such countries as Australia, England, Italy, Mexico, and the United States. Our broad, deeply rooted international base gives us a significant competitive advantage in this area. Our operation on the American market will continue to require large investments during 1986 and 1987. These investments are warranted not only by the growth of the market. The most advanced technological and market-driven developments are taking place in the United States. To maintain our strong position in the world market, we have to participate actively in these developments. The increasingly stringent demands being imposed by American customers in both the public and private sectors of telecommunications will set the future standards that are applied to other markets (LM Ericcson, *Annual Report*, 1985, p. 3).

Finally, asset-global strategies also derive justification from the well-recognized trend towards systems sales and the solving of a customer's problem. A steel company can either stop at exporting rods and sections at the lowest landed cost, or it can go a step further and set up steel distribution and service centers close to its customers in each market, giving them on-time delivery and meeting any special requirements they might have. According to the definition adopted in this chapter, the former would be a typical market-global approach. The latter is a strategy that is equally global in outlook and is consciously based on asset accumulation and deployment abroad rather than just product/market supply at least cost.

Risk. Naturally, asset-global strategies involve a greater measure of risk. They expose a company's assets to all of the foreign business risks such as nationalization, exchange rate movements, and controls of one kind or another that have historically dominated international business. There are also certain aspects that are new to global business. There is, first and foremost, the nature of the exposure itself. Unlike the earlier view of international business, a lot more than just capital resources are at stake. Asset-global strategies involve "exposing" various elements of an organization, creating a certain permeability and risk of "asset leakage" beyond what can be captured by a strictly financial view of risk exposure. This permeability, in turn, results in a symbiotic relationship with the local resources that are being accumulated in the process. Technology is given as much as it is obtained, and this is true for other assets as well. Thus, Toyota's joint venture with General Motors in Fremont, California, is both a financial exposure on the part of Toyota (to foreign exchange and similar risks, not nationalization) and an exposure of its management sytems to a potential competitor. Since the New United Motor Manufacturing, Inc. (NUMMI) started operations in 1984, some 2,000 G.M. staff have apparently already studied there.

Integration and Coordination. Asset-global strategies are also, by their very nature, more dependent on the performance of others. Whether it is business partners, or human resources mobilized in foreign locations, the potential for leveraging assets carries with it the risk of adequately managing them. A global network of assets, more and more of which is represented by knowledge and skills, means paying attention to the people dimension in a world where people continue to think differently and have different aspirations of their own local situation.

As with market-global strategies, building and sustaining competitive advantage rests on the quality and value of the critical asset(s) involved, as much as it does on integrating and coordinating the global system created. The nature and amount of integration, furthermore, cannot be accurately characterized given the multitude of approaches available.

To the extent integration and coordination serve any purpose, it is probably at the level of *each asset* rather than across each stage of the business system or value-chain. The latter, as discussed previously, is more relevant for firms following a market-global approach and, that too, only in one category of cases. Thus, if competitive battles turn around financial resources, it is the financial asset that needs to be closely integrated across countries. If it is manufacturing or technology, those are the assets to be integrated, and so on. As with market-global systems, there are tradeoffs to be made when deciding on integration—not only in terms of flexibility and entrepreneurial freedom but also in terms of asset accumulation.

Barriers to Competition Versus Competition for Barriers

All domestic strategies are ultimately aimed at creating barriers to competition from others. Whether it is proprietary know-how, brand recognition, market share, control over privileged sources of supply, or distribution networks, the purpose of investing in these is to make entry by others difficult and to avoid price competition.

In the international arena, other methods for obtaining protection against competitors are available in addition to those based on market competition. Most of these are in one way or another linked to national protectionist policies or to features unique to local markets. Depending on whether a firm is a well-entrenched incumbent or a potential entrant, it can be seen as a tool of competition or as a barrier to the implementation of a strategy. Either way calls for well-planned investments on the part of the firm.

The protection offered by governments to national and international firms producing and deploying assets locally takes a variety of forms. Apart from the traditional "first entrant" privileges, which seal off the market to import competition once local manufacture begins, indigenous firms usually obtain privileged access to government procurement programs, local R&D grants, subsidies of one kind or another, and incentives to diversify their activities into priority areas. But, as the following quote from the Director of Corporate Planning of Clark Equipment Co. illustrates, these privileges have to be worked for:

> In a Latin American subsidiary, for example, Clark Equipment took a number of steps over the years to shelter the operation from substantial changes in government policy. Early on it was recognized that the only avenue for successfully participating in that market on a continuing basis was to develop an operation indigenous to the country, one which was in concert with the basic aims and interests of the government and which could comfortably adapt to and contribute to changes in policy. This was accomplished through a series of steps, including shared ownership with local investors, local manufacture of virtually all products sold in the market, high local content to provide maximum employment and to develop local suppliers, and export programs to support government trade policies. In short, these steps were taken to establish an operation which was relatively immune from changes in economic policy, directed at outsiders and, in that sense, one which was sheltered from some of the uncertainties of that market (South, 1981, p. 18).

Conceptually, the nature of this protection and the way it is administered are not too different from the regulation of public utilities in most countries. Governments justify their intervention—for job, wealth, and balance of payment reasons—because of certain structural imperfections in product and factor markets, just as regulatory agencies do in invoking natural monopoly considerations. For small countries, even the natural monopoly argument is relevant for otherwise competitive industries and used for convincing companies of the need for controls. Like public utilities, the barriers a government creates around an incumbent imply a quid pro quo in terms of the nature of conduct expected. Price controls, obligations to perform certain services, and to generally conform to the government's notions of public interest are all part of the implicit contract.

Like public utilities in the United States, for example, national regulation also has a political flavor. Once the initial decision to protect is made, the protecting agency becomes "captured" by the very firms it regulates (Stigler, 1971; Posner, 1974). Thus, from being an attempt to serve the national interest, government protection often turns into a product supplied to interest groups; firms constituting the latter provide services when called upon in exchange for barriers to competition. Because of the difficulty in foreseeing future possibilities and requirements, the terms of this implicit contract are kept intentionally open, relying instead on a mutually understood "constitution" governing the ongoing relationship (Goldberg, 1976). Breaking into this complicity and outbidding an incumbent is made all the more difficult because of the personal relationships and a sense of familiarity that develops over time.

As might be expected, companies basing their global strategies on significant asset commitments in the markets they serve stand more to gain from such local barriers. The cost to them, however, is in terms of reduced strategic focus. While they have the possibility of exploiting the public good character of some of their deployed assets over a broad spectrum of local activities, and gaining commensurate financial returns, they become vulnerable to more focused competitors should the local barriers be lifted.

Companies following market-global strategies with minimal local asset deployment are less constrained strategically but more vulnerable to changes in national policies (e.g., the imposition of tariffs or temporary restrictions). The recently publicized funneling of Japanese VCRs through Poitiers by the French government is a case in point. In order to reduce this vulnerability, companies need to think in terms of local alliances, preferably with suppliers or with customers. With respect to suppliers, one might include counter-trade agreements, cross-marketing links, component sourcing, and associations with powerful distribution firms or agents. For customers, apart from long-term supply relations and the building of customer dependence, are relationships linked to product/market adaptation which help to protect against competition from global peers.

Competing With Some, Cooperating with Others

Coalitions with national governments, or their constituencies, is one unique aspect of international strategies; alliances with other international firms is another. Both are admissions of resource dependence—the former

Table 3. The Structure of Inter-Firm Coalitions

Asset Category / Coalition Types	Companies	(1) Finance	(2) Management	(3) Raw Material Access	(4) Product Know-How	(5) Tools and Process Know-How	(6) Manufacturing Capacity	(7) Acquired Market Access	(8) Product/ Market Concept
a. Complementary Market Access (Joint-Ventures)	A	X	X	X	X	X			X
	B	X	X	X	X		X	X	
Technology Access (Licensing)	A					X			
	B	X	X	X			X	X	X
Franchising	A		X	X	X	X		X	X
	B	X	X				X	X	X
Supply Ventures	A				X	X			
	B		X	X		X	X		
Complementary Marketing	A	X	X		X				
	B							X	X
Corporate Venture Investments	A	X	X				X	X	X
	B				X	X			

b. *Supplementary*

Financial Cross-Holding	A	X							
	B	X							
Holding Company Merger	A	X		X					
	B	X		X					
Full-Fledged Functional Merger	A	X	X	X		X		X	X
	B	X	X	X		X		X	X
Raw Material Access	A	X	X	X					
	B	X	X	X					
Joint Product or Process Development and Cross-Licensing	A				X	X			
	B			X	X	X			
Joint Manufacturing	A	X		X			X		
	B	X		X			X		
Joint Market Access	A	X						X	
	B							X	
Product Standardization	A	X							X
	B	X							X

vis-à-vis the environment and the latter in relation to other organizations. As such, they both diminish autonomy but add to the resources available to a firm and insulate it against competition from others.

Complementary Assets. Most of the early international alliances between companies tended to be for the purpose of market entry. A company possessing a new product, or some product-specific asset, typically entered into a joint-venture or license agreement with a local firm possessing access to the market. The assets they brought to the venture were *complementary,* and the managerial role of each partner was reasonably clear. Whereas one partner concentrated on coping with local regulations, getting approvals and helping with market access, the other devoted its resources to product and technology transfer. The first part of Table 3 lists the generic types of coalitions that firms entered into on this basis.

Although such complementary ventures are still popular, the global character of some businesses is giving rise to alliances that are more multinational in terms of mission. As such, they represent a greater global stake for the partners concerned. A notable example is the 1982 joint venture between AT&T and Philips of Holland to commercialize the former's telecommunication products everywhere outside the United States using Philips' distribution capabilities.

Supplementary Assets. A more direct outcome of the globalization of business is the growth in alliances of a *supplementary* nature, some of more temporary duration than others (see Table 3b). Examples of these involving research and development are now commonly seen in the aircraft, automobile, biotechnology, semiconductor, and telecommunication industries. The costs and risks involved in breakthrough innovations or major projects are today such as to make it impossible for a single firm to assume the full burden even if it wished to.

One example in the aero engines field is the 5-nation, 7-company consortium set up in 1983 to jointly develop a new engine (the V2500) for a 150-seat aircraft (Moxon and Geringer, 1985). In addition to assuring political acceptability in all of the national markets represented, the venture aims at spreading the financial cost, estimated at between $1.5 to $2.0 billion, among the consortium members.

Related examples can be found in the automobile industry. One is the joint development and manufacture of automobile engines in Europe among otherwise competing firms. Short product life cycles, expensive tooling, and considerable manufacturing scale economies caused Volvo, Renault, and Peugeot to come together in a jointly owned venture, FSM (France-Seudoise des Moteurs), to make V-6 engines that they all use with minor modifications. The other is the cooperation between Renault and Volkswagen to make a new kind of four-speed gearbox. Each partner takes charge of specific parts of the gearboxes and assembles the finished product for its own use. Renault, whose share of the investment was planned to be $45 million, makes the electronic control system and the converter in addition to specializing in a longitudinal version of the gearbox. Volkswagen, with an $85 million investment, makes the mechanical parts and a transversal version. When initiated, this venture was expected to result in a 20% saving in development costs and 10% economy in production.

Research and development and manufacturing, while the most common, are not the only areas where supplementary coalitions have emerged. As shown in the second half of Table 3, firms can supplement their own resources in all asset categories without a full-fledged merger. In marketing, for example, companies can bring together their respective acquired market access (asset 8) in certain regions for commercializing products made independently. A case in point is the recent agreement between AT&T and Philips to market some medical systems products jointly in the United States. Under the proposed arrangement, the direct-sales operations of both companies would help each other sell diagnostic and medical information systems already manufactured separately by the two companies.

One company that has leveraged itself quickly into a global position, using a mix of complementary as well as supplementary alliances, is Olivetti. As early as 1980, it first sold 33% of its equity to Campagnie de Saint-Gobain in order to establish a link with Saint-Gobain's other electronic holdings, such as CII-Honeywell Bull. The objective was to create a huge European competitor for the world market in data processing and office automation. After a Socialist government came to power in France, Saint-Gobain's holding was reduced to 10% and then transferred to another French company, Compagnie Generale d'Electricite. This was replaced by another alliance, this time with AT&T in 1983. The latter bought 25% of Olivetti's shares for a cash injection of $260 million, with an option to increase the stake to 40% in 1988. In addition to buttressing Olivetti's financial position, this deal called for the two companies to market each other's products in their own geographic markets. Olivetti was to market AT&T's advanced PABX and 3B minicomputers in Europe wile the latter agreed to sell Olivetti's personal computer, the M24, in America. There were other advantages for both parties, too. Carlo de Benedetti, Olivetti's chairman, agreed to a 10-year employment contract, and AT&T gained access to the company's development work in Ivrea. In return, Olivetti gained access to AT&T's telecommunications know-how, having some 15 of its people working with AT&T in Denver on PABX research (Turner, 1986, p. 16).

Apart from asset exchanges with AT&T, Olivetti has opened itself to other alliances as well. In an effort to create a similar link with Japan, it sold 20% of its Japanese company to Toshiba; this too is expected to result in several product exchanges and joint ventures over time. In all, by the middle of 1985, Olivetti had some 30 different marketing and technological links with companies in the United States, Japan, and Europe, including several investments in small high-tech companies such as Stratus Computers, Inc. and VLSI Technology, Inc. that give it a window on new developments and options for product commercialization. These will add to what the company is already getting by way of computers from Hitachi, word processors from Syntrex, Inc., and automated cash machines from Docutel Corp., among others.

Unlike complementary asset ventures, many of these global alliances clearly have an anticompetitive impact. That they are tolerated under national antitrust and cartel legislation is due to their international character but also because of a recognition of the new rules global competition imposes. In fact, some alliances even have the active support of governments, resulting in a dual coalition (one at the interindustry level and the other at the national government level).

The Spectrum of Global Strategies

The distinction between market-global and asset-global strategies, which is summarized in Table 4, and the types of government and company alliances appropriate to each, is intentionally an exaggerated one. Very few companies of any significant size can be recognized today to be following one strategy to the exclusion of the other. What the approach does serve is to define the alternative paths available for small and large firms alike as well as for firms from different industries. Just as any domestic competitive scene consists of a rich and heterogeneous mixture of firms, each occupying a niche and constantly evolving new ways to compete, the global arena too is not the exclusive preserve of the likes of Procter and Gamble, Coca-Cola, IBM, Philips, or Matsushita.

Which dimension of global strategies a firm chooses to emphasize depends on the nature of its main asset, its long-term objectives, and its precommitment of assets in certain countries. Most large companies tend to, in fact, attempt to achieve a combination of market- and asset-global status, if for no other reason than to become less vulnerable to national commercial policies. This is essentially the situation today in color TVs between the two most prominent competitors, Philips and Matsushita. For a variety of historical and strategic reasons, while Philips pursued an asset-global strategy that is now becoming more market-global, Matsushita is evolving in the opposite direction. Matsushita's traditional strategy of sourcing from Japan, where it was fully integrated and had a comparative advantage, while concentrating on deploying marketing assets abroad (asset 8), is gradually giving way to more local production in its main markets

Table 4. A Comparison of Market-Global and Asset-Global Strategies

Characteristics	Market-Global	Asset-Global
1. Product	Universal appeal, essential, source independent, little onsite maintenance and upgrading	Systems requiring maintenance and upgrading, know-how and similar asset application
2. Examples in "Open" Markets	Civil aircraft, VCRs, Coca-Cola, fast-food chains, industrial commodities	Power equipment, retail banking, construction, telecommunication systems, licensing relationships
3. Strategic Objective	End-product market share worldwide	Asset dominance and optimum exploitation of cash flow
4. Basis of Competition	Brand, distribution, logistics, price, quality	Close customer contact, maintenance and upgrading service, problem solving, government/stakeholder protection
5. Main Assets Deployed	7 and 8 (from Table 1)	1-6 (from Table 1)
6. Partner Profile	Supplier, joint-marketing, mostly complementary	Buyer when asset deployment, supplementary when asset accumulation
7. Source of Vulnerability	Tariffs, quotas, voluntary market restrictions, counterfeiting	Restrictions on factor movements, asset leakage, nationalization
8. Nature of Integration and Coordination Across Borders	Across the business system when nonmarket assets drive strategy; otherwise, 7 and 8 only	By asset category

in response to protectionism and appreciation of the yen. Both Philips and Matsushita will ultimately resemble each other in combining market- and asset-globalization, having arrived there via different paths.

Within this convergence of market-global and asset-global approaches, which is unique to large companies, there is nevertheless an element of choice. Companies of similar size, in the same industry, distinguish themselves strategically by the global dimension they emphasize. Thus, in the automobile industry, whereas companies such as Volvo stress the product/market dimension, the large U.S. companies and European companies like Fiat and Renault emphasize the local deployment of assets. General Motors, for example, globalized its sourcing of components but continues to locally assemble and adapt its cars to individual markets quite successfully.

At times, changes in technology or other aspects of the industry may cause a shift from one to the other strategy. Telephone exchanges and turbo generators are two examples of such a shift. In both cases, over time, there has been a trend towards larger units and higher minimum production volumes. In telecommunication main-exchange switchgear, the evolution from crossbar to electronic exchanges led to a diminishing value-added in assembly, which is relatively more labor intensive and less subject to scale economies, and a near doubling of the scale economies at the parts manufacture level. Not only that, far more expensive and sophisticated equipment is needed for testing and quality control that further increases the penalty of decentralized manufacture. By one estimate, if local integration abroad reaches a level of 50%, the cost penalty for electronic switchgear can be as high as 30% for production volumes of 120,000 lines per year. In turbo generators, the shift from 1,300 MWe sets running at 1,800 rpm in the early 1970s had a similar effect. Because of experience effects, economies in design and assembly, and long setup times, the critical plant size increased more than four times in terms of output (Doz, 1979, pp. 85-87). For both telecommunications and turbo generators, technological change induced a shift from an asset-global to a market-global approach on the part of large companies.

The more interesting question, however, is whether there is a general trend towards one or the other form of global strategy in a relative sense. Although most of the writing on the subject and discussions within companies seem to indicate a relatively greater role for market-global approaches, the question is hard to answer unequivocally.

Favoring market-global strategies are all of the trends having to do with trade liberalization, converging demand patterns, and the growing opportunities for product sourcing on a worldwide basis. Whereas scale economies in production are now becoming less of a compelling factor, because of downsizing and the emphasis on scope, their role is being taken over by other, more intangible assets. Investments in R&D, product/market concepts, and advertising are, if anything, not only as large but more susceptible to scale economies by virtue of their public-goods character.

Also pointing in the same direction are some of the things made possible by new information technologies. Not only do these allow more rapid market information and control over logistics, sometimes they also diminish the need for deploying complementary assets in each location where products are sold. The obvious example is that of product servicing and upgrading. Although some of this can be telecommuted or sent in modularized packages, referred to by some as "know-ware," other knowledge functions can be built into the hardware itself instead of being imparted by skilled people on site.

A case in point are the wire and spark erosion machines made by Ateliers des Charmilles, S.A. of Geneva, Switzerland. In view of the high level of skill required to operate these machines, the company previously spent a great deal of effort in operator training and transferring new techniques. Recently, it incorporated some 60 software modules on cassette which operators can use to optimize the machine's capabilities themselves.

The fact that the need for local asset deployment has diminished in certain cases, either because of trade liberalization or the possibilities offered by new technologies, does not, however, mean that asset-global strategies have any less of a future. Apart from the growing emergence of small firms with unique assets, especially technological, the trend in most industries towards system sales promises to maintain this dimension of strategy, too.

Also compelling firms to become asset-global is the asset accumulation dimension of such strategies described earlier. After all, access to local universities, R&D facilities, finance, and talent is as much a part of the global arena as the selling of products.

IMPLICATIONS FOR ORGANIZATION STRUCTURE

Global Structures of U.S. and European Companies

Because international business has often followed a pattern of diversification, multinational structures have been designed mainly to cope with the added complexity generated by geographic and/or product diversification. U.S. companies, in the early stages of their international-ization, first grouped all foreign activities under a so-called International Division. As more products were introduced in a greater number of countries, and as significant asset commitments abroad resulted, most U.S. multinational companies disbanded their International Divisions in favor of worldwide Area Divisions or Product Divisions. If product diversity was proportionately greater than area diversity, Product Divisions became the basis for organizing the worldwide business. Conversely, if the company was represented in a large number of countries, with a narrow product or business range but a high proportion of sales generated abroad, the preferred structure was an Area Division (Stopford and Wells, 1972). Companies having both area and product diversity, to follow the logic, ended by adopting some form of product-area matrix. A third dimension, usually consisting of functions, was added to the matrix in cases where dominance was required in particular functions or where investments made in these functions offered a potential for realizing scale economies.

There were, however, certain exceptions to this evolutionary structure. Some companies in health care and food processing, for example, continued to cope with product and geographic diversity with an international division. Rather than changing structure, they concentrated instead on management systems, policies, and processes, including the use of teams, task forces, and the encouragement of broad skills and perspectives among key managers (Bartlett, 1982). This preference for an international division has also been vindicated by performance. Thus, of the 85 companies in the Harvard Multinational Enterprise Project that retained a particular structure between 1970 and 1980, companies with an international division increased foreign sales by an average of 435%; those with a global matrix structure saw international revenues rise by 371%. But the foreign sales of companies organized by global product divisions grew only 259% even though they started from a lower base of sales (Davidson and Haspeslagh, 1982).

European companies, by and large, followed the U.S. pattern except in the early stages. Rather than group their first international ventures under a special organization such as an international division, they preferred to keep foreign subsidiaries relatively autonomous and have them report in a less formal manner to the chief executive or certain executive directors constituting the management committee of the parent company (Franko, 1976; Jolly, 1985). Once the need for closer integration between the parent and its subsidiaries was felt, however, the structure changed to a worldwide area, product, or matrix structure.

Global Structures of Japanese Companies

Japanese multinationals, the third major group of companies dominating the international scene, tended to employ an international division to manage their foreign operations well beyond the point of product or area diversification when U.S. and European companies changed. Typically, they first divided their division into two departments, one handling exports from Japan and the other overseeing subsidiaries and affiliates in which capital or technology had been deployed (Business International Corporation, 1981). In a number of companies, these two departments were later merged as exports from Japan needed to be coordinated with local manufacturing operations and the trade flows originating from them. Apparently, language difficulties, the predominantly export or import nature of international business, and inexperience in foreign manufacture, all favored concentrating in one place whatever international expertise the company possessed. The natural predisposition to horizontal and vertical communication already in place meant that coordination within the domestic product divisions (the predominant form of the parent company's structure) was done without a formal matrix structure. If one takes into account the process at work within large Japanese multinational companies, most of them today have features of product-area-function matrix without the formality or rigidity inherent to such structures in U.S. or European companies.

Global competition, and the strategies that companies have designed to meet it, have until now largely been handled within these structures. To the extent that certain adaptations have been made, they have mainly consisted of strengthening the "product" dimension of the matrix organizations already in place. Although some companies have indeed reorganized to focus on products or strategic business units, making them the *only* worldwide profit centers, most have chosen to use policies and other mechanisms to shift the power from country and regional offices to head office units while maintaining an additional profit responsibility and some entrepreneurial freedom at the country level (Prahalad, 1976).

Mixed Structures

Naturally, all product groups or strategic business units have not had the same global imperatives imposed on them. This has meant in practice a greater recourse to mixed or differentiated structures, with some parts of the company organized along worldwide centrally managed product divisions and others sharing responsibility and accountability between products and areas. For example, when ASEA of Sweden moved from a functional to a business unit structure in 1981, business units became responsible for the worldwide profitability of their products and services without changing the profit center status of country organizations. However, one exception to this conventional product-area matrix was made. The newly formed Robots Division was given complete control over its worldwide results. Rather than share this responsibility jointly with country organizations, independent Robot Divisions (or companies) were established outside the scope of the existing national organizations and made to report exclusively to the parent company division in Vasteras (Jolly, 1985).

Another example of a differentiated multinational structure is that of General Electric. Rather than defining all its strategic business units (SBUs) by product categories, it has designated a number of countries (including Brazil, Canada, and Spain) as SBUs in their own right. This allows the company to give proper attention to unique local market conditions or a unique portfolio of businesses in a particular country. Although such country SBUs may not serve the purpose of a coherent market-global strategy, they at least ensure global *presence,* an especially important ingredient in the implementation of asset-global strategies. In order not to dilute the focus of product-based, worldwide SBUs, intracompany joint ventures between them and the country SBUs are sometimes entered into, thus allowing for an asset-global strategy in some countries to be pursued along with a market-global strategy in others.

Current Problems in Global Organization

Whereas the differentiated structures, and changes in the relative power of product and country units in multinational matrix organizations, have allowed companies to cope with some of the requirements imposed by global strategies, they are only part of the answer. Judging from recent discussions on the subject with executives in several multinational companies, a number of problems still remain, and the previous normative guidelines on structures need to be looked at afresh.

Part of the problem stems from the sheer complexity of the decision about the appropriate prototype structure. Which businesses are to be organized as worldwide SBUs or product groups and which as essentially area organizations is harder to determine than the rules established by past empirical research might suggest. Variables such as foreign product diversity and the proportion of sales generated abroad (Stopford and Wells, 1972), or those that capture forces for global integration versus national responsiveness (Prahalad, 1976; Doz, 1979), are neither fully representative of the information and transaction needs of companies today nor do they adequately spell out normative transition points for moving from one prototype to another.

Staying with a chosen unidimensional structure, such as a worldwide product organization, but breaking up functional responsibilities or the amount of integration of particular stages of the company's value chain (Bartlett, 1984; Porter, 1985) has its drawbacks. Centrally directing, for example, research and manufacturing, but decentralizing the authority and resources for marketing to country organizations, implies a divisibility of functions and value chain stages that is seldom obtainable or even desirable. Neither, for that matter, do such structural adaptations take into account issues of motivation, performance measurement, and entrepreneurial freedom that are equally important as the cohesion of strategy. The observed success of worldwide product divisions in reducing costs, but at the expense of reduced foreign sales, is symptomatic of this weakness in unidimensional structures that otherwise seem obvious candidates for a global strategy (Davidson and Haspeslagh, 1982).

Building multiple foci into a matrix remains conceptually appealing, but the experience of many global firms has been disappointing. Today, with rapid change and the consequent fast obsolescence of information gathered for central decision making, the weaknesses of matrix structures, if anything, are more apparent.

A final dilemma is the trend towards vertical disaggregation within organizations and the increase in outside alliances mentioned earlier. The "dynamic networks" that are increasingly appearing in international business need to be viewed simultaneously from the perspective of their individual components, some of which lie outside the firm's traditional boundaries and sphere of control, and from the network as a whole. For a given organization, this suggests a heavier reliance on self-managed workgroups internally, more external subcontracting and other co-venture schemes, and a greater willingness to view organizational boundaries and membership as highly flexible (Miles and Snow, 1986).

Some Structural Guidelines

How then *should* organizations structure themselves for pursuing global strategies? As previously discussed, the fundamental aim of such strategies is to exploit, on a global basis, particular assets a firm possesses while the opportunity lasts. Structural guidelines that follow from this general objective are essentially: (a) placing the locus of entrepreneurship where the critical assets are deployed, (b) integrating and coordinating selectively such that the full exploitation of an asset is not unduly compromised, (c) allowing for organizational interdependence with coalition members, and (d) permitting asset accumulation to take place as effectively as asset deployment.

Looking at global strategies in this manner inevitably means departing from some of the traditional strategy-structure prescriptions that evolved from a purely domestic context and then extended, with minor modifications, abroad. It also means looking at global companies as organic systems, forcing managers to design all-purpose, or at least multi-purpose, structures that permit the exercise of a wide range of strategic options at the same time.

How many and what kinds of degrees of freedom are to be built into such multi-purpose structures depends on the nature of assets being exploited and the role a particular firm sees for itself in its industry. The broad prescription, however, is to configure primarily along asset lines or functions (which are their nearest surrogate). Within this primary structure lies a *network of asset nodes* representing deployed assets and the loci of entrepreneurial activity. These are the growth poles of the firm, reflecting the freedom to exploit assets in certain domains.

Such a view of a global enterprise is not too different from Hedlund's (1985) analogy of a hologram to describe the role and status of subsidiaries within a global network—each part contains information sufficient to reproduce the whole original image, albeit somewhat blurred. Rather than being tools for the implementation of a product/market strategy only, these asset nodes are centers for strategic initiative in their own right. Thus, a firm pursuing a global strategy on the strength of its investments in market access (asset 7) might find a number of unexploited regional opportunities for that asset merely because the asset has been dedicated to another, more limited, use. Allowing the subsidiary to "pull" other products and complementary assets into its sphere is what the notion of a network of asset nodes implies. Although it runs counter to the conventional wisdom of staying with what the firm knows best, it is based on the argument that what the parent knows and sees may not be the same as what subsidiary management does. Freedom to source from either within or outside the organization's boundaries in response to changes in comparative advantage is another concrete implication.

For asset-global strategies, this network view is even more compelling. Giving subsidiaries too narrow a mission based on some preconceived notion of *between-country* competition not only constrains their potential for accumulating local resources but diminishes their potential for competing *within* their country. Why, for example, should two subsidiaries be connected together in solving the same R&D problem when the country-specific capabilities of one could be better used elsewhere? A more centrally-directed organization would be both less aware of what these country-specific assets are and what problems can be most profitably tackled.

Naturally, such a loose network does not allow for cross-border integration at the product level, the level at which global competition seems to be defined in most instances. But this is an intentional disagreement. Most assets, in today's context, are only of temporary worth. Building and extending a uniform generic strategy, such as differentiation, cost leadership, or focus (Porter, 1980), across countries, and sustaining competitive advantage by an optimally configured and integrated value chain, assumes a certain stability and homogeneity in product/market scope that seldom obtains, except probably in certain commodities. Even for these, fluctuations in exchange rates, energy prices, protectionist barriers, and labor costs make any configuration suboptimal long before the investments are amortized.

Apart from the lack of flexibility, the organization structure prescription that integration implies—central, hierarchical direction from heads of product groups or SBUs regardless of where these might be located—is hard to justify. If cost minimization and standardization is what is required, the pressures for it will emerge automatically as subsidiaries themselves perceive the advantages offered. These can be coped with nonhierarchically through horizontal coordination among those concerned without loss of entrepreneurial freedom. If another global firm is found to be more successful in certain markets, the same pressure for strategic change will automatically feed through, as long as subsidiaries see it in their best interest. It is ironical, in fact, that global strategies should be associated with central direction and control just when organizations themselves are being encouraged to become more decentralized and less formal—in a word, more entrepreneurial.

Global Structures in Practice

What then is the nature of coordination required, and how does the "network of asset nodes" view differ from multidomestic organizations of the past? To some extent it is the *need* for coordination itself that is different. If subsidiaries are all made to think globally, they will automatically establish points of contact with other units in the network. After all, if the sources of change are global, no subsidiary can expect to remain domestic on its own, regardless of whether it has been traditionally treated that way for reasons of national responsiveness by the parent. Provided the network is adequately exposed to market forces, the search for synergy itself becomes internalized. A primary structure aligned by asset or functional category, and open to initiatives, is best prepared to accommodate such requests because that is where the sources of synergy lie. As for subsidiaries getting into each other's way at the product/market level, which product division structures have been expected to avoid, the possibility is as real as it is exaggerated. After all, if two subsidiaries cannot compete with one another, how can they expect to compete with an outsider in their own domain? Planning for synergy, in other words, can be tantamount to a lack of trust in subsidiary management or, worse, a repudiation of natural markets and competitive forces.

If the above sounds Darwinian in its connotation, it is only to highlight the contrasts with the earlier prototype structures firms have been using to cope with global competition. It does, however, conform to the population ecology view of organizational forms (McKelvey and Aldrich, 1983), though only to the extent that it allows for unintended variations to occur *within* the global network of a single firm. Also, in terms of the typology of organizational roles proposed by Miles and Snow (1978), the implication for subsidiaries is that most assume either a "prospector" or "analyzer" role. Only this will allow for the kind of "pull" for resources and self-coordination that the notion of a network demands. Even the "defender" role, in which primary attention is devoted to improving the efficiency of existing operations, calls for at least some proactive behavior in response to market and comparative advantage changes.

An organic structure of the type described is, of course, only an ideal. Apart from omnipresent market imperfections, it runs counter to the natural predisposition of managers to consciously direct and control their organization's future. Its practical manifestation, therefore, is likely to consist of hybrid solutions. In terms of subsidiary roles, for example, there will inevitably be some that exercise more leadership than others based on the extent of their market domain and the assets vested in them. When Procter and Gamble launched its Vizir detergent in Europe, for example, it transferred some coordination tasks previously implemented by headquarters to one qualified subsidiary (Bartlett and Ghoshal, 1986). Similarly, after Matsushita had created a network of mini-Matsushitas (producing a broad range of products mainly for the local market) in a number of Southeast Asian countries, each of which then began wishing to export, it strengthened its regional coordination and assigned specific export products to each country, making them, in a sense, lead subsidiaries for those products. The business system for these products was, however, configured more as a network rather than as a functionally divided and tightly-knit global organization. Malaysia not only became the principal export base for room airconditioners but a competence center for that product as well, with more and more design and production expertise transferred to it.

The organizational changes taking place within Matsushita in Southeast Asia are, in fact, a good example of how far a global network can go today and how a company can structure around asset nodes. Matsushita's philosophy of "National Service Through Industry," and an international policy emphasizing local orientation, brought about a network of subsidiaries each of which drew on the assets it needed from the parent and accumulated others in its national environment. When the subsidiaries began to get into each other's way in the export market, it was Matsushita's trading company, MET, which arbitrated on the strength of its global market access, not the respective product divisions at headquarters. This allowed country organizations to continue investing and building competence to meet global competition in their markets (such as imports from other Japanese companies) long after it would have been the case in a centrally-directed company. Most of the resources were generated locally.

Matsushita's subsidiary network, coordinated by vesting foreign acquired market access in a trading company rather than in product divisions, is not an isolated example. A host of other companies have realized that the foundation of a global strategy ultimately rests where the customers are, as do the resources needed to implement it. Royal Dutch Shell's geographically decentralized structure with the centralization of some key functions and assets (notably finance, certain procurements, and exploration and production know-how), is another example from a different industry. It is the company's strength in critical assets, more than its cross-border strategy and integration, that makes it a strong global competitor. Digital

Equipment's recent move to a country-level focus, within a primarily functional structure, is yet another illustration of looking at global strategies as essentially asset exploitation rather than uniformly focused product/ market competition.

Managing such multi-purpose structures and making sure that various units do possess hologram characteristics, however, requires considerable investments in the design of appropriate policies and management systems. If the "anatomy" of the organization is to be flexible, to use Bartlett's (1982) analogy, special attention needs to be paid to its "physiology" and "psychology." Foremost are the policies guiding resource allocation and performance evaluation. These need to address global strategic issues at the level of each subsidiary while bearing in mind the uniqueness of locally accumulated assets and their special competitive circumstances. Criteria based solely on, for example, the parent's cost of capital, or operating standards, imposes biases and time frames that are unrealistic and can even be counter-productive. What is needed are evaluation criteria that encompass a wide range of parameters, each adapted to a subsidiary's mission and ambitions. The replacement of "profit centers" by "performance centers," as some propose, is a step in this direction (Business International Corporation, 1986, p. 35). Judging from various companies' experience in applying different criteria for evaluating individual businesses in a domestic portfolio, it is also feasible. Planning systems, adapted to each subsidiary's environment, obviously need to be developed to serve this purpose (Chakravarthy and Perlmutter, 1985).

Adaptation of formal management systems is, of course, only part of the challenge. Decentralization of the locus of entrepreneurship to where assets are deployed calls for mechanisms whereby local initiatives can be aligned to the overall direction of the company. For this, managers need to be induced to apply a global perspective from the start and to be willing to share costs and resources with other units. Reward systems that relate compensation to subsidiary as well as company-wide performance is one way to achieve this. A system for compensating a subsidiary for its assistance rendered to other units is another. These are both "culturally neutral" systems and avoid the need for more normative control methods, such as those based on a commonly shared corporate culture and business principles. As such, they are easier to design and implement.

TYPES OF MANAGERS REQUIRED
BY GLOBAL STRATEGIES

Global strategies and the structures that are evolving to support them clearly affect all aspects of human resource management. Proper attention to human resources is also now well recognized as a key to successful strategy implementation (Edstrom and Lorange, 1984; Hrebiniak and Joyce, 1984; Tung, 1984). Rather than trying to explore this topic comprehensively, a more modest question can be posed: What kind of manager is required by today's global firms?

With respect to *cognitive orientation,* global strategies clearly involve far greater degrees of freedom in their formulation and implementation than domestic ones. Not only is there a wider variety of generic strategies but different competitor types, cultural traits, and national business environments to be taken into account. Compared to traditional approaches to international business, furthermore, the shorter time frame for action and the interdependence of decisions across national boundaries force a simultaneous consideration of many complex factors.

Yet, to ask managers to have breadth and depth of knowledge in every conceivable area, and the skills to do something about it as well, is as unrealistic as it is platitudinous. So how can this pluralism be handled by more or less average managers?

The traditional way of handling plurality has been to simplify and order it by classification and by imposing a mind-set that enables one to interpret what all the signals mean. However, as is said of architecture, "we shape our buildings; thereafter they shape us." Global managers need to recognize plurality for what it is and resist classifying it in the hope of "managing" it. Formalized models with detailed calculations of costs, benefits, and time frames worked fine in a more leisurely and less competitive world. Today, within the market-global and asset-global categories described in this chapter, is an entire spectrum of strategies, getting more finely tuned all the time and being designed by people with a very heterogeneous mind-set. Managers need to widen their cognitive horizons, absorb and retain new perspectives and information, much like a sponge, and learn to react in spontaneous and unconventional ways if necessary. This is no more than what individual entrepreneurs have always done.

If one accepts the description of a global company in the previous sections, this expanded cognitive scope includes not just environmental sensitivity but also an *aptitude for looking at networks as holographic structures.* It means seeking and possessing a global view of a network while managing only a small part of it. Because there are no automatic conflict resolution mechanisms, such as in hierarchical structures, the multiple foci need to be internalized by a wide cross-section of managers. Network managers need to become as comfortable with geographic diversity as they have traditionally been with product diversity at home. Just as they learned to identify the critical sources of success for domestic strategies, they need to learn what it is, beyond political and cultural empathy, that determines successful management of a geographically dispersed system.

Clearly, the starting point for such an assessment is an *attitudinal change*. Certain country nationals and, within them, a select minority, are more global in their outlook than others. The smaller a country, and the more export dependent it is, the greater the proportion of such managers willing to overcome cultural and linguistic barriers. These also happen to be countries that build up trade surpluses vis-à-vis the more inward-looking ones. Although managers can become cognitively aware of global competition, they also need to be sufficiently motivated to do something about it.

Another success factor is clearly *personality*. In addition to a predisposition to cooperate, share perspectives, and appreciate the points of view of those managing in different environments, global managers need to become comfortable with conflicting demands and unplanned changes in the system they are part of. A dynamic network, in which the locus of entrepreneurship is widely dispersed, necessarily means ambiguity in the direction of change. Coping with this ambiguity and the stresses it creates is a real need today.

Because only broad strategies can be set in most types of global businesses, perhaps the other most important managerial aptitude required is that of *policy and system design*. This characteristic, particularly the acceptance of a widespread authority to transact, means constant review of all of the systems and means by which an organization is held together and performs smoothly. More managers need to become familiar with planning systems, transfer price mechanisms, financial criteria, human resource policies, and the structure of businesses and information systems. In brief, the successful manager in today's global firm is more likely to be an organization builder than a strategy analyst.

CONCLUSIONS AND FUTURE RESEARCH DIRECTIONS

How realistic the notion of global competitive strategies is in today's context depends largely on how it is conceptualized. The approach taken in this chapter has been to search for a credible framework—one which admits the existence of sovereign nations, protectionist policies, and socioeconomic differences—that, at the same time, helps distinguish these strategies from earlier forms of international competition. While discussing strategies in terms of their "degree of globalness" may have reflected reality more closely, the discussion was couched in terms of "alternative approaches to globalization" instead. This approach, it was felt, provides the conceptual watershed needed for preparing strategies for the future without, in the meantime, being too far removed from the pragmatic concerns of today.

Looking at global competitive strategies as the worldwide exploitation of assets, rather than of products and services, has the virtue of encompassing a wide range of possible approaches that are within the reach of large as well as small firms. It includes, within the market-global dimension, strategies based on extending a product/market concept and its delivery from a domestic to a global level, approaches already being pursued by global marketers. In its asset-global dimension, it has room for companies that do not have the needed universal products, nor the reputation and infrastructure to commercialize them, but which have some other unique asset with which they too can participate on a global basis.

One important conclusion from adopting such a framework is that global competitive strategies are a lot more than the global extension of domestic generic strategies based on product/market competition. While configuring a firm's value chain for minimum cost within a chosen generic strategy may indeed be relevant in some instances (Porter, 1985), it is not always the recommended strategy. Not only can firms adopting an asset-global approach break into this chain on the basis of some dominant asset, but the requirements for integration and internalization themselves can prove to be onerous. The way in which firms transact their assets and participate internationally, in other words, is as important as the nature of competition in end products and services.

A direct corollary of this conclusion applies to firms that are considering embarking on a global business. They need to concentrate on the development of some unique asset, whether or not it is manifest as a product/market concept. They have to become globally known for something—whatever it is. With the growing search for alliances of a complementary and supplementary nature on the part of other firms, they need to feel no compulsion to build all of the related assets themselves. They too can see their assets commercialized globally, and have their sales and profits grow geometrically, as many have shown in recent years, by teaming with others.

A third conclusion, which has to do with the environment for international business itself, concerns the role of national governments. Because it is unrealistic to assume a laissez-faire attitude on the part of governments any time in the near future, global competitive strategies *have* to be designed to take into account the possibility of government intervention. Business is only one of the constituents of elected governments, however powerful it may be.

The final and perhaps most perplexing conclusion to be drawn from the discussion in this chapter concerns the organizational and human resource management implications of global strategies. The current tendency to integrate and centrally coordinate (direct would be a better term) so-called global businesses within multinational companies—in the hope of gaining sustainable advantage from an optimally configured global value chain—run counter to everything else that appears to be influencing the way organizations are evolving. Most trends point to the direction of dynamic networks, decentralized structures, and greater authority for resource commitment to more managers. When coupled with the special requirement of global companies to cooperate with other organizations and stakeholders, centrally-directed integration needs to be viewed with caution. Surely, advances in management information systems that permit loose structures in a domestic setting, while still meeting standards of cost, quality, and service, can achieve the same ends abroad.

Like most reviews of a phenomenon that is constantly evolving, this chapter raises more issues of both a conceptual and an empirical nature than it comes to grips with. At the level of strategy classification, because of the greater degrees of freedom and the alternative participation modes available, generic structures defined in a product/market sense are probably too limiting. A great deal more research needs to be done on how companies approach the global market and the strategies that have proved to be successful under different circumstances. For this, one needs to focus longitudinally and cross-sectionally on companies in the same industry and with a similar global scope in their operations. Drawing parallels from domestic strategies is useful but does not give adequate insight into international competition as it is practiced today.

Whereas an attempt has been made here to break from traditional approaches to international competition, the proposed concept of "global asset exploitation" clearly needs to be refined and elaborated upon. This concept is already being applied to some extent in a domestic setting, notably the United States, under the pressures of financial restructuring. New insights can be drawn from a cross-sectional study of the "de-conglomeration" phenomenon now in progress that have direct relevance to global strategies. Because both product/market diversification and functional diversification (or asset accumulation as the concept is employed here) is involved, such a study would need to address both dimensions of restructuring to see how U.S. conglomerates have begun to focus their activities in the 1980s. Particularly helpful would be an examination of the relationship between product/market concentration and asset concentration as firms have gone about focusing their activities. If the hypotheses developed in this chapter have any merit, there ought to have occurred a relatively greater emphasis on asset utilization, particularly of the inexhaustible intangible ones, than on product/market concentration, as was the case in earlier restructuring efforts.

The second major area of research concerns the relative merits of a market-global over an asset-global approach, and when and for which firms a particular approach is relevant. Up to now, at least, it has been the smaller companies that have pursued asset-global strategies. Larger companies, though they may have backed into an asset-global mode on account of protectionism, have tended to establish product/market dominance early. Yet, judging from the activities of small, innovative startup companies, the barriers to entry on account of market dominance are no longer as forbidding as they may have been in the past.

A more in-depth study of asset-global strategies themselves is also needed. While the asset-accumulation dimension is key, as manifest in today's proliferation of so-called strategic alliances, very little work has been undertaken regarding the risks involved, the possibilities of "asset leakage" to others, and the strategic compromises and rigidities these alliances might bring about in the future.

Finally, the organizational implications of global strategies provide a rich area for new concepts and for policy-oriented research. One of these is the design of appropriate systems to cope with global business. Information systems, for example, all have the limitation of primarily serving *internal* needs. With an increasingly large proportion of transactions of strategic significance shared with others outside the firm's boundaries, each with their own objectives, criteria for success, and cultural predispositions, this can hardly be useful.

The same self-defeating internal orientation applies to the way management development and organizational cohesion are being attempted. The domain of intervention of global managers, and consequently their knowledge and skills, is more external than is true of domestic managers and less bound to a single environment as was the case with international managers in the past. Yet, most management training programs within global companies are geared to improving things within the company, making it function better, and not toward how managers can relate better to the people and assets they are really managing—those outside. Corporate culture, and all that goes with building and maintaining it, is in this situation just like any other culture—it only tells you what your peers expect.

REFERENCES

Abernathy, William J., and James Utterback (1978). "Patterns of Industrial Innovation." *Technology Review* 80:41-47.
Ayal, Igal (1981). "International Product Life Cycle: A Reassessment and Product Policy Implications." *Journal of Marketing* 45:91-96.
Ayres, Robert U., and Steven Miller (1982). "Robotics, CAM, and Industrial Productivity." *National Productivity Review* 1:42-60.
Bartlett, Christopher A. (1982). "How Multinational Organizations Evolve." *Journal of Business Strategy* 3:20-32.

_____(1984). "Organization and Control of Global Enterprise: Influences, Characteristics and Guidelines." Boston: Harvard Business School, Working Paper 8-785-046 (Revised January 1985).

Bartlett, Christopher A., and Sumantra Ghoshal (1986). "Tap Your Subsidiaries for Global Reach." *Harvard Business Review* 64:87-94.

Bartling, D., and H. Hadamik (1982). *Development of a Drug: It's a Long Way From Laboratory to Patent.* Basel: Buchdruckerei, Gasser and Cie.

Bradbury, Frank R. (ed.) (1978). *Technology Transfer: Practice of International Firms.* Alphen Aan Den Rijn: Sijthoff 7 Noordhoff International Publishers BV.

Buckley, Peter J., and Mark Casson (1976). *The Future of the Multinational Enterprise.* London: MacMillan Press.

Business International Corporation (1981). *New Directions In Multinational Corporate Organization.* New York: Business International Corporation.

_____(1986). *New Thinking: A Guide to Corporate Survival and Growth.* New York: Business International Corporation.

Business Week (1986). "And Now, The Post-Industrial Corporation." March 3, p. 60.

Caves, Richard E. (1971). "International Corporations: The Industrial Economics of Foreign Investment." *Economica* 38:1-27.

Chakravarthy, Balaji S., and Howard C. Perlmutter (1985). "Strategic Planning for a Global Business." *Columbia Journal of World Business* 20:3-10.

Coase, Ronald H. (1937). "The Nature of the Firm." *Economica* 4:386-405.

Davidson, William H., and Philippe Haspeslagh (1982). "Shaping a Global Product Organization." *Harvard Business Review* 60:125-132.

Dean, James W., Jr., and Gerald I. Susman (1989). "Strategic Responses to Global Competition: Advanced Technology, Organization Design, and Human Resource Practices." In Charles C. Snow (ed.), *Strategy, Organization Design, and Human Resource Management.* Greenwich, CT: JAI Press, pp. 297-331.

Doz, Yves (1979). *Government Control and Multinational Strategic Management: Power Systems and Telecommunication Equipment.* New York: Praeger.

_____(1986). *Strategic Management in Multinational Companies.* Oxford: Pergamon Press.

Dunning, John H. (ed.) (1985). *Multinational Enterprise, Economic Structure and International Competitiveness.* New York: Wiley.

Edstrom, Anders, and Peter Lorange (1984). "Matching Strategy and Human Resources in Multinational Corporations." *Journal of International Business Studies* 15:125-137.

Franko, Lawrence G. (1976). *The European Multinationals: A Renewed Challenge to American and British Big Business.* London: Harper & Row.

Gluck, Frederick W. (1982). "Meeting the Challenge of Global Competition." *The McKinsey Quarterly* Winter:2-13.

Goldberg, Victor P. (1976). "Regulation and Administered Contracts." *The Bell Journal of Economics* 7:426-488.

Hamel, Gary, and C.K. Prahalad (1985). "Do You Really Have a Global Strategy?" *Harvard Business Review* 63:139-148.

Hayes, Robert H., and Steven G. Wheelwright (1979). "The Dynamics of Process/Product Life Cycles." *Harvard Business Review* 57:127-136.

Hedlund, Gunnar (1985). *The Hypermodern MNC—A Heterarchy?* Stockholm: Institute of International Business, Stockholm School of Economics (RP 85/5, August).

Hrebiniak, Lawrence G., and William F. Joyce (1984). *Implementing Strategy.* New York: MacMillan.

Huszagh, Sandra M., Richard J. Fox, and Ellen Day (1986). "Global Marketing: An Empirical Investigation." *Columbia Journal of World Business* 20:31-43.

Hymer, Stephen (1960). "The International Operations of International Firms: A Study of Direct Investment." Ph.D. Dissertation, Massachusetts Institute of Technology.

Jo, Sung-Hwan (1981). "Overseas Direct Investment by South Korean Firms: Direction and Pattern." In Krishna Kumar and Maxwell G. McLeod (eds.), *Multinationals From Developing Countries.* Lexington, MA: Lexington Books, pp. 53-71.

Johnson, Harry G. (1970). "The Efficiency and Welfare Implications of the International Corporation." In Charles P. Kindleberger (ed.), *The International Corporation.* Cambridge, MA: MIT Press, pp. 35-56.

Jolly, Vijay K. (1979). "Transformation Regimes, Product Cycle Distortions and the Export of Manufactures from Large Developing Countries." Ph.D. Dissertation, Harvard University.

──────── (1982). *FM-21 Membrane Cell (A) and (B)* (case studies). Geneva: International Management Institute.

──────── (1984). *The Matsushita Group in Malaysia* (case study). Geneva: International Management Institute.

──────── (1985). *ASEA (A) and (B)* (case studies). Geneva: International Management Institute.

Kaplinsky, Raphael (1982). *Computer-Aided Design: Electronics, Comparative Advantage and Development.* London: Frances Pinter.

Kindleberger, Charles (1969). *American Business Abroad.* New Haven, CT: Yale University Press.

Knickerbocker, Frederick T. (1973). *Oligopolistic Reaction and the Multinational Enterprise.* Cambridge, MA: Harvard University Press.

Levitt, Theodore (1983). "The Globalization of Markets." *Harvard Business Review* 62:92-102.

LM Ericcson, *Annual Report,* 1985.

McKelvey, William, and Howard Aldrich (1983). "Populations, Natural Selection, and Applied Organizational Science." *Administrative Science Quarterly* 28:101-128.

Miles, Raymond E., and Charles C. Snow (1978). *Organizational Strategy, Structure, and Process.* New York: McGraw-Hill.

──────── (1986). "Organizations: New Concepts for New Forms." *California Management Review* 28:62-73.

Moxon, Richard W., and J. Michael Geringer (1985). "Multinational Ventures in the Commercial Aircraft Industry." *Columbia Journal of World Business* 20:55-62.

OECD (1986). *OECD Science and Technology Indicators: No. 2.* Paris: OECD.

Porter, Michael E. (1980). *Competitive Strategy: Techniques for Analyzing Industries and Competitors.* New York: Free Press.

──────── (1985). *Competitive Advantage: Creating and Sustaining Superior Performance.* New York: Free Press.

Posner, Richard A. (1974). "Theories of Economic Regulation." *The Bell Journal of Economics and Management Science* 5:335-358.

Prahalad, C.K. (1976). "Strategic Choices in Diversified MNCs." *Harvard Business Review* 54:67-78.

Qualls, William, Richard W. Olshavasky, and Ronald E. Michaels (1981). "Shortening of the PLC—An Empirical Test." *Journal of Marketing* 45:76-80.

Quelch, John A., and Edward J. Hoff (1986). "Customizing Global Marketing." *Harvard Business Review* 64:59-68.

Quinn, James B. (1977). *Pilkington Brothers Ltd.* (case study). Geneva: Centre d' Etudes Industrielles.

South, Stephen E. (1981). "Competitive Advantage: The Cornerstone of Strategic Thinking." *Journal of Business Strategy* 1:15-25.

Stigler, George (1971). "The Theory of Economic Regulation." *The Bell Journal of Economics and Management Science* 2:3-21.

Stopford, John M., and Louis T. Wells, Jr. (1972). *Managing the Multinational Enterprise.* New York: Basic Books.

Swanger, Clare C. (1984). *Apple Computer, Inc.—Macintosh (A)* (case study). Stanford, CA: Graduate School of Business, Stanford University.

The Economist (1983). "Big Is Not So Bad After All." February 19, p. 84.

Thackray, John (1985). "Much Ado About Global Marketing." *Across The Board* 22:38-46.

Tung, Rosalie L. (1984). "Strategic Management of Human Resources in the Multinational Enterprise." *Human Resource Management* 23:129-143.

Turner, Graham (1986). "Inside Europe's Giant Companies: Olivetti Goes Bear-Hunting." *Long Range Planning* 19:13-20.

Vernon, Raymond (1966). "International Investment and International Trade in the Product Cycle." *Quarterly Journal of Economics* 80:190-207.

———— (1979). "The Product Cycle Hypothesis in a New International Environment." *Oxford Bulletin of Economics and Statistics* 41:255-268.

Watson, Craig M. (1982). "Counter Competition Abroad to Protect Home Markets." *Harvard Business Review* 60:40-42.

Wells, Louis T., Jr. (1972). *Product Life Cycle and International Trade.* Cambridge, MA: Harvard University Press.

Williamson, Oliver (1975). *Markets and Hierarchies.* New York: Free Press.

A THEORY OF THE OFFERING: TOWARD A NEO-INDUSTRIAL BUSINESS STRATEGY

Richard Normann and Rafael Ramirez

Services are no longer what they used to be. This is, in short, the lesson that recent developments in Western economies has taught us, for the massive growth in services has not taken place in the tertiary (service) sector of these economies. On the contrary, services are growing fastest in the secondary (production) sector, implying that whatever distinguished goods from services must be rethought.

In our view, the notion of neo-industrialism, characterized by a "service-intensive" industrial sector, is more likely to depict emerging business than the notion of postindustrialism that has dominated thinking over the last 20 years. The extent to which we believe this to be the case is evident in the fact that the invitation to write this chapter found us in the middle of the most comprehensive R&D project which the organization in which we work has undertaken since its inception. The project is designed to provide a new perspective of business theory and practice in this period of neo-industrialism, for it is clear that existing theories are unable to grasp, let alone manage, the complexity that is emerging.

Since we began in 1980 as consultants in service business management, it has become clear that the basic distinction between "services" and "goods" upon which our work was originally based is changing. The standard criteria used to distinguish the two kinds of economic activity are, as Gershuny and Miles (1983) showed, so problematic that calculating economic activity by sector figures entails making a large number of subjective and/or arbitrary choices. Even more importantly, our opinion is that the emerging pattern in business is making the sectoral distinction between goods and services irrelevant from a strategic point of view. This is so because what companies offer in the market in effect is made up of mixes (or systems made up) of both goods and services (see Figure 1).

In our view, examining business strategy in a way that takes the "offering" (a product-service-information mix defined by a given price) as the basic unit of analysis presents important advantages over existing theories that use the "firm" as their point of departure (e.g., Porter, 1985). The first advantage is that, precisely because the offering consists of different mixes of goods, services, and information, a theory using this concept should, in principle, hold for any kind of business. As Miller and Friesen (1986) have shown, this is something that Porter's (1980) framework fails to do.

A second advantage is that the theory of the offering we propose automatically takes into account the "new" assets that companies need to manage strategically in order to keep or obtain competitive advantage. These assets include know-how, information, and customer "access control"— assets that traditional theories either do not allow for or ignore.

A third advantage of the theory of the offering is that it provides an explanation as to why the distinction between services and goods is so difficult to assert, and simultaneously, it delimits the situations in which such a distinction is appropriate.

It is important to point out that the theory of the offering introduced in this chapter does not, in and of itself, constitute a strategic framework. The overall strategic framework of which it forms a part also includes an "ecological" framework that provides a systematic understanding of the industry (or industries) that make up the offering provider's context. The ecological framework includes dimensions of the business environment such as level of fragmentation, extent of regulation, stage of development, and so forth.

In this chapter, we limit ourselves to presenting the theory of the offering, which builds on and develops state-of-the-art service management theory and practice. The theory is largely focused on the relationship that the provider has with the buyer or consumer, which is the place where the sustained profitability of the business strategy is actualized. In the first section, we briefly discuss why the distinction between goods and services is becoming increasingly ambiguous. The second section derives the strategic implications of the neo-industrialist characteristic of seller-client

Figure 1. Typical Elements of a Product-Service Mix
from the Customer's Point of View

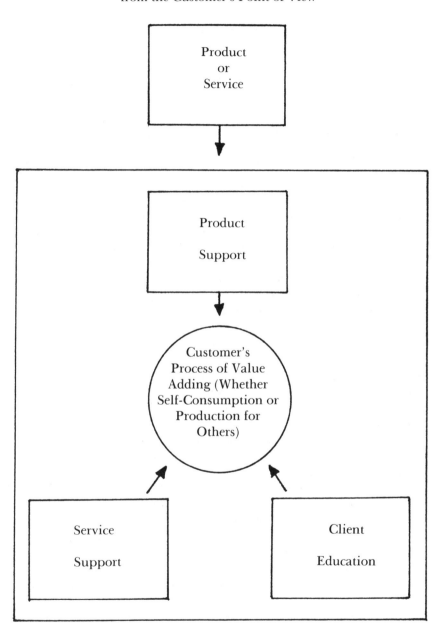

collaboration in the co-production of an offering. The third section presents three important dimensions along which an offering can be designed, and the fourth section introduces the "offering cube," a diagrammatic means of showing composite offerings. The final section presents some conclusions and suggestions for further research.

THE DISTINCTION BETWEEN GOODS AND SERVICES

The Service Management Group (SMG) originated in the service sector and indeed played a role in shaping the so-called "Service Wave" that Western economies have been riding in recent years (Normann, 1984). Yet, since 1983, when a brick company called one of our offices because it realized that its success depended on developing what came to be known as a "service-intensive" strategy, things have been changing a lot. The different mix of companies that are today seeking our services is only one of the many indicators of the changing nature of business. We believe that the changes are as fundamental as those which the Industrial Revolution brought about. For example, the then-revolutionary achievement of the ability to mass produce standardized goods is today matched by the newly-acquired capacity to mass produce nonstandardized goods.

Technological and other changes have resulted in many goods-production enterprises becoming more "service loaded" and many service companies being able to manage their services as goods. A few years ago, Normann (1984) noted some of the basic differences between manufacturing and service businesses (see Table 1). This table, which characterizes the "conventional wisdom" regarding the difference between service and nonservice companies as it was at the beginning of the 1980s, is useful to illustrate the extent of change which has occurred.

The first thing to note is that many of the characteristics attributed mainly to manufacturing businesses are becoming characteristic of services as well. For example, an increasing number of "services" can now be stored, largely due to innovative applications of microprocessing technology. Thus, an "expert system" in the French Minitel menu of offerings stores train reservation services that are available on (electronic) "tap" at any time. Also, it is now possible to spatially separate production and consumption in an increasing array of services. For example, some corporate head-offices occupying expensive Manhattan real estate have placed various clerical and bookkeeping services in cheaper suburban or offshore locations that are electronically (or optically) connected to the "consumer" in the head office. Finally, increasing numbers of services can now be "exported." For example, one of our clients "exports" home-based computer processing for underwriting operations abroad.

Table 1.   Basic Differences Between Manufacturing and Service Businesses

Manufacturing	Service
The product is generally concrete	The service is less tangible
Ownership is transferred when a purchase is made	Ownership is not generally transferred
The product can be resold	The service cannot be resold
The product can be demonstrated before purchase	The service cannot usually be effectively demonstrated (it does not exist before purchase)
The product can be stored by sellers and buyers	The service cannot be stored
Consumption is preceded by production	Production and consumption generally coincide
Production, selling and consumption are locally differentiated	Production, consumption, and often even selling are spatially united
The production can be transported	The service cannot be transported (though "producers" often can)
The seller produces	The buyer/client takes part directly in the production
Indirect contact is possible between company and client	In most cases direct contact is necessary
Can be exported	The service cannot normally be exported, but the service delivery system can

Source: Adapted from Normann (1984).

In a similar manner, an even larger number of manufacturing processes are acquiring "service" characteristics. At least two reasons account for this. The first reason, the arbitrariness of accounting practices, became particularly evident when "outsourcing" became common. It turned out that what was considered a *goods* production "cost" if done "in-house" became a "business to business" *service* when bought in the market. Thus, one of our colleagues calculated that a North Sea oil platform's cost was made up of between 55% to 67% worth of "services" (depending on the model and on accounting practices).

The second reason that much manufacturing is becoming more service-like is technological change. This characteristic is more complex and subtle, and has to do with the transformation of work that automated production involves. Thus, Hirschhorn (1984) pointed out that "line" operators in businesses such as steel rolling, who have traditionally been considered to be "goods" manufacturing personnel, become "service" providers when they oversee a battery of robots that do the "primary manufacturing tasks." Such "service" roles in goods manufacturing exemplify how the distinctions between service and manufacturing with which we are familiar are breaking down. No longer fitting either of the accepted definitions, the emerging pattern is a phenomenon of a fundamentally different nature that needs to be understood from an alternative point of view.

Much of the change, as noted, is due to the diffusion of microtechnology. But as Emery (1978) and others (Hirschhorn, 1984; Wiseman, 1985) have described, technological transformations have social and managerial implications, so the phenomenon is more properly portrayed as sociotechnical (Trist, 1981). New sociotechnical configurations call for a fundamental revision of the managerial assumptions, practices, and orientations left over from industrialism if they are to be effectively and profitably managed. This implies that the traditional management logic may have to be surpassed and the issue dealt with at the level of strategic choice.

STRATEGIC IMPLICATIONS OF NEO-INDUSTRIALISM

The service perspective developed by SMG contains the important lesson that, strategically, it is crucial to consider a company from the customer's point of view. Although traditional service management concepts are still valid, we have come to realize that the only difference between the "service" and the "nonservice" sector that really counts for the customer is the role (or roles) that the seller plays in helping customers to create value for themselves. This perspective effectively transforms the traditional definition of a client as a customer, for it leads one to consider clients not only as buyers but also, to a greater or lesser extent, as *co-producers* of their own value-producing activity. It is, of course, their interest in getting help to produce value that leads customers to sellers in the first place. However, the extent of value co-production that clients carry out may mean that customers are not only buyers and co-producers but potential *competitors* of the seller as well. This implies that the kind of management perspective that "services" calls for is also now relevant in nontertiary economic activities.

Apart from transforming a provider's relationship with its "market," this perspective has another, and perhaps more important, result. It is that the traditional distinction of a firm as being either a "services" or a "goods" producer depends at least as much on what it charges the client for as upon its production logic. Thus, from a *strategic* perspective, the traditional classification of companies into "goods" and "services" categories loses relevance. What *is* relevant is that the mix of things that a seller offers helps it clients to help themselves in ways that fulfill their expectations.

We thus paradoxically found out that developing the logic of the original service orientation led to dissolving the strategic relevance of the service-good classification. It provided for a strategic vision that is much more dependent upon managing a complex set of variables relating to the *client* than on defining and meeting predetermined operational objectives. In this sense, it fits with what Morgan (1982, 1983) termed a "cybernetic" corporate strategy—widening the array of options in order to avoid "noxious" areas of the environment. This is so because a client-oriented strategy in its ultimate form consists of enabling the client to choose from as many possible value-adding (or, more exactly, self-help-supporting) options as possible.

It is important to note that by emphasizing the "widening" dimension of the strategy we do not mean that an offering-producing system should go from providing a few things to either all or a few clients to providing all services to all clients. Being "client-oriented," which is here taken to mean very "business oriented," means offering as many services as possible to "core" clients. This means that the successful offering-producing system will tend to be one that has moved into the "B" quadrant of Table 2. Note that the idea of an "offering producing system" allows the strategy to be applicable not only to the single firm but also to systems of firms such as the "strategic alliances" that are now common in high-tech industries (Astley and Brahm, 1989) and the "syndicates" found in financial services (Venkatraman, 1989).

Four factors in the emerging sociotechnical reality support pursuing this suggested client-based strategy. First, clients—particularly if they are businesses—are increasingly better informed vis-à-vis sellers. Therefore, the seller can no longer base its relative advantage vis-à-vis the client on simply having superior information. Instead of relying on strategic notions such as "market differentiation" (e.g., Porter, 1985), sellers must establish a relationship of continuous mutual co-learning with their clients (Ramirez, 1983). Sellers collaborate with their clients in developing ever better "offerings" of products and services, allowing the relationship to adapt so that clients are continuously supported in helping themselves under different conditions.

Second, because of this co-learning process, the "commercial role" of the successful offering-providing system must be defined according to client perspectives and not on client-independent criteria of "what it does." Because of the capacity that each offerer has of putting a price on different items in its own way of relating to its clientele (in ways which are explored later), the classification of offering-producing activities based on any client-independent criteria will, as Gershuny and Miles (1983) showed, be subject to much error.

Third, the sociotechnical changes in the relationships among stakeholders transform not only the commercial roles of individual offering

Table 2.   Achieving A Successful Relationship
Between A Provider and Its Clients

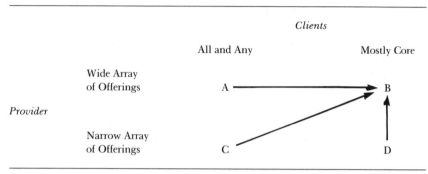

systems but also the "rules of the game" whereby sustained profitability is obtained. For example, because of the importance of meeting client expectations, firms are collaborating in new and unexpected ways. Competing fiercely in one situation, they will join forces in another to help their clients in ways that their respective competitors cannot match. An example is the collaboration between Siemens and Ericsson to produce mobile phones in Nordic countries while at the same time competing for telephone switching contracts elsewhere. (See Perlmutter and Heenan [1986] for a good overview of this phenomenon.)

Finally, the intensification of the "information content" of almost all business processes due to microprocessing technology implies that "new" assets need to be understood and managed. Two of these new assets are control over customer bases and control over access to the relationships among different customer bases. Dun and Bradstreet, for example, manages to treat wholesalers as information sources for retailers (a customer base) while at the same time using the knowledge it has from its relationships with retailers as a resource for providing value to wholesalers (which in effect is another customer base).

From this strategic perspective, the so-called "moment of truth" (Normann, 1978, 1984)—a physical and psychological meeting between a customer and an offering provider—becomes an element in a larger, more complex, continually evolving "process of truth." In such a process, the relationship between seller and buyer before and after the moment of truth establishes the long-term viability and sustainability of that relationship. This means that a lot of attention will have to be given to the "pre-core" and "post-core" moments of truth that make up the client's survival process. In the air transport business, for instance, this implies that a lot of attention must be given to what happens on the ground—as Jan Carlzon, the president of SAS and perhaps the most important figure in making the moment of truth concept extensively known, recently put it in describing his business during the 1990s.

THREE STRATEGIC DIMENSIONS OF AN OFFERING

According to established distinctions between "secondary" and "tertiary" commercial activity, the company that puts a large proportion of the price of its offering on the presale, sale, or postsale supporting activities by which a client uses something (anything!) to create value for itself is a "service" company. The company that does not put a large proportion of its overall pricing on these supporting activities is a "nonservice" company. Note that while there is a lot of discussion among theorists as to the extent of "goods-dependent" services vis-à-vis those which are not (e.g., Guinjoan, 1986), the fact of the matter is that all services (including nude massages!) require some sort of good in order to be delivered (the massage table). In the same way, all goods need some sort of service, including "self service" (Normann, 1984: Chapter 6), in order to be consumed. Thus, the traditional distinction does not rest, as it is often supposed, upon the activities of the companies but on their pricing strategies—and these, we have argued, in being tied to the clients' particularities, vary greatly even across the same offering range. In the remainder of this section, we identify three important dimensions of offerings that are made available in the market.

Depth

The *deepening-shallowing* dimension of an offering is the one along which the extent to which a company helps its clients to create value for themselves is determined. The "shallower" the offering, the more the company helps the client to be a co-producer; the "deeper" the offering, the less a company does in helping clients to do things for themselves (instead doing it for them). Thus, the strategy followed by the Swedish furniture company IKEA was one of "shallowing" its furniture offering by creating a system that relies heavily on customer self-service. As should be evident from this example, there is nothing negative about developing a "shallowing" relationship with the client through the offering; shallowing often is a successful way to adapt the offering in situations where self-help is attractive or acceptable for the relevant clientele.

By contrast, offerings in which complex or "tightly coupled" elements must be made to interact under carefully controlled conditions that are normally difficult to obtain, as is true for the production of steel alloys, may not permit "shallowing." This is also the case in situations where the capital/labor or know-how/labor ratios are high.

As a consequence, it can be seen that "depth" is positively correlated with doing things *for* clients, increasingly with client-defined specifications. "Shallowness," on the other hand, is positively correlated with managing a set of learning and support relations *with* clients.

Range

A second dimension to consider (always from the client's point of view) is the range of offerings that an offering provider is able and/or willing to make available to the client. The greater the range offered by a seller, the more products and services the client will be able to choose from it. This second dimension can be called the *broadening-narrowing* dimension. The greater the range, the "broader" the offering; the smaller the range, the "narrower" it is.

Choice

The breadth of the offering range is (from the client's perspective) not necessarily equivalent to the number of options provided by a seller. The number of options among which a client can choose given a fixed range (which in effect is a ratio of choices to range) is what the third and last dimension of the offering measures. We term this dimension the *bundling-unbundling* dimension. If there is a small number of options from which to choose, the offering is "bundled"; if there is a relatively large number of choices, the offering is "unbundled."

It should come as no surprise that the bundling dimension is closely related to how the offering is priced. In an unbundled offering, clients can freely choose which options they want, without being obliged to buy "A" if they only want "B" (e.g., choosing flavors at a Baskin and Robbins ice cream shop). An unbundled offering means that a price is attached to each item chosen, allowing clients not only to "tailor make" their choices but also implying that they will pay for each and every item chosen while not paying for what they do not want.

On the other hand, the same range of offerings can be available but bundled into packages. Thus, if you want "A," you can have it—but only with "B." Even if you do not want "B," you still pay for "A" *and* "B" in order to buy "A" only. An example would be a bank offering only checking-savings accounts. If you want only a savings account, you also get—and pay for—the unwanted checking account.

The bundling-unbundling (or choice) dimension, therefore, is not only a way of "packaging" the offerings but also a way of determining both market niche (Freeman and Hannan, 1983) and, importantly, pricing strategy (Normann and Haikola, 1985). The "leveraging" of one money-making item that may not sell well on its own with another that does, and pricing both together, is illustrative of this approach. An example is offering "free" car washes with a gas fill-up.

THE OFFERING CUBE

The three strategic dimensions—deepening-shallowing, broadening-narrowing, and bundling-unbundling—can be combined into one integrative framework that we call the *offering cube* (see Figure 2). In total, the offering cube allows for 26 possible ways of transforming the offering: 6 single changes (keeping two dimensions fixed), 12 dual changes (keeping one dimension fixed), and 8 triple changes (keeping no dimension fixed).

Fitting a change in the offering onto the cube from any one apex to any other apex depends on the competitive logic of the ecologic situation and on the particularities of the client or group of clients, for a "client-independent" move cannot be meaningfully mapped onto the cube. Thus, for example, if a mechanical engineering firm that has done work only on a turn-key (i.e., finished plant) basis decides to offer consulting services, it will be "shallowing" its offering for those clients that used to buy the turn-key projects and now do some of the work themselves; but it will be "broadening" for those that used to hire engineering consulting firms to install, operate, or maintain the turn-key plants they used to buy.

Figure 2.   The Offering Cube

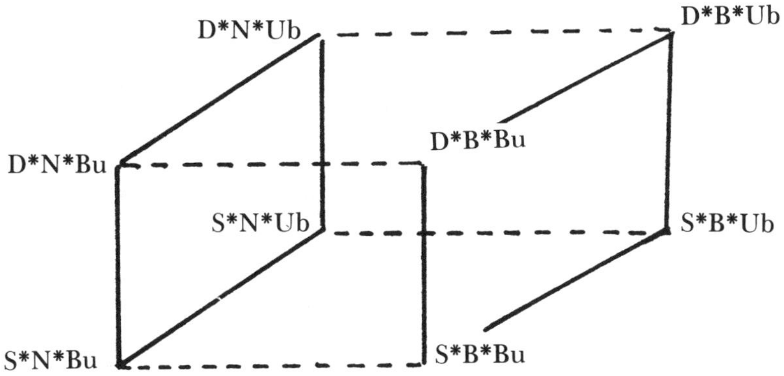

Code: S Shallowing   —   D Deepening
           N Narrowing   —   B Broadening
           Bu Bundling   —   Ub Unbundling

Table 3. The Twelve Possible Composite (Dual) Changes in the Offering Cube

	Strategic Dimension That Is Fixed	Change in Remaining Dimensions	Effect of Change on Clients	Examples of Applicable Business Situations
1.	Broadening-Narrowing (Range Unchanged)	Deepening and Bundling	Do more for client but with fewer options while range unchanged	Some options unprofitable but needed, profitable opportunity to do more for client without broadening range
2.	Broadening-Narrowing (Range Unchanged)	Deepening and Unbundling	Do more for client, more options, range unchanged	Little cross-option subsidization, difficult to broaden range yet profitable opportunity to do more for client
3.	Broadening-Narrowing (Range Unchanged)	Shallowing and Bundling	Do less for client, fewer options, range unchanged	Some options profitable, self-help movement strong, cannot broaden range
4.	Broadening-Narrowing (Range Unchanged)	Shallowing and Unbundling	Do less for client, more options, range unchanged	Little cross-option subsidization, strong self-help movement, cannot broaden range
5.	Bundling-Unbundling (Options Unchanged)	Deepening and Broadening	Do more for client, expand offerings, options unchanged	Clients have less time to consume but more money to spend, want to shop on least number of occasions
6.	Bundling-Unbundling (Options Unchanged)	Deepening and Narrowing	Do more for client, fewer offerings, options unchanged	Client demands more help on fewer things, client heterogeneity has not changed
7.	Bundling-Unbundling (Options Unchanged)	Shallowing and Broadening	Do less for client, expand offerings, options unchanged	Strong self-help movement and profitable opportunity in separate field (not "bundleable") or included in existing bundles

8.	Bundling-Unbundling (Options Unchanged)	Shallowing and Narrowing	Do less for client, fewer offerings, options unchanged	Strong self-help on fewer things, existing bundling attractive to change
9.	Deepening-Shallowing (Depth Unchanged)	Bundling and Broadening	Expand offerings, narrow options, depth unchanged	Profitable opportunities with high cross-option subsidization, need to organize clients into "clubs" to restrict access
10.	Deepening-Shallowing (Depth Unchanged)	Bundling and Narrowing	Narrow offerings and options, depth unchanged	Unprofitable offerings and high cross-option subsidization
11.	Deepening-Shallowing (Depth Unchanged)	Unbundling and Broadening	Expand offerings and options, depth unchanged	Profitable opportunities and little cross-option subsidization
12.	Deepening-Shallowing (Depth Unchanged)	Unbundling and Narrowing	Narrow offerings, expand options, depth unchanged	Unprofitable offerings but little cross-option subsidization

Note: "Triple" changes along the dimensions of the offering cube would involve the following 24 combinations of "dual" changes: 1 and 5; 1 and 6; 1 and 9; 2 and 5; 2 and 6; 2 and 11; 2 and 12; 3 and 7; 3 and 8; 3 and 9; 3 and 10; 4 and 7; 4 and 8; 4 and 11; 4 and 12; 5 and 9; 5 and 11; 6 and 10; 6 and 12; 7 and 9; 7 and 11; 8 and 10; and 8 and 12.

The following among these 24 possibilities are equivalent, leaving eight possible "triple" changes. They can be respectively denoted by the following eight letters (see text): 1 and 9, 1 and 5, and 5 and 9 (A); 6 and 10, 1 and 6, and 1 and 10 (B); 2 and 5, 5 and 11, and 2 and 11 (C); 2 and 6, 6 and 12, and 2 and 12 (D); 3 and 7, 7 and 9, and 3 and 9 (E); 3 and 10, and 8 and 3 and 10, and 8 and 10 (F); 4 and 7, 7 and 11, and 4 and 11 (G); and 4 and 8, 4 and 12, and 8 and 12 (H).

We believe that the way to make the offering cube an integral part of a strategic framework is to relate the 26 possibilities to the clientele situation and, more generally, to the ecologic state of the business environment. While we are developing a systematic way of doing this, as indicated at the end of the chapter, here we limit ourselves to outlining illustrative conditions presented at the right end of Table 3 (one strategic dimension is fixed while the other two can be changed). A supermarket in an urban area with a changing ethnic mix is used as the basis for these examples (the numbers below refer to the transformations shown in Table 3).

1. The store decides to provide a "free" home-delivery service for people who used to carry their groceries home. It thus offers to do more for clients, and the extra offering is bundled into the price of the core offering (groceries and other goods). Even if you want to carry the groceries home yourself, you must in effect pay for this service which would otherwise likely be a money loser on its own.

2. The store decides to offer an optional home-delivery service that involves paying a surcharge for it separately. It calculates that it will not lose money on this service and that it will help to keep clients. (This example applies only to those clients not engaging another seller, such as a taxi service, to get their groceries home.)

3. For this example to be realistic there needs to be at least three potentially separable parts in the original offering. Thus, the store might cut its previous home deliveries, but the parking lot, which used to involve a charge, is now free (i.e., its price is bundled into that of the core offering).

4. The store announces that it will discontinue its home-delivery service and will begin to charge for parking.

5. The store announces that it will offer a home-ordering service that comes with its existing home-delivery service.

6. The store will offer a home-ordering service to accompany its home-delivery service but will no longer offer kosher foods, because the Jewish people in the area are moving elsewhere and the proportion of the store's market which they now represent is so small that it is no longer profitable to cater to them.

7. The supermarket will no longer offer the home-ordering and delivery service but, on the other hand, it will now offer a store credit card.

8. The supermarket will no longer offer its home-ordering and delivery service, and, given the unprofitability of the kosher food segment, it will no longer offer these foods.

Table 4. "Triple" Changes Using the Offering Cube

Type of Strategic Change	From	To
A	shallow-narrow-unbundled	deep-broad-bundled
B	shallow-broad-unbundled	deep-narrow-bundled
C	shallow-narrow-bundled	deep-broad-unbundled
D	shallow-broad-bundled	deep-narrow-unbundled
E	deep-narrow-unbundled	shallow-broad-bundled
F	deep-broad-unbundled	shallow-narrow-bundled
G	deep-narrow-bundled	shallow-broad-unbundled
H	deep-broad-bundled	shallow-narrow-unbundled

9. The store, which up to now has not had a parking lot, opens a new one, and it is "free" (i.e., the price is including in the core offering). Perhaps it is "free" only for those buying more than a minimum quantity at a time or per month.
10. The store decides to make its existing parking lot "free" (i.e., clients pay for it in paying for the core offering whether they use it or not) and decides to get rid of kosher foods for the reasons stated above.
11. The store, which up to now has not had one nearby, decides to open a parking lot for those who want to pay for it.
12. The store, which has had a "free" parking lot, decides that it will make those customers who want to use it pay for it (they will use it anyway) and will simultaneously cut its kosher food line.

Table 4 lists the eight "triple" changes factored out at the bottom of Table 3. As seen, these changes involve modifications along each of the strategic dimensions simultaneously (or going from one apex to its opposite one in the offering cube). Thus, for example, the conditions in which an "F"-type change (shallowing, narrowing, and bundling) would be recommended are those in which it was decided that the clientele would find it attractive to do more of the value-adding production by itself (shallowing); where some of the parts of the offering on their own have so little demand that they are not worth providing (narrowing); and that yet other options, while not profitable on their own, need to be provided as part of the total package in order for this one to be more attractive (bundling). In the supermarket example, it would mean something like doing away with both the home delivery (shallowing) and the kosher foods (narrowing) but making the parking free (bundling).

CONCLUSIONS AND SUGGESTIONS FOR FURTHER RESEARCH

In our consulting-based research, we have seen how the foregoing analysis of the offering can be used as a way of thinking through the problems that firms and systems of firms face in running their businesses. While the concept of the offering is in principle applicable to all kinds of businesses, further empirical research will be needed to more precisely determine the extent to which this is so.

Our current research (the beginning of which is reported in Normann and Haikola, 1985; see also Normann, 1977) focuses on the development of the ecologic framework that complements the offering framework and encompasses factors such as industry fragmentation, regulation, and maturity. The fitting together of both frameworks provides not only a set of strategic options but also the basis for redefining the offering-producing system's most desirable boundaries. Basing the definition of the producing system's boundaries upon the overall effectiveness of the co-producing relationship with clients is a promising basis, we believe, for a critical and constructive reexamination of the theory of the firm (Normann and Ramirez, 1988).

An interesting research direction that we are currently pursuing with our colleagues at SMG is developing methods to quantify the "deepening-shallowing" and the "bundling-unbundling" dimensions (the third one being easier to measure). Of course, upon having developed quantification techniques, historical analysis of the framework will be made possible. This research will permit us to better correlate different mixes of strategic options with the profitability and other characteristics of business actors and their environments, allowing us to identify under what conditions and in what domains different aspects of both frameworks are of greatest value.

It may be that the problem of generalizability will present itself not in terms of kinds of companies but in terms of international situations. The fact that the theory of the offering has emerged from our observations of mostly European contexts should be taken into account when applied to other situations. We have found, for example, that many of the "leading edge" theories of strategy and management coming out of U.S. situations are not adaptable to European companies, and thus it is fair to assume that the converse could also be the case.

In closing, it can be said that the transformation of sociotechnical systems that is occurring during the neo-industrialist period requires a concomitant transformation of business theory. As advisers to the senior managers of some of Europe's most sophisticated companies, we have come to learn that the development of new business practices poses a challenge to those whose task it is to design or even describe, understand, or evaluate these practices.

We hope the offering framework introduced here is a helpful step in meeting this challenge.

ACKNOWLEDGMENTS

We would like to acknowledge the help of many of our colleagues at the Service Management Group in developing the concepts discussed in this chapter. The Service Management Group was founded in 1980, consists of a group of companies with offices in eight countries, and provides strategy consulting to top managers of service-intensive organizations.

REFERENCES

Astley, W. Graham, and Richard A. Brahm (1989). "Organizational Designs for Post-Industrial Strategies: The Role of Interorganizational Collaboration." In Charles C. Snow (ed.), *Strategy, Organization Design, and Human Resource Management.* Greenwich, CT: JAI Press, pp. 233-270.

Emery, Fred E. (1978). "The Assembly Line: Its Logic and Our Future." In William A. Passmore and John J. Sherwood (eds.), *Sociotechnical Systems: A Sourcebook.* La Jolla, CA: University Associates, pp. 339-347.

Freeman, John H., and Michael T. Hannan (1983). "Niche Width and the Dynamics of Organizational Populations." *American Journal of Sociology* 89:1116-1145.

Gershuny, Jonathan and Ian Miles (1983). *The New Service Economy: The Transformation of Employment in Industrial Societies.* London: Frances Pinter.

Guinjoan, Modest (1986). Los Servicios en la Economia Espanola. Doctoral Dissertation, Escuela Superior de Administracion y Direccion de Empresas, Barcelona, Spain.

Hirschhorn, Lawrence (1984). *Beyond Mechanization.* Cambridge, MA: MIT Press.

Miller, Danny, and Peter H. Friesen (1986). "Porter's (1980) Generic Strategy and Performance: An Empirical Examination With American Data (Part 2: Performance Implications)." *Organization Studies* 7:255-262.

Normann, Richard (1977). *Management for Growth.* London: Wiley.

_____ (1978). "Kritiska Factorer Vid Ledning av Serviceforetab." In J. Arndt and A. Friman (eds.), *Legning, Produktion, and Marknadsforing av Tjanster.* Stockholm: Liber. (Taken from "Utvecklingsstrategier for Svenskt Service Kunnade," SIAR, 1978.)

_____ (1984). *Service Management: Strategy and Leadership in Service Businesses.* London: Wiley.

Normann, Richard, and Bengt Haikola (1985). Winning Strategies in Financial Services: A Multi-Client Report. Working Paper. The Service Management Group.

Normann, Richard, and Rafael Ramirez (1988). Business Logics for Innovators: A Multi-client Report. Working Paper. The Service Management Group.

Morgan, Gareth (1982). "Cybernetics and Organization Theory: Epistemology or Technique?" *Human Relations* 35:521-538.

_____ (1983). "Rethinking Corporate Strategy: A Cybernetic Perspective." *Human Relations* 36:345-360.

Perlmutter, Howard V., and David K. Heenan (1986). "Cooperate to Compete Globally." *Harvard Business Review* 64:136-152.

Porter, Michael E. (1980). *Competitive Strategy.* New York: The Free Press.

_____ (1985). *Competitive Advantage.* New York: The Free Press.

Ramirez, Rafael (1983). "Action Learning: A Strategic Approach for Organizations Facing Turbulent Conditions." *Human Relations* 36:725-742.

Trist, Eric L. (1981). "The Evolution of Sociotechnical Systems as a Conceptual Framework and as an Action Research Program." In Andrew H. Van de Ven and William F. Joyce (eds.), *Perspectives on Organization Design and Behavior.* New York: Wiley, pp. 19-75.

Wiseman, Charles (1985). *Strategy and Computers.* New York: Dow Jones-Irwin.

Venkatraman, N. (1989). "Strategic Management and Information Technology: Evolutionary Linkages and a Research Framework." In Charles C. Snow (ed.), *Strategy, Organization Design, and Human Resource Management.* Greenwich, CT: JAI Press, pp. 131-159.

PART II

ORGANIZATION DESIGN

STRATEGIC MANAGEMENT AND INFORMATION TECHNOLOGY:
EVOLUTIONARY LINKAGES AND
A RESEARCH FRAMEWORK

N. Venkatraman

Over the years, information technology (or, more simply, IT[1]) and its impact on various facets of the economy has been a subject of considerable speculation and discussion but relatively little research. Recently, however, management professionals, as well as academic researchers from a wide variety of disciplines (e.g., computer science, communications technology, sociology, psychology, history, communications, and management) are increasingly focusing their attention on this rather general subject. Futurists have painted interesting but perhaps scary scenarios of the information society in the twenty-first century (e.g., Naisbitt, 1982). Others have contrasted the emergence of the information age with that of the industrial age (e.g., Strassman, 1985). Still others have called IT the most significant force yet in the transformation of society. The following quote from Diebold is particularly telling:

> Information technology . . . is becoming increasingly the key to national economic well being, affecting virtually every industry and service. One would be hard pressed to name

a business that does not depend on the effective use of information: to design products and services, to track and respond to market demands, or to make well-informed decisions. Information technology will change the world more permanently and more profoundly than any technology so far seen in history and will bring about a transformation of civilization to match (1984, p. 10).

Even if one does not subscribe to these rather extreme views, it is necessary to recognize that information technology is currently a major force that has the potential to affect a range of organizations in fundamental ways. For example, the impact of information technology on how work is performed at different levels of the organization, and its influence on organization structure, management process, and labor force displacement, have been of concern to many observers. Similarly, several striking examples of strategic advantages realized through innovative uses of information technology capabilities call attention to the critical linkage between strategic management and information technology (*Business Week*, 1985, 1986; Wiseman, 1985; Keen, 1986).

This chapter is primarily concerned with the likely impact of various information technologies on theory, research, and practice of strategic management. The reason for adopting such a perspective reflects a fundamental belief that information technologies have the potential to influence the core of a firm's activities: choices pertaining to products, markets, and technologies (the corporate strategy level) as well as competitive methods within each of the product-market segments (the business strategy level). Since strategic management as a research discipline is concerned with the general management task of organization-environment alignment and arrangement (Andrews, 1980; Bourgeois, 1980; Snow and Miles, 1983), the impact of information technologies on the organization can best be analyzed from the vantage point of strategic management rather than from one of the operating functions such as the management information system, marketing, or production. In addition, from a practitioner's perspective, we agree with Porter and Millar's view: "The management of information technology can no longer be the sole province of the EDP department . . . general managers must be involved to ensure that cross-functional linkages, more possible to achieve with information technology, are exploited" (1985, p. 159).

At the outset, it should be noted that the available literature on the interrelationships between strategic management and information technology is not extensive. Indeed, the literature base is barely five years old, consisting mostly of anecdotes, normative frameworks that presumably aid in exploiting IT-based advantages, and widely scattered speculative writings. The purpose of the chapter, therefore, is to begin to integrate these views and findings in order to develop a set of research issues that reflect important strategic management concerns—both from a theoretical and a managerial perspective. The hope is that the chapter will serve as a launchpad for systematic research efforts aimed at incorporating emerging IT issues into the strategic management literature.

The chapter is divided into two major sections. In the first section, the emerging interrelationships between strategic management and information technology are examined using a set of three linkages that have evolved over a period of time. Initial steps toward the development of a research framework are taken in the second section with specific attention devoted to four research themes and their corresponding methodological problems.

THE RELATIONSHIP BETWEEN STRATEGIC MANAGEMENT AND INFORMATION TECHNOLOGY: THREE LINKAGES

This section provides the necessary background to conceptualize the relationship between strategic management and various information technologies. The discussion is organized around three linkages that connect three important dimensions: strategic management, information technology, and the management information systems (MIS) function. The last dimension is critical both from a historical point of view (IT was traditionally viewed as belonging to the MIS function) as well as an organizational point of view (to discuss changing roles and responsibilities). The linkages are diagrammatically represented in Figure 1, with the numbering scheme reflecting the chronological evolution of the linkages.

Link 1: *Management Information System <—> Information Technology*

This link is best understood against the backdrop of the classical role of the management information system. According to the traditional view, MIS is a service function (just as accounting, human resources, industrial relations, or legal), and it is charged with the administration of the management reporting and control systems as well as the efficient processing of relevant data. This is exemplified by numerous definitions found in the MIS literature. For example, MIS has been defined as "a set of facilities and personnel for collecting, sorting, retrieving, and processing information which is used, or desired, by one or more managers in the performance of their duties" (Ein-Dor and Segev, 1978, p. 1631) or as "a computer-based organizational information system which provides information support for management activities and functions" (Ives et al., 1980, p. 910). According to such definitions, MIS systems are designed to cater to the informational requirements of different managerial roles, and they are evaluated using

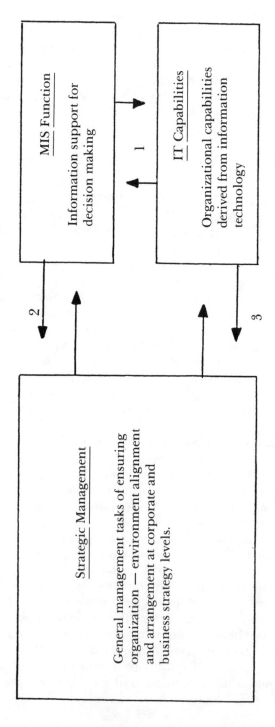

Figure 1. The Relationship Between Strategic Management and Information Technology: Three Linkages

criteria such as timeliness, format quality, and reliability (Gallagher, 1974). The traditional view emphasized the *technical capability* of the MIS system, and information technology was largely conceived as the "technical core" of the MIS function.

Consequently, the important characteristics of this linkage are: (1) hardware and software support for information dissemination for decision making, and (2) flexibility of design to facilitate modifications in information requirements or to respond to the fast-changing technical core of the system's hardware. MIS was generally seen as a collection of subsystems for specific decision areas such as payroll accounting, cost accounting, inventory control, financial accounting, and traditional management control (variance-reporting) systems. Thus, in terms of Anthony's (1965) levels of management activities—strategic planning, management planning and control, and operational planning and control—MIS mostly supported the third level and, to some extent, the second level. The strategic planning level, by virtue of its unstructured decision making, received minimal support from the traditional conceptualizations and role definitions of MIS.

Consequently, MIS designers and managers were essentially concerned with managing this link from an efficiency perspective: developing the best possible configurations and operations of the system given the level of resources allocated. Success was usually measured in terms of cost-savings directly attributable to the system. In sum, the traditional view of MIS suggested that it was "a service function that is periodically turned on and off as needed, much as the hot water and air-conditioning are turned on and off as needed" (King, 1983, p. iii).

Link 2: Strategic Management <—> Management Information System

The description of Link 1 reflects the view that the charter of the MIS function was derived directly from operational information needs and had no explicit connection with strategic choices at corporate and business levels. This was largely the case until the late 1960s and early 1970s when the belief that MIS needed to be tailored to the organization's strategy gained currency. In 1968, McKinsey and Co. published a report, *Unlocking the Computer's Profit Potential,* that called for a formal link between the design and implementation of MIS and the firm's strategies and objectives. This report urged managers to visualize computers in business organizations as something more than a data-processing tool at the operational level of the organization. The MIS ought to support business and corporate strategy as well (Kriebel, 1968; Zani, 1970).

King (1978) proposed that the link between strategic management and information systems be composed of an "information system strategy set" (information system objectives, constraints, and design strategies) that is derived from the "organization's strategy set" (mission, objectives, and strategies). This type of arrangement has been used in IBM's Business System Planning which involves a four-stage sequence as follows: (1) definition of business objectives, (2) definition of business processes and activities, (3) definition of data requirements, and (4) definition of the information architecture. These four stages reflect a fundamental belief that information systems should support the goals and objectives of the business and that BSP should be viewed as a vehicle for translating business strategy information needs into an MIS (for a detailed description of this methodology, see International Business Machines Corporation, 1981).

The importance of systematic linkages between strategic planning and MIS planning is underlined by preliminary empirical support. For example, Pyburn's (1983) study of MIS planning practices, despite its small sample size, established the criticality of the link between MIS planning and the firm's corporate strategy. Broader support for this relationship was provided by Venkatraman and Raghunathan (1986) in a large-sample study of the MIS planning practices of over 300 leading U.S. corporations. Specifically, they found that a strong linkage between MIS planning and business planning was an important determinant of overall MIS planning effectiveness.

Transformation of the Role. Although there is awareness within the MIS discipline that a management information system should be designed in accordance with a firm's strategy, a similar awareness does not exist among strategy researchers. Attention to characteristics of management information systems in strategy research is still a rarity. This can be understood by focusing on the widely-shared conceptualization of the strategy hierarchy: corporate, business, and functional. These levels are formally linked through planning and control systems (Lorange and Vancil, 1977; Camillus and Grant, 1980), and functional strategies are derived from the "higher-level" strategies. Hofer and Schendel's view is typical of this position: [A]t the functional area level, the principal focus of strategy is on the maximization of the resource productivity . . . (and) functional area strategy (is) to be constrained by business strategy, and is, in turn, to be constrained by corporate strategy" (1978, p. 29).

Thus, MIS strategies flow from business and/or corporate strategies, and since functional strategies typically do not attract much attention from strategic management researchers, consideration of information systems in strategic management research has been limited. This is a bit curious, however, since there also is widespread agreement that strategic choices require a systematic analysis of organizational strengths and weaknesses, presumably including the MIS function.

In recent years, there has been a growing belief that a business's functional areas should possess a strategic as well as operating perspective. In this emerging tradition, key themes include: "strategic marketing management" in which marketing activities are more closely tied to business planning (Wind and Robertson, 1983); "strategic human resource management" whereby human resource planning is woven into the early stages of strategy formulation (Fombrun et al., 1983); and the notion of "manufacturing as a competitive weapon" which illustrates potential sources of strategic advantage that lie within the production function (Wheelwright, 1984).

Similarly, several authors have called attention to the possibility of using information systems to gain strategic advantage (e.g., Benjamin et al., 1984; Ives and Learmonth, 1984; McFarlan, 1984; Rockart and Scott-Morton, 1984; Wiseman, 1985). As King noted in an editorial comment in the *Management Information Systems Quarterly*, "Information (and IS) has the potential to be a primary source of comparative advantage in the marketplace rather than merely as a resource to be efficiently managed or a service that is periodically turned on and off as needed" (1983, pp. iii-iv). Thus, today the link between strategic management and MIS is becoming bi-directional, with a "strategic" role for the MIS function.

Strategic Information Systems. In making a transition towards a strategic role, the goals and tasks of the management information systems function undergo an important transformation. The MIS system is no longer viewed in terms of informational support for operational decisions but rather as a means of realizing organizational objectives, especially the achievement of competitive superiority in the marketplace. Accordingly, information systems whose character is to achieve competitive superiority are termed "strategic information systems" (Ives and Learmonth, 1984; Wiseman, 1985), and these are differentiated from more operationally-focused MIS. Strategic information systems are designed to support relatively unstructured decision processes, especially those that are intricately tied to the activities of the marketplace. Usually such decisions require a combination of internal and external data that are neither obvious nor completely specified. Although a perfect demarcation between management information systems and strategic information systems can seldom be made, the conceptual distinction is important for management practice just as is the conceptual distinction between strategic and operational decisions.

Anecdotal evidence and trade publications indicate that the number and diversity of strategic information systems are on the increase. This is not an appropriate forum to discuss each of these systems individually, but a partial listing of such systems with their corresponding benefits (in terms of strategic advantage) is provided in Table 1.

Table 1.   A Partial List of Well-Known Strategic Information Systems

Firm	Description	Ascribed Benefits
American Airlines	SABRE Reservation System— installed in over 11,000 travel agencies for booking airline, hotel, and rental car reservations	Provides American Airlines with critical operating data that can be used for strategic decisions; travel agents hooked on to SABRE are likely to book on American more than other airlines
American Hospital Supply Company	ASAP-order entry system— installed in over 4,500 medical establishments to order supplies on-line. The system is internally connected to several supporting systems	Streamlined order-processing operations; captive customers who are likely to place orders through ASAP rather than with competitors
Bancone Corporation	Several systems that support strategies for electronic banking services	Helped Bancone to differentiate in a fiercely competitive marketplace and perform well
Citicorp	Extensive use of automated teller machines and global transaction network	Streamlined operations; supported Citicorp's strategy for global banking
McKesson Corporation	Economost—order entry system that supports customers with inventory control and analysis of sales	Fully integrated system that allows McKesson to be an efficient low-cost producer in a fiercely competitive industry
United Airlines	APOLLO—Travel agency reservation system with several augmented services installed in about 7,000 agencies	Broadly similar benefits as SABRE provides to American (with additional revenues because of augmented services)

Strategic information systems achieve their objectives largely through the following: (1) reconfiguration of the information flows within an organization to provide comparative advantages relative to competition, and/or (2) development of interorganizational systems that extend beyond the traditional boundaries of a single organization. These modes are not mutually exclusive but are discussed independently below using illustrative examples.

Reconfiguration of Information Flows. Consider the case of an airline that uses timely data to increase its load factor, perhaps the single most critical factor for achieving success in the airline industry. By developing a strategic information system that is designed not only to continually collect data on flight bookings, but also to compare current sales against historical patterns, the airline can recommend to its own ticketing agents (as well as travel agents) to shrink or expand the number of discount seats available on a particular flight depending on the current level of advance bookings. Similar benefits can accrue to a hotel where a key determinant of competitive performance is the occupancy ratio. Using a system that provides data on current occupancy, historical patterns, and anticipated bookings, pricing levels can be modified and communicated to travel agents to derive additional bookings through tour-packages. In both these cases, the "perishability" of the service makes the "timeliness" of information (in addition to its accuracy and reliability) a critical determinant for achieving success in the marketplace. Indeed, one can generalize this mode of achieving comparative advantage to any service which has perishable inventory and which can be sold at prices close to marginal cost.

The basic notion of timeliness of information can be extended from the context of the service sector to the manufacturing sector. Consider the case of an oil company which is able to communicate with its dealers directly and instantaneously as oil prices change to ensure that there is minimum delay in the setting of prices at headquarters and the adjustment of prices at diverse retail outlets. While the concept may appear to be intuitively obvious and simple, the advantage realized can be better understood by comparing this way of communication to the traditional system—that headquarters communicate prices to regional offices, which in turn pass on the information to sales representatives and finally to the outlets.

Yet another illustration of this scheme is seen in the case of a large company that linked its field sales units to its main office through an "electronic bulletin board" so that updated information inventory, price changes, and schedules could be obtained to support sales calls.

These illustrations share one common theme: it is that information technologies did *not* influence fundamental strategic choices. However, the implementation of such decisions through organizational hierarchy and channels is facilitated through the use of IT, leading to improved strategic results. Indeed, such examples reinforce the importance of strategy implementation by highlighting the possibilities opened up by recent developments in information technology.

A question that arises at this stage is: Why should such a system provide any source of strategic advantage in the marketplace? The answer perhaps lies in the *differential capability* of firms to reconfigure their information flows to obtain an additional (favorable) degree of freedom in the competitive game. It is well accepted that a "me-too" strategy is unlikely to yield any sustainable long-term advantages. As Rumelt argued, "a strategy that does not either create or exploit an asymmetry consitituing an advantage must be rejected" (1979, p. 205). Since informational asymmetries (relative to other players) can be deliberately created using strategic information systems, they are potential sources of comparative advantage in the marketplace. All the examples discussed (airlines, hotels, oil companies, etc.) can be understood in terms of the differential capability to reduce information "float" or "lag" (through the design of the strategic information system) and translate informational advantages into market advantages.

Interorganizational Systems. The discussion thus far has shown that informational efficiency achieved through system reconfiguration can provide comparative advantages in the marketplace for a single organization. This may not be anything new except that it is now possible to design and deploy such innovative systems less expensively than ever before because of the rapid decline in the cost of computing and communication. By contrast, interorganizational strategic information systems have the potential to achieve competitive success by exploiting different types of information-based links with many diverse actors in the marketplace.

In simple terms, an interorganizational strategic information system can be thought of as an "electronic marketplace." The potential to develop interorganizational links, and consequent competitive advantages, is perhaps the single most important reason for the increased attention to informational systems in the strategic management literature. Recent theory and research have addressed interorganizational systems (Barrett and Konsynski, 1982; Cash and Konsynski, 1985), the emergence of "electronic markets" (Malone et al., 1986), and a new organization form called the "dynamic network" (Miles and Snow, 1986).

One can conceptualize and discuss the role of interorganizational systems at two different levels. For example, if one is interested in the functioning of "electronic marketplaces" (rather than on any particular player), then the focus will be on understanding the diversity and density of communication flows across different sets of organizations as well as the relative power or benefits that accrue to different actors through their differential use of information technologies in the marketplace. This is analogous to the well-known "industry analysis" using industrial organization economics concepts (e.g., Porter, 1980). On the other hand, if the focus is on a particular organization to investigate how information systems achieve competitive superiority, it is necessary to examine the various links that the organization has with the electronic marketplace. The latter perspective is more pertinent for a strategy researcher and hence is adopted here.

Using this perspective, a focal organization can be conceptualized as having links to other organizations in the general environment (suppliers, buyers, competitors, stakeholders such as financial institutions, unions, and so forth). In a more restricted sense, the focal organization can be conceptualized in relation to its suppliers (input) and buyers (output) as a value-delivering system. Traditionally, the focal firm has maintained communication links with its buyers and suppliers using media such as the telephone, telex, and postal service. But, due to the increase in computing and communication capabilities and the reduction in their cost, several firms have found it attractive to develop electronic links with their key suppliers and/or buyers. A relevant question from a strategy perspective becomes: Do these electronic links merely improve efficiency (due to reduction in errors and the substitution of machines for people), or do they provide an additional set of mechanisms for achieving competitive advantages in the marketplace?

The expected benefits from the design and use of such a strategic information system can be understood through the case of American Hospital Supply Corporation (AHSC). Its Automated System for Analytical Purchasing, deployed in 1976, is often cited to illustrate the potential for achieving competitive advantage in the marketplace. The reason for the popularity of this system is that when it was designed, the general view was that information systems could be used only to improve operational decision making. AHSC extended its use of an information system to achieve strategic advantages as well.

AHSC manufactures and distributes health care products to hospitals, laboratories, and medical specialists. Given the increasing cost of processing customer orders, the company considered the use of dedicated electronic terminals at the location of its major customers. The introduction of electronic terminals can be visualized at one level as substituting fixed costs (electronic terminals) for variable costs (operators who manually process orders), with the primary benefit accruing from the high volume of transactions. If this were the case, AHSC's system serves mainly to illustrate the operational efficiency of the transaction-processing tasks. But, an added strategic benefit developed (which incidentally the company had not foreseen)—namely, that hospitals where the terminals had been installed were virtually locked into AHSC's purchasing system. Customers found it easier to send their order through these terminals than to choose the relatively inefficient option of using the telephone-ordering systems of competitors. By 1984, over 4,500 customers were electronically linked into the AHSC system, and they could order any of over 100,000 products. It is widely accepted that this system has provided American Hospital Supply Corporation with a formidable advantage in the competitive health care business.

This system not only provided operational efficiency for American Hospital Supply Corporation, it also allowed AHSC to differentiate its services from those of competitors. AHSC is able to guarantee better service (reliable delivery and confirmation of orders after ascertaining stock availability), and the system serves as a barrier against the possibility of customers switching to competitors because of the initial investment in training employees how to use the system.

Has this information system improved AHSC's performance? The benefits must be measured in terms of increased market share since profits attributable to this specific innovation are not known. Specifically, it was found that (1) hospitals linked to the system were more likely to buy from AHSC than from its competitors, (2) the average hospital purchase order in this system averaged 5.8 items compared to the industry average of 1.7 items per order, and (3) revenues during 1978-1980 were as much as three times more than the corresponding three-year period prior to the introduction of the system (*Business Week,* September 8, 1980). And, during 1981-1986, the company doubled the installation of the system in its client locations, and there was a steady increase in the proportion of total sales received through the system versus traditional channels.

Another illustration of a strategic information system is airline reservation systems, where the customer is the travel agent and the airlines are the service providers.[2] During the period of airline regulation, when ticket price was not a primary differentiating factor, travel agents played a key role in influencing travelers' choices. Within this context, American Airlines introduced its SABRE reservation system that is installed on travel agents' desks to assist them in the ticketing process. Although this system displayed nearly all flights, it gave priority to American flights by displaying them first on the terminal. It is estimated that between 70-90% of airline bookings are made from the first set of flights shown on the screen, and more than 50% are made from the first line shown on the screen. While some have questioned this practice as a violation of fair trade,[3] others consider this to be a significant strategic move that has parallels with the American Hospital Supply system. American Airlines maintained that any built-in "bias" in the display of flight schedules over that of its competitors was justified given the level of investment (over $300 million) the firm committed to this venture.

The SABRE system helped American Airlines in its relative market position in the airline industry. Although exact data are not available, it is widely acknowledged that the proportion of tickets booked through the SABRE system was much higher for American Airlines flights than for any other airline whose schedules were also displayed by the system. Similar patterns can be observed with United Airlines' APOLLO system in which travel agents linked through this system booked more flights on United than any other airline. Not only did these airlines benefit from this type of system ahead of their competitors in an era of regulation, but they had a significant head-start on the competition when the industry was deregulated. This is because their information systems provided them with critical market data on travelers that could be used for strategic decisions pertaining to pricing and promotional packages.

Realizing the strategic importance of such a system, several other airlines developed and even tested their own versions before deciding that it would be difficult to compete against SABRE and APOLLO. In recent years, American Airlines has forged ahead with its commitment to exploit its system for competitive advantage. For example, it has announced a personal-computer-version of the reservation system that enables travelers to book flights directly rather than use travel agents. Indeed, automation of the ticketing process through personal computers, as well as the use of automated ticketing machines at airports, could seriously transform the basis of competition in the airline industry in the next decade and threaten the existence of the current network of travel agencies.

Similar interpretations can be made for the other information systems summarized in Table 1. The common underlying theme in the successful use of these systems appears to be that one pioneering organization develops and deploys a strategic information system with an intent to create favorable asymmetries in the marketplace. Such systems—either confined to the boundaries of a single organization or more often extended beyond a single organization—usually provide the pioneering organization with significant operating (efficiency-related) benefits as well as strategic (marketplace or competitive) advantages. While it is premature to predict the long-term benefits from such systems (especially in view of the possible standardization of system configurations which may offset firm-specific advantages), early indications clearly support the realization of short-term benefits by pioneering organizations.

It is necessary at this point to recognize that the discussion thus far has been limited to those strategic management issues that do not involve significant changes in a firm's product-market scope. Indeed, the aforementioned examples serve to illustrate the role that strategic information systems play in developing and implementing business (competitive) strategies rather than any role they may play at the corporate level (i.e., choice of businesses to pursue). However, information technologies and information systems can play an important role in corporate strategy, too, which is discussed next as the third link.

Link 3: Strategic Management <—> Information Technology

Peter Keen was one of the first to call attention to the direct link between information technology and strategy. He noted: "As yet there is no field entitled 'telecommunications and business policy.' Discussions on the impact of communications technology usually focus on hardware, public policy, and regulation, or on specific applications such as office automation, teleconferencing, and electronic banking" (1981, p. 54). Since this statement was made, however, several new and powerful forces in the technological and market environment compel one to recognize the link between strategic management and information technology in terms of the fundamental role played by IT in influencing the formulation of a firm's strategy rather than merely supporting its implementation.

"IT Push" versus "Business Pull." The radical transformation of the strategy-IT link can be viewed as a combination of two concurrent (and perhaps equally powerful) forces, referred to here as "technology push" and "business pull." The characteristics of the first force are fairly well understood. Over the years, rapid advances in and the convergence of related technologies have resulted in continuous improvements in the sophistication and price-performance ratio of information technologies. These developments now make it possible for companies to utilize IT-based applications at a fraction of the cost that would have prevailed just a few years ago. Figure 2 illustrates some basic data to support the point that cost trends in computation (cost per million transactions per second) and communication have been steadily declining, while the annual cost of manual information processing has been on the increase.

The nature of the second force, "business pull," can be explicated by focusing on the degree of competitiveness in various markets. Managers are constantly looking for ways to compete in today's fast-changing and complex marketplace. The potential for innovative ways of competing, as well as new products and services made possible through information technology, provides managers with an entirely different spectrum of opportunities and threats. Given the general explosion of computing power and communications capabilities (e.g., integrated voice and data), several new business applications can be (and have been) developed that directly enhance efficiency and effectiveness in the marketplace.

Over the last five years, several normative frameworks have been proposed to enable managers to conceptualize and exploit information technology for strategic advantage. For example, Parsons (1983) highlighted this relationship using Porter's (1980) competitive forces and generic strategies. Benjamin et al. (1984) discussed the strategic opportunities presented by IT using two basic dimensions: domain of change (competitive versus internal operations) and domain of influence (structural change versus traditional products and services). The four cells of the two-dimensional matrix thus generated imply differences not only in terms of the nature of opportunities but also in terms of the modes available for exploiting them. Wiseman (1985)

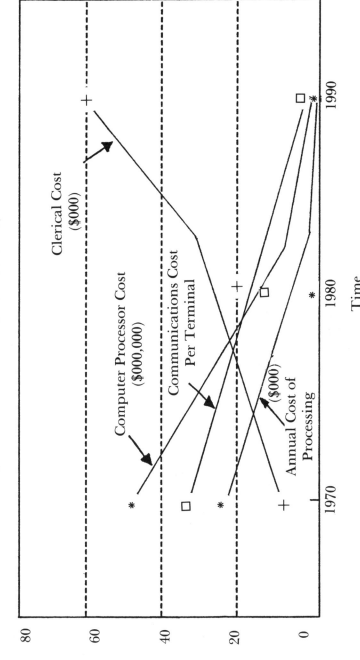

Figure 2. Cost—Performance Trends
(Processor and Communication Economics)

Source: Robert I. Benjamin (1982), "Information Technology in the 1990s: A Long Range Planning Scenario." *MIS Quarterly,* 6: 11-32.

proposed an options generator using four basic questions: (1) What is the strategic target (supplier, customer, competitor)? (2) What is the strategic thrust (differentiation, cost, innovation, growth, alliance)? (3) What is the mode (offensive, defensive)? and (4) What is the direction (use, provide)? For a detailed discussion of these different normative frameworks, see Ives and Learmonth (1984).

The connection between strategic management and information technology is discussed here by addressing three strategy issues with appropriate examples. These are: (1) substitute products and the blurring of market boundaries (illustrated through the development of the Cash Management Account by Merrill Lynch to compete against established financial institutions); (2) the understanding of corporate diversification (Dun & Bradstreet's radical change of its corporate portfolio over the last decade away from a set of loosely-linked activities toward one that is centered on the concept of exploiting information as a product and the use of current technologies as the medium of distribution); and (3) strategy development and implementation using IT-based capabilities (Batterymarch Financial Management's corporate strategy that was conceived and implemented through information technology). These three examples collectively highlight the complexity and importance of the role played by information technologies in influencing the fundamental strategic choices of a firm.

Substitute Products and the Blurring of Market Boundaries. The first example illustrates the potential offered by information technologies to develop superior substitute products (or services) as well as altering the definition and domain of business operations. The introduction of the Cash Management Account by Merrill Lynch in 1978 represented a revolution in terms of redefining the concept of financial services in a marketplace that was dominated by traditional banking institutions. This new business concept integrated diverse financial instruments under one common umbrella so that the individual investor could enjoy the convenience of moving money across various accounts as well as benefit from the "float" that banks traditionally enjoyed. This account integrated four basic investor services: (1) automatic investment of cash and dividends in a money-market account, (2) credit through a standard-margin account, (3) cash withdrawal by check or debit card, and (4) investment advice in managing and diversifying the account.

This concept could not be operationalized without the use of information technology given that it requires daily swaps across different accounts so as to post credit card charges, checks, securities, and deposits to develop an updated credit limit for each account holder. This complex data-processing operation is not incidental to the business concept but is fundamental to its conceptualization and implementation. The importance of information technology to this business strategy is perhaps best reflected by the fact that in 1982 Merrill Lynch sought and obtained a patent for its Cash Management Account system (including the complex web of data processing). The annual fees generated by the new account system were approximately $60 million in 1983, and several variations (circumventing the patent protection) of this basic concept have been offered by Merrill Lynch's competitors in recent years.

"Dominant Logic" of Diversification. The second example focuses on the diversification approaches of modern corporations and the concern within the strategic management discipline to explain the motives and effects of diversification. Corporate diversification and its impact on organizational performance is a central concern of strategic management, but it has been largely researched from an industrial economics perspective such as product and market extensions (e.g., Rumelt, 1974). However, a more recent view is that the diversification-performance relationship can be understood in terms of general management's "dominant logic"—defined as the way in which managers conceptualize the business and make critical resource allocation decisions (Prahalad and Bettis, 1986). The example of Dun & Bradstreet serves as a partial illustration of a firm that has transformed its portfolio significantly over the last decade. Indeed, the additions and deletions to its portfolio can best be understood in terms of the notion of dominant logic and a strategic vision of the role of information technology in the larger economy.

In 1978, Dun & Bradstreet was a $763 million diversified information services company with four major divisions. The Business Information Services division contributed 38% of revenue but only 27% of operating income. By 1983, Dun & Bradstreet had become a $1.5 billion information services giant with 45% of revenues and 34% of operating income derived from Business Information Services. Changes in the composition of the firm's portfolio represent an interesting example of a fundamental commitment to information technologies as a central pillar of strategic choice and redirection. In 1979, Dun & Bradstreet acquired a computer services company and a software company to develop new product offerings based on the basic data that it collects as part of its traditional operations, but these offerings can be sold through different channels. It divested its broadcasting stations and merged with A.C. Nielsen and Co. in order to exploit economies of scale and scope in the collection, packaging, and marketing of data for different purposes. Other new product offerings that are rooted in information technology include an airlines guide (electronics edition); DunsPlus, an alliance with IBM and Lotus; and DunsNet which enables Dun & Bradstreet users to access a wide range of databases. So, in essence, the basic data of "credit rating"—which was sold in one standard form without IT—could be converted into 30 different "products" (such as Dunsquest, Duns Million Dollar Lists, Duns Financial profiles, etc.) each targeted at specific customer groups. Thus, while none of its services was sold "electronically" in 1978, over 70% of Dun & Bradstreet's business is now organized around information technology.

Strategy Development and Implementation Through IT Capabilities. The third example illustrates the fundamental connection between the development and implementation of strategies and the role of information technologies. Indeed, the case of Batterymarch Financial Management highlights the way IT can drive as well as support strategy and how it can help determine a company's place in the value chain of a given business.

The company's main business is to manage pension funds, and its investment philosophy (which is its business strategy) is best summarized using four adjectives: (a) contrarian, (b) value-oriented, (c) conservative, and (d) opportunistic. "Contrarian" reflects a belief that excess returns can be obtained from investment postures that are contrary to conventional wisdom (e.g., the company buys stocks that belong to the "hated" category). "Value-orientation" reflects a belief that information-gathering is a competitive activity and that the consensus view of the value of new information may not be correct. This is perhaps best reflected in the following quote: "We have not increased cyclical exposure . . . based on a forecast or expectation that real growth will be more than other investors are predicting. We have emphasized cyclical stocks because they are usually bargains when news is poor" (Batterymarch Financial Management Annual Report, 1983). "Conservatism" reflects a concern with "downside risk as well as upside potential," while "opportunism" stems from a belief that no formula or model will always be right.

All these views (especially the contrarian philosophy) can only be operationalized using a well-integrated computing and information-gathering system that allows investment managers to look for trends that reflect their beliefs. It also requires an organization that is different from the traditional pyramidal structure, one that is "flat" and can accommodate close and quick information exchanges across value-adding activities. Figure 3 compares Batterymarch's value-chain with that of a typical financial management firm. The traditional view of operations in this market is illustrated in the top half of the figure, along with the typical allocation of personnel (support and professional staff). Traditionally, over 100 support staff are required throughout the entire value-chain. In such a configuration, the cost incurred by the value-chain would be expected to go up significantly over the years (see Figure 2). On the other hand, Batterymarch minimizes support staff and places greater emphasis on the professional investment manager—with requisite computer support. The

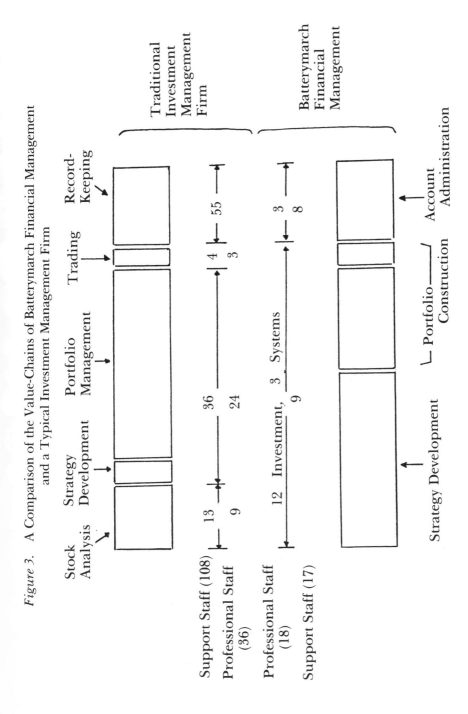

Figure 3. A Comparison of the Value-Chains of Batterymarch Financial Management and a Typical Investment Management Firm

lower half of Figure 3 is intended to provide a broad view of the relative efficiency enjoyed by Batterymarch due to its reconfiguration of the value-chain in light of its investment philosophy. Finally, Batterymarch's financial performance has recently been in the upper quartile of the industry (Clarke, 1985).

TOWARDS A RESEARCH FRAMEWORK FROM A STRATEGIC MANAGEMENT PERSPECTIVE

In this section, the main objective is to develop a preliminary research framework that highlights important research themes reflecting the relationship between strategic management and information technologies. The aim is to develop a framework using a strategic management perspective, the general thrust of the chapter. The framework is seen as an initial but critical first step in the movement away from the present state of isolated case descriptions toward a coherent and systematic understanding of the impact of current and expected developments in information technology on the practice and research of strategic management.

The proposed framework is based on three fundamental components: (1) an external environment characterized by the emergence of the electronic marketplace, (2) firm-level strategic choices and responses to exploit IT-based opportunities and threats, and (3) assessment of short- and long-term benefits attributable to these specific strategic actions. Figure 4 is a schematic representation of the research framework, and it highlights four research themes (numbered A through D). The ensuing discussion is an elaboration of these research themes with particular attention to methodological problems and issues.

Emergence of the Electronic Marketplace

The importance of this research theme stems from a fundamental axiom of environment-strategy alignment or fit (Snow and Miles, 1983; Venkatraman and Camillus, 1984). That is, a systematic representation of environmental characteristics is necessary to assess the appropriateness of strategies and their effects on performance. Hence, the first research theme deals with the characteristics of the emerging electronic marketplace. The basic task here is to address the question: How can we describe a particular market characterized by electronic (communication and computer) linkages, and how can we discriminate among different types of markets?

Current strategy research portrays the external environment using concepts from related disciplines such as industrial organization economics (e.g., degree of product differentiation, concentration ratio, advertising

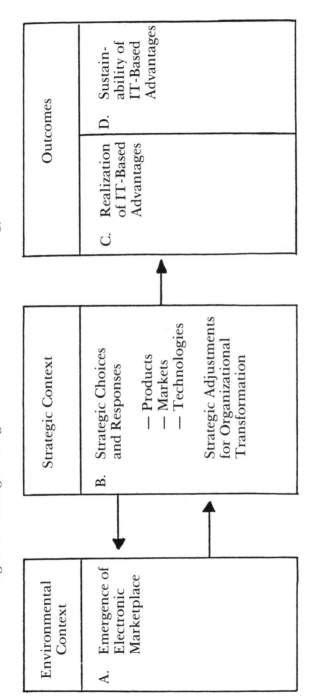

Figure 4. Strategic Management and Information Technology: A Research Framework

intensity, entry and exit barriers, bargaining power, substitute products); marketing (e.g., product life cycle); or organization theory (e.g., uncertainty, hostility, dynamism, heterogeneity). These constructs are reasonably clear to researchers both at a theoretical and an empirical level. However, it is not clear whether such environmental attributes are adequate for reflecting the nuances that emerge from electronic communication and computer-based linkages. This is because IT-based developments could alter the traditional sources of advantages in a marketplace (attributable to concepts such as entry barriers or scale economies). For example, in banking services, IT-based access to services has seriously eroded the traditional entry barriers enjoyed by many smaller, regional banks. It is possible to integrate a geographically-dispersed market into a single unified market through information technologies, thus turning what is traditionally considered to be a structural weakness into a firm-specific advantage. For an overview of the role played by information technologies in influencing industry characteristics, see Parsons (1983).

Nevertheless, it is premature to suggest that these extant concepts are not useful. Indeed, it is probably necessary for strategy researchers to conceptualize the key characteristics of electronic markets by appropriately building from the current base of constructs and their measures. This is a challenging task at two levels. At one level, the task is to delineate the market in some common way since the traditional product-based classification (Standard Industrial Classification Codes) may be inappropriate given the power of information technology to substitute a range of products and services. At another level, the task is to derive a parsimonious set of concepts such that a typology of electronic markets can be developed. This task is complicated by the fact that the traditional manufacturing versus service distinction may be limited given that many corporations are increasingly reconfiguring their value-chain to increase the service component of their product-offering.

Methodological Issues. While the identification of this research theme is relatively simple, specific research designs to address it are not straightforward. Presently, there are at best a handful of markets that have witnessed a true electronic transformation. Given the embryonic stage of understanding of IT forces and the innovative strategies firms have developed to change the rules-of-the-game in the marketplace, it may be premature to aim for a typology now. Alternatively, it may be more realistic to first identify the key concepts that describe electronic markets. One promising avenue would be to examine the forces that propelled the transformation. As mentioned earlier, these could reflect both technology-push as well as business-pull. Such descriptions could then be aggregated to achieve common characteristics across different markets. Subsequently, such characteristics might be refined using a Delphi-style expert panel.

The author is currently conducting a research study to understand and describe the market for tax-preparation services. This market is undergoing a radical metamorphosis from a mature market dominated by H&R Block and its franchises toward one that is characterized by a state of flux. This is because of the recent decision by the Internal Revenue Service to accept electronic filing of tax returns (Wedick, 1986). Thus, in addition to the traditional tax preparers, the market is now opening for financial institutions (direct deposit of refunds), credit-card companies (possibility of payments with credit cards), software manufacturers (because of the market for electronic filing-ready software required every year to handle that year's tax laws), and telecommunication companies like MCI, Western Union, and AT&T (because of the market for transmission of tax forms as well as other critical information). The study in progress aims to arrive at a parsimonious description of this emerging electronic market as well as calibrating the likely strategic responses of the different players given the new opportunities.

Strategic Responses to IT-Based Opportunities and Threats

This theme relies on an accurate portrayal of the electronic market and focuses on the strategic responses of different firms. It is reasonably clear that developments in IT provide a set of opportunities (in terms of new products/services or superior implementation capabilities) as well as threats (possible exploitation of these developments by competitors to realize first-mover advantages). Current thinking and research in strategic management would suggest that the strategic choices and response patterns of different firms competing in the same marketplace are unlikely to be uniform. Indeed, a fundamental assumption within strategic management is that strategic actions and resource commitments are unique to a firm's situation (Andrews, 1980). For example, Citibank's global banking strategy is highly dependent on its IT-based capabilities while its competitor, Bank of America, puts far less emphasis on IT capabilities in its strategy. Also, not all airlines emphasize information technologies equally in their competitive strategies. Hence it may be safe to conclude that the use of information technologies will vary in all markets subject to electronic transformation. The research question then becomes: What are the key characteristics that explain or predict variations in emphasis on information technology? One possible approach would be to use the Miles and Snow (1978) strategy typology to test for differences in IT usage in different markets. Alternatively, a taxonomy based on dimensions of strategic response such as risk-taking, proactiveness, etc., could be employed (e.g., Miller and Friesen, 1984; Venkatraman, 1985). In this way, the strategic choice perspective is invoked to explain variations in response patterns given a set of common external stimuli (i.e., potential opportunities and threats posed by IT).

Methodological Issues. A promising approach for exploring this theme is a field study of a sample of organizations within a given market. The study would focus on the competitive strategies of key industry participants and their type and degree of emphasis on information technology. By limiting the sample frame to a well-defined market, extraneous conditions could be largely controlled. Data could include (1) managerial perceptions of the environment, strategy, and IT emphasis (based on the premise that managers' actions are consistent with their perceptions of opportunities and threats); (2) objective indicators of strategy and the level of resource commitment to IT; and (3) specific organizational actions (such as alliances, acquisitions of IT firms, redefinition of functional roles, etc.) taken in response to opportunities and threats.

The previously mentioned study of the tax preparation business intends to probe this theme as well. Specifically, the response patterns of different firms will be related to their distinctive competencies. In this way, issues pertaining to information technologies are integrated into basic strategy research themes and questions.

Realization of IT-Based Advantages

The third theme focuses on the benefits of strategic actions, especially the realization of IT-based advantages. In the literature, there appears to be a widespread but implicit belief that information technologies provide significant and universal advantages to all major firms in the business. Normative frameworks portraying the connection between strategic management and information technologies are built around this position. However, empirical research supporting such a position is rather weak. Nearly all the discussions of this topic invoke the well-known examples (such as those listed in Table 1) in a rather general way to argue that IT-based actions in the marketplace provide strategic advantages.

While we do not discount the benefits realized by companies such as American Hospital Supply Corporation or Merrill Lynch, it is necessary to underscore the fact that it is difficult (if not impossible) to generalize from these isolated descriptions and assessments. Given that only the "success stories" get reported in the popular press (*Business Week*, 1985, 1986) and in normatively-oriented writings (e.g., Wiseman, 1985; Keen, 1986), it is not clear how or to what extent IT-based advantages accrue to various firms in a particular business.

Research pertaining to this theme should focus on documenting two issues. The first, and perhaps easiest, problem is to show that firms have realized significant advantages from using information technologies (measured by accepted performance indicators such as increased market share or profitability). This can be done by using either a *pre* (prior to the use of information technology) or *post* (subsequent to the introduction of such systems) research design controlling for external trends. Although a precise determination of the benefits obtained by Merrill Lynch and American Hospital Supply is not possible, the magnitude of the increase in market share and revenues would lead one to conclude that these firms realized some IT-based benefits. The other, more difficult problem is the need to systematically rule out rival explanations for various outcomes. This is necessary to precisely attribute benefits to IT-based actions. Before we enthusiastically extol the virtues of information technology for competitive advantage (like we seem to have done prematurely with strategic planning and market share, to name two), we need stronger research support in order to develop normative guidelines.

Methodological Issues. This theme presents a challenge for strategy researchers since it calls for the documentation of a definitive (perhaps causal) link between strategic actions and the realization of IT-based advantages. As mentioned before, one possible approach lies in the use of pre- versus post-designs with adequate controls. Another useful approach is a quasi-experimental design (with experimental and control groups). The author is evaluating the possibility of employing such a design to ascertain the degree of IT-based advantages in a service firm. The setting is attractive in that the firm has several homogeneous markets. While some business units are expected to take specific strategic actions to exploit IT-based opportunities, others are likely to continue along their traditional strategic path. This situation presents an opportunity to carry out a "natural" experiment with pre and post assessment across both "control" and "experimental" groups of business units. The expectation is that such a study would provide systematic evidence on IT-based strategic advantages.

Sustainability of IT-Based Advantages

Even if IT-based advantages are realized in the short-run, are they sustainable? Although these advantages arise from innovative ideas, and can be somewhat protected by patents, what prevents competitors from imitating IT-based approaches and reaping their own benefits? Proponents argue that the lead-time is sufficiently long for pioneers to reap supernormal profits, and they often cite the example of Merrill Lynch's Cash Management Account which existed for over four years before being swamped by "me-too" products (despite a patent). However, the general pervasiveness of IT capabilities may make it very difficult for pioneers to emulate Merrill Lynch's success. Therefore, the key question becomes: What determines the level of sustainability of IT-based advantages in the marketplace, and is it uniform across all types of IT innovations?

Methodological Issues. This theme is perhaps the most difficult to investigate because it requires longitudinal research designs. It is difficult to assess sustainability using a cross-sectional design unless one carries out a post-hoc analysis of the time lag between the innovative use of IT in a particular business and the subsequent, more widespread use of the same idea in other businesses. For example, it took about four years before a serious competitive product emerged for Merrill Lynch's Cash Management Account and a similar time lag before competition developed for American Hospital Supply's purchasing system. While Merrill Lynch had some protection because of its patent, AHSC did not. Several reasons have been proposed for the inevitable time lag. By systematically accumulating such data, one can understand the cause of variations in time lags along the lines of MacMillan et al. (1985). They studied competitors' responses to easily imitated products in the banking industry through an innovative research design that called for self assessments of lag time based on industry experience. By using a panel of industry experts and a Delphi approach, one can compare predicted and actual lag times. Such an approach could provide initial, albeit crude assessments of the sustainability of IT-based advantages. However, a true assessment of sustainability can only be made longitudinally.

CONCLUSION

This chapter provided an overview of the relationship between strategic management and information technology. Essentially, it argued that characteristics of information technologies should be reflected in strategic management research. More specifically, it traced the forces underlying the intrinsic nature of this relationship and identified a set of research themes using a strategic management perspective. A preliminary framework was developed around these research themes so that strategy researchers could begin to address them in a systematic way.

ACKNOWLEDGMENTS

Michael S. Scott-Morton and John H. Grant read previous versions and made useful comments, but the usual disclaimer applies.

NOTES

1. The term *information technology* (or IT) is used in its broadest sense to refer to computer systems, information processing software and services, telecommunications, microchip technology, fiber optics, and robotics.

2. For an overview of airline reservation systems, see Harvard Business School note #0-184-009 titled, "Note on Airline Reservation Systems."

3. Both American Airlines and United Airlines were required by the Civil Aeronautics Board on November 14, 1984 to change the display rules to ensure parity among airlines.

REFERENCES

Andrews, Kenneth R. (1980). *The Concept of Corporate Strategy.* Homewood, IL: Irwin.

Anthony, Robert N. (1965). *Planning and Control Sytems: A Framework for Analysis.* Boston: Harvard Business School.

Barrett, Stephanie, and Benn R. Konsynski (1982). "Inter-organizational Information Sharing Systems." *MIS Quarterly* Special Issue:93-105.

Benjamin, Robert I., John F. Rockart, Michael S. Scott-Morton, and John Wyman (1984). "Information Technology: A Strategic Opportunity." *Sloan Management Review* 25:3-10.

Bourgeois, L. Jay, III (1980). "Strategy and Environment: A Conceptual Integration." *Academy of Management Review* 5:25-39.

Business Week (1985). "Information Power." October 14:108-114.

_____ (1986). "Information Business." August 25:82-90.

Camillus, John C., and John H. Grant (1980). "Operational Planning: The Integration of Programming and Budgeting." *Academy of Management Review* 5:369-379.

Cash, James I., Jr., and Benn R. Konsynski (1985). "IS Redraws Competitive Boundaries." *Harvard Business Review* 63:134-142.

Clarke, Raymond (1985). The Application of Information Technology in an Investment Management Firm. Master's Thesis, Sloan School of Management, Massachusetts Institute of Technology.

Diebold, John (1984). "Six Issues that Will Affect the Future of Information Management." *Data Management:*10-12, 14.

Ein-Dor, Phillip, and Eli Segev (1978). "Strategic Planning for Management Information Systems." *Management Science* 24:1631-1641.

Fombrun, Charles, Noel Tichy, and Mary Ann Devanna (1983). *Strategic Human Resource Management.* New York: Wiley.

Gallagher, Charles A. (1974). "Perceptions of the Value of a Management Information System." *Academy of Management Journal* 17:46-55.

Hofer, Charles W., and Dan E. Schendel (1978). *Strategy Formulation: Analytical Concepts.* St. Paul, MN: West Publishing Co.

International Business Machines Corporation (1981). *Business System Planning.* New York: IBM Corporation.

Ives, Blake S., Scott Hamilton, and Gordon B. Davis (1980). "A Framework for Research on Computer-Based Management Information Systems." *Management Science* 26:910-934.

Ives, Blake S., and Learmonth, G.P. (1984). "The Information System as a Competitive Weapon." *Communications of the ACM* 27:1193-1201.

Keen, Peter G.W. (1981). "Communications in the 21st Century: Telecommunications and Business Policy." *Organizational Dynamics,* Autumn:54-67.

_____ (1986). *Competing in Time: Using Telecommunications for Competitive Advantage.* Cambridge, MA: Ballinger.

King, William R. (1978). "Strategic Planning for Management Information Systems." *MIS Quarterly* 2:27-37.

_____ (1983). "Information as a Strategic Resource." *MIS Quarterly* 7:iii-iv.

Kriebel, Charles H. (1968). "The Strategic Dimension of Computer Systems Planning." *Long Range Planning* 1:7-12.

Lorange, Peter, and Richard F. Vancil (1977). *Strategic Planning Systems*. Englewood Cliffs, NJ: Prentice-Hall.

MacMillan, Ian, Michael L. McCafferty, and George Van Wijk (1985). "Competitors' Responses to Easily Imitated New Products." *Strategic Management Journal* 6:75-86.

Malone, Thomas W., JoAnne Yates, and Robert I. Benjamin (1986). "Electronic Markets and Electronic Hierarchies: Effects of Information Technology on Market Structures and Corporate Strategies." Working Paper, Sloan School of Management, Massachusetts Institute of Technology.

McFarlan, F. Warren (1984). "Information Technology Changes the Way You Compete." *Harvard Business Review* 62:98-103.

McKinsey & Co. (1968). *Unlocking the Computer's Profit Potential*. New York: McKinsey & Co.

Miles, Raymond E., and Charles C. Snow (1978). *Organizational Strategy, Structure, and Process*. New York: McGraw-Hill.

——— (1986). "Organizations: New Concepts for New Forms." *California Management Review* 28:62-69.

Miller, Danny, and Peter H. Friesen (1984). *Organizations: A Quantum View*. Englewood Cliffs, NJ: Prentice-Hall.

Naisbitt, John (1982). *Megatrends*. New York: Warner Books.

Parsons, Gregory L. (1983). "Information Technology: A New Competitive Weapon." *Sloan Management Review* 25:3-14.

Porter, Michael E. (1980), *Competitive Strategy*. New York: Free Press.

Porter, Michael E., and Victor E. Millar (1985). "How Information Gives You Competitive Advantage." *Harvard Business Review* 63:149-160.

Prahalad, C.K., and Richard A. Bettis (1986). "The Dominant Logic: A New Linkage Between Diversity and Performance." *Strategic Management Journal* 7:485-501.

Pyburn, Phillip J. (1983). "Linking the MIS Plan with Corporate Strategy: An Exploratory Study." *MIS Quarterly* 63:149-160.

Rockart, John F., and Michael S. Scott-Morton (1984). "Implications of Changes in Information Technology for Corporate Strategy." *Interfaces* 14:84-95.

Rumelt, Richard P. (1974). *Strategy, Structure, and Economic Performance*. Boston: Harvard Business School Press.

——— (1979). "Evaluation of Strategy: Theory and Models." In Dan E. Schendel and Charles W. Hofer (Eds.), *Strategic Management: A New View of Business Policy and Planning*. Boston: Little, Brown, pp. 196-212.

Snow, Charles C., and Raymond E. Miles (1983). "The Role of Strategy in the Development of a General Theory of Organizations." In Robert Lamb (Ed.), *Advances in Strategic Management*, Vol. 2. Greenwich, CT: JAI Press, pp. 231-259.

Strassman, Paul (1985). *The Information Payoff*. New York: Free Press.

Venkatraman, N. (1985). Strategic Orientation of Business Enterprises: The Construct and Its Measurement. Doctoral Dissertation, Graduate School of Business, University of Pittsburgh.

Venkatraman, N., and John C. Camillus (1984). "Exploring the Concept of Fit in Strategic Management." *Academy of Management Review* 9:513-525.

Venkatraman, N., and T.S. Raghunathan (1986). Strategic Management of Information Systems Function: Changing Roles and Planning Linkages. Working Paper #1743-86, Sloan School of Management, Massachusetts Institute of Technology.

Wedick, John L., Jr. (1986). "Electronic Filing at the IRS: The Goal is Global." *Journal of Accountancy* 162:110-116.

Wheelwright, Steven (1984). "Manufacturing Strategy: Defining the Missing Link." *Strategic Management Journal* 5:77-91.

Wind, Yoram, and Thomas S. Robertson (1983). "Marketing Strategy: New Directions for Theory and Research." *Journal of Marketing* 47:12-25.

Wiseman, Charles (1985). *Strategy and Computers: Information Systems as Competitive Weapons.* Homewood, IL: Dow Jones-Irwin.

Zani, William (1970). "Blueprint for IS." *Harvard Business Review* 48:97-99.

A FRAMEWORK FOR THE DESIGN AND IMPLEMENTATION OF COMPETITIVE INTELLIGENCE SYSTEMS

John E. Prescott and Daniel C. Smith

The rapid ascendance of competitive intelligence in both strategy formulation and implementation can be attributed primarily to an increased awareness by managers of the role that competitive forces play in determining firm success. While much has been written concerning processes of collecting and analyzing competitive information (Porter, 1980; 1985; Washington Researchers, 1983; Hax and Majluf, 1984; Fuld, 1985; Prescott, 1987; Prescott and Grant, 1988; Smith and Prescott, 1987), little guidance has been provided to managers responsible for implementing the competitive intelligence function. Although the techniques of competitive analysis and their refinement continue to be relevant, emerging concerns lie with the management of the competitive intelligence function. Accordingly, the purpose of this chapter is to provide an overview of a systematic approach to the design and implementation of competitive intelligence systems.

The chapter is divided into three major sections. In the first section, the purposes and uses of competitive intelligence are described. The second section presents a framework for designing competitive intelligence systems based on past research and practitioner insights. The final section outlines directions for future research.

THE NEED FOR COMPETITIVE INTELLIGENCE SYSTEMS

Perhaps the most significant indication of the need for a more systematic approach to the management of competitive intelligence activities is the recent formation of the Society of Competitor Intelligence Professionals. The Society is essentially a trade association with the goals of developing, improving, and promulgating the methods, techniques, and standards of individuals involved in competitor intelligence. Such individuals include managers with the responsibility of developing a competitive intelligence function within their business, analysts who are currently conducting competitive intelligence and desire to improve their current skills and develop new ones, and information vendors who want to continue to provide their customers with state-of-the-art products.

Examples of Competitive Intelligence

The need for competitive intelligence systems can be illustrated more specifically by exploring how competitive intelligence is currently being used, identifying unresolved issues, and suggesting how these issues can best be addressed. As the following examples illustrate, competitor intelligence is used by companies to address a wide variety of issues. Duquesne Light Company, an electrical utility, has recently begun to study the changing dynamics of its industry to better position itself if deregulation becomes a reality. A division of an aerospace company has begun to examine competition in the simulator industry as part of a search for alternate markets for its lucrative flight simulator training business which will soon decline due to the introduction of a new type of plane. Ford Motor Company purchased competitors' automobiles and employed "reverse engineering" to more fully understand the design and cost of its competitors' cars. A division of Textronics has developed closer relationships with its suppliers to build both stronger ties and to better understand how its competitors are dealing with their suppliers. Competitors of Proctor and Gamble regularly scan the P&G Alumni Directory searching for managerial talent. The domestic food industry is studying and developing responses to growing threats from global competition. Many competitors in the health care industry are monitoring Humana's decisions as it enters the insurance business to learn from that company's accomplishments and mistakes. A casket manufacturer has developed detailed profiles of its main competitor's cost structure, managerial talent, and merger activity in order to better position itself in the business.

This diverse set of examples suggests that many companies acknowledge the value of competitive intelligence. Yet, in virtually every organization, the competitive intelligence function has not developed in a way that addresses several concerns regularly raised by managers responsible for this activity. Some of the more prominent of these concerns include: When do I know that I have collected enough information about competitors? How should I measure effectiveness? What resources are most critical to successful competitive intelligence? What should be the roles of corporate versus divisional levels? How do we get people to share information when they consider information to be a source of power? What are the products of competitive intelligence, and how do I put them in a format that managers will use? What are the ethical and legal issues involved? How much of a budget should I devote to this activity? These and other concerns highlight the need for a logical and comprehensive approach to the design and implementation of a competitive intelligence system.

Purposes and Definitions

The overall purpose of a competitive intelligence system is to facilitate *management* of the processes of collecting, analyzing, interpreting, and disseminating information about industries and competitors. Two broad outputs of these processes are improved decision making and managerial training. Decision making is improved by avoiding surprises, better inputs to both short- and long-term planning, more focused marketing and R & D, and by the identification and assessment of potential acquisition and divestiture candidates. A competitive intelligence system contributes to ongoing training and development by exposing managers to the techniques of competitor analysis, encouraging the sharing of information and thus the cross-fertilization of ideas, and increasing managerial sensitivity to the implications of both strong and weak competitor signals.

Before beginning a discussion of the elements of a framework for designing competitive intelligence systems, it is necessary to place the competitive intelligence activity into a proper perspective. Intelligence is not synonymous with data or information (Rodriguez and King, 1977; King, 1978; Zaltman and Deshpande, 1979). *Data* refers to a factual description of the competitive environment and represents the raw input to the competitive intelligence system. Industry concentration ratios; industry profit, cost, and capacity utilization levels; and competitor advertising levels, pricing tactics, and general operating philosophies are typical types of competitive data. *Information* is data that have been given meaning. Of particular concern for managers is that the data be evaluated and interpreted in light of specific types of decisions (e.g., capacity expansion, new product development, acquisitions). For instance, knowledge of relatively high industry profit levels coupled with low entry barriers may signal managers to further differentiate their product to guard against the erosion of market share in the event of entry by outside firms. A particular interpretation, however, may not be accepted as true. *Intelligence* is information whose credibility and meaning have been established. Thus, information suggesting a need to further differentiate a firm's product offering is credible only if high profit and low entry barriers are likely to prompt entry by new firms.

With respect to the domain of competitive intelligence activity, traditional literature on this topic has, at least implicitly, been concerned primarily with the competitive environment faced by firms in their immediate product markets. This focus is understandable given that (1) changes in the competitive fabric of product markets typically have a direct effect on performance, and (2) most managers are involved primarily with formulating and/or implementing product-market strategies. Such a focus, however, is inherently shortsighted; long-term success requires that a firm interact effectively with a variety of stakeholder groups (Freeman, 1984). As such, the design of a competitive intelligence system that will provide effective strategic and tactical intelligence must be based on a broader definition of competitive environments. Thus, the domain of competitive intelligence activity should be viewed as any point in the value chain where a firm must "bid" against other firms in order to obtain a particular resource (Porter, 1985). The value chain is comprised of five major activities: (1) inbound logistics, (2) operations, (3) outbound logistics, (4) marketing and sales, and (5) service and support activities including the firm's infrastructure, human resource management, technology development, and procurement (Porter, 1985). This broad definition of competitive intelligence activity both sets it apart from narrower disciplines such as market research and necessitates close interfunctional coordination for success.

The following section of the chapter develops a framework for the design and implementation of competitive intelligence systems. The primary goal is to assist managers as they address the above-mentioned design issues.

A FRAMEWORK FOR THE DESIGN OF COMPETITIVE INTELLIGENCE SYSTEMS

Although the field of marketing has long stressed the need to systematically identify and examine the behavior of competitors (Adler, 1967), the

Figure 1. A Framework for Designing Competitive Intelligence Systems

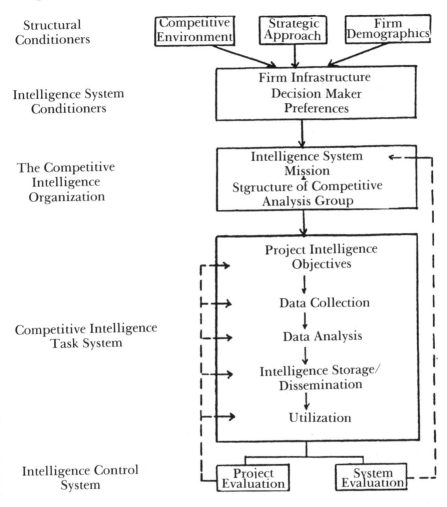

publication of Michael Porter's (1980) *Competitive Strategy* marked the beginning of an intensified effort by both practitioners and researchers to better understand competitor behavior. Since that time, most of the effort in this area has been focused on methodologies for analyzing industries and competitors (Hax and Majluf, 1984; Sammon et al., 1984; Prescott and Grant, 1988) and on strategies to take advantage of competitive gaps and/ or minimize competitive threats (Grant and King, 1982; Day, 1984; Porter, 1985).

While great strides have been made in developing the tools and techniques of competitive analysis, little has been done in the way of understanding the role, organizational structure, and processes that such activities entail. Some insights can be obtained from research on environmental scanning units which has examined scanning techniques, the overall sophistication of these units, and the problems encountered in acquiring and using environmental information (Aguilar, 1967; Fahey and King, 1977; Steiner, 1979; Porter, 1980, 1985; Jain, 1984; Lenz and Engledow, 1986). However, what has been characterized as environmental scanning units are, in most organizations, synonymous with planning departments. Competitive intelligence, by contrast, can be thought of as one element of environmental analysis. Further, competitive intelligence exists, often in a very informal and unsystematic state, throughout an organization (Wall, 1974; Porter, 1985).

The absence of a framework for the design of competitive intelligence systems has hindered the advancement of the competitive intelligence function in many firms. The framework proposed here is based on previous research and on discussions with managers who are currently attempting to build competitive intelligence systems in their organizations.

A competitive intelligence system is comprised of two subsystems, the intelligence task system and the intelligence control system, both of which are administered by the competitive intelligence organization (see Figure 1). The competitive intelligence organization is, in turn, determined by two intelligence system conditioners: the firm's infrastructure and the decision makers' preferences. These conditioners are influenced by three broad structural characteristics: (1) the nature of the competitive environment, (2) the general strategic approach of the firm, and (3) the level of sophistication of the firm's strategic planning and support systems.

Structural Characteristics

Traditionally, academics have suggested that a firm's environment, its strategy, and other firm demographics impose contingencies upon the design of environmental scanning units (Thompson, 1967; Camillus, 1986). Empirical research, however, has found little support for the contingency perspective. Aguilar (1967) found no relationship between functional area, hierarchical level, or organizational size and scanning. Kefalas and Schoderbeck (1973) found no significant patterns between environmental dynamism and scanning. Hambrick (1982) found little evidence to support the contention that strategic emphasis influenced environmental scanning. Lenz and Engledow (1986), in their field study of "leading edge" corporations, concluded that managerial preferences played a major role in determining the structure of environmental scanning departments while the environment played a minor role. Other researchers have arrived at similar conclusions (Hambrick, 1981; Boulton et al., 1982).

However, other researchers have found that such structural factors affect the process of interpreting (Janis and Mann, 1977), analyzing (Miller and Friesen, 1983; Fredrickson and Mitchell, 1984; Fredrickson, 1985), disseminating (Rogers and Agarwala-Rogers, 1976), and politicizing (Allison, 1971) information. These various studies suggest that the environmental, strategic, and demographic factors do not directly affect the design of a firm's competitive intelligence system but rather operate indirectly through their influence on the framing of decision makers' perceptions. We argue that the key contingencies for the design of competitive intelligence systems are the firm's infrastructure (its existing systems, modes of decision making, conflict resolution approach, etc.) and decision makers' preferences.

Firm Infrastructure

A firm's infrastructure, or integrating mechanisms (Miles and Snow, 1978), is the existing set of management systems and procedures for addressing recurrent issues and managing individuals and groups. Examples include planning and control systems, reward systems, communication systems, conflict resolution styles, and recruiting and selection systems. A firm's infrastructure is relatively permanent and typically changes in incremental steps (Quinn, 1980). The significance of the infrastructure for competitive intelligence system design is that it acts as a filter for the flow of information into, through, and out of the firm. In addition, it establishes norms for how information will be processed and politicized.

The sophistication of the firm's infrastructure plays an important role in the design of a competitive intelligence system. As Miles and Snow (1978) note, the various integrating mechanisms of a firm must be consistent with one another. Inconsistencies across the systems will lead to conflicts and effectiveness problems. Therefore, a competitive intelligence system must be designed to fit the complexity and sophistication of existing administrative systems. Designers must resist the temptation to develop the "ideal" system or one that has the goal of changing or improving the other systems. In this sense, a firm's infrastructure can be thought of as a constraint on the design of a competitive intelligence system.

Decision Makers' Preferences

The process of decision making involves problem recognition (Janis and Mann, 1977; Cowan, 1986), diagnosis (Shrivastava and Grant, 1985), and implementation (Bower, 1972; Mintzberg et al., 1976; Donaldson and Lorsch, 1983). Throughout the decision-making process, managers attach meaning to information according to their perceptions (Weick, 1979).

Information-gathering is a perceptual process by which an individual organizes diverse verbal and nonverbal stimuli. Individuals tend to have a dominant style of sensing data from their environment which is either sensation or intuition (Jung, 1953). Sensing types pay particular attention to the facts of a situation and break down information into small bits. Intuitive types, on the other hand, take in data by examining the whole situation. They tend to draw relationships between various concepts that they bring to the situation, specifically looking for conformities and deviations from their expectations. Jung (1953) contended that individuals cannot easily apply both styles simultaneously.

Information evaluation, according to Jung (1953), is the process used in formulating a decision. Two prominent styles of information evaluation are thinking and feeling. Thinking types are characterized by use of the scientific method which brings logic and analytical techniques to structure a problem. Feeling types, in contrast, arrive at their decisions based on how they feel about the situation surrounding a decision or the people involved. Feeling types tend to stress the uniqueness of every situation and thus rarely structure any two problems the same. Researchers have used Jung's typology to study a variety of organizational decision-making issues (Hellriegel and Slocum, 1986).

In an ongoing study that can shed some light on the way that managers gather and interpret information, Weber (1986) has begun to track the strategy-making process in terms of the way that managers scan, interpret, and evaluate information. Results of this study indicate that in terms of competitive information, managers scan their suppliers, competitors, and technological environment in an irregular mode. The focus of most of their scanning is on internal performance, products, customers, and general economic conditions. While managers appear to scan a broad array of data, they typically rely on easy-to-get information for decision making.

The scanning activity of managers is closely tied to the sources of information they employ. Heavy reliance is typically given to routine reports and casual meetings with personal contacts. The reliance on personal contacts supports Mintzberg's (1973) research on managerial work in which he found that little reliance was placed on formal meetings and special reports done within the company or by consultants. The network of relations developed by an executive seem to influence greatly the sources of information that are used.

Weber (1986) further found that managers use a past orientation to interpret data about markets and suppliers and a future orientation when scanning internal performance and the technological environment.

The evaluation of information, according to Weber's (1986) study, was conducted through numerical analysis for internal performance. All other evaluation was strongly based on personal perceptions and convictions. In short, this study found that managers relied heavily on the intuition/feeling dimensions in their decisions. This conclusion has several important implications for the design of competitive intelligence systems. First, given intuitive/feelers' preference for examining the overall picture, both the mission of the function and individual projects should be positioned in a way that illustrate how they fit into the overall scheme of the organization. Secondly, intuitive/feelers look for conformation and deviation from their prior expectations. Thus, the system and its outputs need to consider these beliefs and expectations carefully to avoid political problems (Zaltman and Deshpande, 1979). Third, personal considerations and contacts play a strong role in the decision-making processes of intuitive/feelers. Therefore, using sources, data, and analytical techniques that decision makers find credible and comfortable is essential. This poses an interesting opportunity for training decision makers in the techniques of gathering, analyzing, and disseminating competitive intelligence. Finally, intuitive/feelers tend to view every situation as unique. One approach for handling this potential problem is to identify the uniqueness of the situation but also draw on relevant experiences that can be generalized to other firms facing a similar situation. One technique is to use firms in other industries as benchmarks for comparison (Tucker et al., 1987).

THE COMPETITIVE INTELLIGENCE ORGANIZATION

The competitive intelligence organization is the administrative component of a competitive intelligence system. The design of this function entails the development of the intelligence mission and the determination of the structure of the competitive intelligence group.

Intelligence System Mission

While every competitive intelligence system is somewhat unique, missions can be classified as either comprehensive or project based. The two types of missions differ in their scope, individual involvement, and outputs (Prescott and Smith, 1987). Comprehensive missions are broad in scope, centralized in the organization, and provide outputs that are integral to the strategic planning efforts of the entire corporation. Kodak, for example, uses such an approach. A project-based mission is narrow in scope, decentralized and autonomous, and provides outputs that are directly related to individual programs or projects. Upjohn uses the project-based approach. Figure 2 illustrates a classification scheme for examining competitive intelligence missions. The two dimensions shown in the figure, the *comprehensiveness*

Figure 2. A Classification of Competitive Intelligence Missions

Comprehensiveness of Assignment

	One Fact or Figure	Partial Company or Industry Profile(s)	Complete Company or Industry Profile(s)	Comprehensive System
Offensive				
Informational				
Defensive				

Type of Assignment

ot assignments and the *type* of assignments, are useful factors for examining competitive intelligence missions. The comprehensiveness of assignments can be broken down into four categories. The first three represent a project format whereas the fourth is an ongoing comprehensive system. These categories are:

1. *One Fact or Figure.* The objective is to find one piece of information. For example, what is the size of the fast-food market? How many distribution outlets does a drug retailer have? How many R & D personnel are employed by a particular steel firm? What is the business philosophy of a certain CEO?

2. *Partial Company or Industry Profile.* The objective here is to understand one particular area of an industry or company in depth. For example, what are the barriers to entry in the watch industry? How have service dealerships for stereos changed over the last five years? What is the financial position of a competitor? Which competitors will be most affected and how by a particular technological change?

3. *Complete Industry or Company Profile.* The objective is to understand, in depth, an industry or company. The assignment would cover every major aspect of a company or industry. For example, a competitor profile would encompass all the functional areas, administrative systems, management's goals and profiles, the organization's culture, its corporate and business strategies, position in the industry, and so on.

4. *Comprehensive System.* A comprehensive system would include complete profiles for every competitor, potential competitors, and the industry. Ideally, the system would be an interactive, computerized network in which decision makers could conduct in-depth strategic analyses. Alternatives could be analyzed and compared in real time. The on-line capabilities would also permit continual updating of information. An important distinction between a comprehensive system and the other three is that the comprehensive system is ongoing whereas the other three are projects that have a definite beginning and end.

The comprehensiveness dimension concerns the depth of the analyses and the degree to which they are interrelated and continuous. The second dimension, type of assignment, focuses on the purposes that the analysis will serve for the organization. Three general types of assignments are offensive, informational, and defensive. These types are not mutually exclusive. Typically, a particular assignment will contain aspects of all three types, and the outputs of one often can serve as a starting point for another.

Offensive assignments are conducted to evaluate the impact of a strategic or tactical move on the industry and competitors. Another aspect of an offensive assignment is to determine potential competitor responses that might influence the success of the move. A new distribution system, a new product introduction, an attempt to develop a product that would become the industry standard, or a new warranty policy are all examples of where an offensive assignment would be appropriate. Before Honeywell introduced a new product in the gyrostabilizer business, it conducted an extensive offensive analysis of the existing competitors to evaluate their strengths, weaknesses, and possible responses.

Informational assignments are neutral in the sense that no apparent action is being taken by the firm conducting the analysis to gain an immediate competitive advantage. The results of the assignment, however, may lead to actions that may be either offensive or defensive. Informational assignments primarily have a purpose of gaining a better understanding of the industry or competitors. These types of analyses often arise as a result of a manager wanting to check out a rumor. For example, Whirlpool encourages its personnel to send rumors related to its competitors to its competitive intelligence unit. The unit evaluates, codes, and inputs the rumor into an information system accessible to a wide variety of managers.

Periodically, the rumors are reevaluated as to their veracity and usefulness. Informational assignments are also a good starting point for organizations with little experience in conducting competitive analysis.

Defensive assignments are oriented toward understanding the potential moves that a competitor can make that would threaten the competitive position in the firm and developing responses to minimize or neutralize the threat. Examples of situations requiring a defensive analysis include two competitors discussing a merger to gain a dominant position in the industry, a technological breakthrough in another industry that results in a substitute product having a very favorable price-performance relationship, and a weak competitor whose parent has disclosed a commitment to market leadership. The low entry barriers and increased price competition in the after-market for automobiles has led at least one U.S. automobile manufacturer to conduct a defensive competitive analysis to evaluate its position and determine how it can best compete.

Managers can use this classification system to determine the type of mission that best fits the needs of the organization. By examining the comprehensiveness and types of assignments that the organization will typically carry out, managers can determine whether the project or comprehensive mission better fits their needs and thus assist them in resource allocation decisions. For example, many managers justifiably ask how long a project should take. One aerospace firm allocates ten working days to develop an overall profile of a competitor. Through prior experience, it found that 80% of the necessary information was located and analyzed in 20% of the allocated time and that allocating resources beyond a two-week period (except in special situations) was not cost-effective and did not increase the effectiveness of the project. The experiences of this firm (and others) illustrate that, over time, competitive intelligence personnel should be able to gauge the time requirements of a typical project and establish standards that can be conveyed to clients.

Designing the Competitive Intelligence Group

The second component of the intelligence organization is the organizational structure of the competitive intelligence unit. Since the mission statement defines the objectives and domain of the unit's "clients," it plays a significant role in determining the hierarchical location and design of the unit.

The design of the administrative component of a competitive intelligence unit involves careful consideration of the following five design parameters: (1) structure and location of the unit in the organizational hierarchy; (2) tasks and outputs; (3) recruitment, selection, and training of individuals; (4) reward systems; and (5) interfunctional relationships. Each of these design issues is examined below.

Figure 3. Alternative Locations for Competitive Intelligence Units

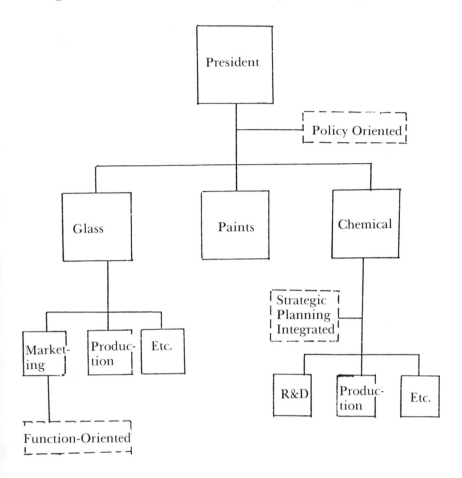

Location and Structure of the Competitive Intelligence Unit

Decisions concerning the placement of the competitive intelligence unit in the organizational hierarchy are complicated because competitive intelligence often exists at the corporate, business unit, and functional levels and within many staff groups. The selection of a site(s) will have profound impact on its legitimacy, tasks, and relationships with other organizational units. Organizations have generally placed their competitive intelligence units in three locations. Building on the work of Lenz and Engledow (1986), competitive intelligence units can be classified as policy-oriented, strategic planning-integrated, and function-oriented (see Figure 3).

Policy-Oriented.   This type of unit is located at the corporate level and reports directly to senior-level management. The focus of the policy-oriented unit is on identifying broad changes in the industry and competitors, stimulating the thinking of the top management team, and conducting special projects at the discretion of top management. While a full-time staff may exist, typically the unit is comprised of a staff manager who carries out assignments with the assistance of a cross-functional team. The central location of the unit provides legitimacy and, typically, cooperation from other organizational units. A regulated utility began its competitive intelligence program with a policy-oriented group because top management felt that the lack of any formal program in the past required close attention and support from the president's office. The company plans to move the unit to the marketing function upon the completion of several projects which will establish its legitimacy and methods of operation.

Strategic Planning-Integrated.   A competitive intelligence unit can be integrated into the strategic planning process at any level in the hierarchy. As part of the planning effort, the focus of activity centers on industry and competitor studies which are an integral input to the development of a strategic plan. Therefore, the unit is subject to the constraints of the planning process. The staff often will be involved in activities related to environmental scanning and other planning efforts. Since the focus is different than traditional environmental scanning which focuses on broad economic, social, political, technological, and international issues that cut across all businesses, each planning department typically needs to conduct its own studies unless there is a central unit which can cut across business boundaries. Its location provides a ready outlet for its tasks, but the legitimacy and cooperation from other units can become difficult. Westinghouse requires that all of its business-unit plans have a section devoted to the competition. As a result, each unit has discretion over the emphasis it places on competitive intelligence, and the planning department is the natural location for conducting competitive analysis. Westinghouse thus conducts competitive intelligence activities at the corporate, division, and business-unit levels.

Function-Oriented.   This type of unit is attached to a particular functional unit such as marketing or R & D and addresses specific issues relevant to the individual function. The focus of the activity tends to be relatively narrow although cross-functional projects can occur. While industry and competitor profiles sometimes are developed, it is more common to have projects that examine more specific issues such as product modifications, cost and performance characteristics of new technologies, and the impact of selection, training and reward systems of competitors. The typically close interaction with line managers provides the advantage of assisting with the solution to immediate problems. However, unless there is a clear vision of the business's strategy, solutions that emerge from a function-oriented unit are susceptible to suboptimization. Further, intergroup cooperation can become a problem unless the groups perceive a benefit to their unit. General Electric's Lighting Business Group has begun a competitive intelligence program in the market research department. The program has quickly moved from an emphasis on pricing, a key aspect of this business, to a broad set of topics. Its location in marketing has facilitated both an acceptance of the program (because of its historical involvement with pricing) and its expansion (due to its perceived relevance given the increased competition from Philips and other firms).

The focus of activity becomes narrower as one moves from the policy-oriented to the function-oriented unit. As a result, some corporations such as Eastman-Kodak have developed competitive intelligence units at each hierarchical level.

Tasks and Outputs

The tasks of competitor intelligence involve the gathering of information, the analysis of the information to develop intelligence, and the management of the process to ensure that competitive intelligence is disseminated to appropriate managers on a timely basis. Two key aspects of any job are its technology (Woodward, 1965) and interdependence (Thompson, 1967). The technology of competitor intelligence is characterized by moderate-to-high uncertainty, diversity, and products that are tailored to customer specifications. This "job shop" production process is further characterized by high labor skills and costs, high flexibility, and moderate levels of efficiency.

The activities of the job involve reciprocal interdependence, meaning that the activities of the unit flow back and forth between other units. For example, while conducting a competitor profile for a client in the organization, competitor intelligence personnel might have to contact several organizational units as well as outside organizations or sources. As a result of the contacts, the units providing information may want something in return. The net result is a network of interrelationships developed to address the assignment, and the final output could be provided to several of the units that supplied information. These units may then use the information as an input for another task. (This aspect of competitive intelligence system design will be discussed further in the sections below on people and interfunctional relationships.)

The outputs of a competitive intelligence unit can be classified into two broad groups: tangible products and training. The tangible products of a competitive intelligence unit can include:

- Industry analysis reports;
- Competitor reports;
- Newsletters and bulletin boards;
- Position papers related to:
  a. resource needs,
  b. key industry or strategy assumptions,
  c. policy issues;
- Project reports;
- Presentations;
- Data bases.

Regardless of the output, the results should address implications in such a way that the inevitable "So what?" question is addressed, and direction should be provided to the "What do I do?" question.

Training is a second class of outputs and may include knowledge, skill, or experience with:

- Analytical techniques of competitive intelligence, interviewing, and listening skills;
- Different strategic or functional perspectives;
- The process of information sharing;
- The avoidance of surprises;
- Activities planning;
- Creativity.

People

Ultimately, it is people who conduct competitor intelligence activities. While this is an obvious statement, little has been written concerning the roles of these individuals in the organization or the training and types of skills required to successfully generate competitive intelligence. Camillus (1986) has identified six major roles that can be modified to portray competitive intelligence positions: coordinator, analyst, consultant, integrator, instigator, and decision maker. The coordinator role involves monitoring the execution of the competitive intelligence process and consolidating all of the various tasks. The analyst role primarily involves technical capabilities related to the gathering of data and its subsequent conversion into information. Operating in a consulting role, competitive intelligence personnel are available to address the concerns of decision makers with respect to any aspect of the competitive intelligence process. As integrators, competitive intelligence personnel serve as a channel of communications between different levels of management and between departments. When an individual serves as an idea generator, gadfly, or identifier of significant issues, he or she is taking on the role of instigator. The final role is that of a decision maker where the person is actively involved in decisions concerning strategic goals and action plans.

The six roles have been presented in a particular order. The initial roles are technical, process related, passive, and advisory, while the latter roles are more managerial, output related, active, and decision oriented.

Training and development is another major aspect of the "people" dimension. Individuals bring diverse skills to the competitive intelligence function. Often these skills need to be refined and new ones developed. There are several areas of expertise that an individual involved with competitive analysis needs to develop. The first, and arguably most important, are interpersonal skills. Interpersonal skills are of particular importance during the stages of data gathering and information dissemination. Specifically, individuals need to develop interviewing skills, and they need to be aggressive in following leads and probing for additional details. The ability to develop a network of contacts is also essential to becoming an efficient and effective intelligence manager and gatherer.

An often overlooked aspect of working as a competitive intelligence professional is the need to have a systematic understanding of the industry, organization, and operations of the firm. This knowledge must go beyond an economic perspective and incorporate behavioral and political dimensions.

Individuals can develop some of the above-mentioned skills by becoming familiar with the disciplines of strategic management, information systems, operations research, behavioral sciences, finance, economics, statistics, and marketing. All of the above disciplines and skills lead to the ultimate ability required for successful competitor intelligence. In the final analysis, it is the ability to draw implications that will ultimately determine the value of the competitive intelligence function. Implications are drawn not only from the analysis but from the weak signals that are identified during the analysis. Implications thus assist managers in identifying courses of action and establishing priorities.

Reward Systems

Jobs related to competitive intelligence, like many staff positions, are difficult to evaluate. Ideally, any reward system has a series of dimensions on which to evaluate performance, standards indicating "good" performance, and a time frame identifying what period and how often the dimensions should be measured. While it is widely recognized that managers of a competitive intelligence unit should explicitly address performance indicators, standards, and time frames, little hard evidence is available regarding the types of rewards currently used. Washington Researchers

(1983), a competitive intelligence-gathering organization, has conducted a salary survey of 120 individuals currently employed in intelligence activities. The results revealed that 66% earned over $40,000 per year with 28% earning over $60,000 and only 14% earning under $30,000. Information about nonmonetary rewards is sparse and primarily anecdotal.

Interfunctional Relationships

In virtually all competitive intelligence projects there is a need for collaboration with other functional units of the organization. Managers working in this situation must determine how much integration is required and how it should be achieved (Gupta et al., 1986; Ruekert and Walker, 1987). In general, three types of interfunctional interaction must be developed and managed: (1) transactions between competitive intelligence personnel and others, (2) communication flows between the intelligence unit and other units, and (3) coordinating mechanisms across organizational units (Ruekert and Walker, 1987).

Required integration is determined by the amount and type of transactions between the functions. Three common types of transactions are: (1) resource flows which are primarily financial in nature, (2) work flows, and (3) assistance flows such as technical and staff services (Ruekert and Walker, 1987). As resource dependencies increase, Ruekert and Walker (1987) found that resource flows increase, and the function that controls the needed transactions begins to influence the decisions and actions of the other unit. Within a competitive intelligence system, as an assignment moves through the stages of data collection to analysis to dissemination, the resource dependencies shift from the competitive intelligence group to the other function(s). During the initial stages of gathering the information, the competitive intelligence unit is often dependent on individuals to supply the necessary information. Thus, coordinating mechanisms between the parties are necessary (Lawrence and Lorsch, 1967).

Coordinating mechanisms may include rules and procedures, informal influence, and conflict resolution mechanisms. In general, as the frequency of interaction between groups increases, the development of standard operating procedures to address coordination should increase. While rules and procedures are effective for recurring issues, they are less effective for novel issues. In the novel situation, informal influence can be an efficient approach. For conflicts, cooperative approaches appear to produce the best results in terms of employee satisfaction and overall solution (Blake and Mouton, 1969; Ruekert and Walker, 1987). However, cooperative solutions generally are less efficient.

Communication flows between organizational units appear to be facilitated when the objectives and tasks of the units are similar (Ruekert and Walker, 1987). Competitive intelligence personnel should attempt to ensure that various other groups are aware of the unit's mission, projects, and capabilities as well as how they can assist the operations of other groups and the overall corporation.

THE COMPETITIVE INTELLIGENCE TASK SYSTEM

As illustrated in Figure 1, the competitive intelligence task system is the central element in the competitive intelligence system. The competitive intelligence task system operates on a project basis. In the context of competitive analysis, projects may be routine and ongoing, as in the case of monitoring an industry's capacity utilization, profit, and cost levels. More often, however, competitive analysis projects are ad hoc in nature and are related to activities associated with the formulation and implementation of strategy. Examples of ad hoc projects which may benefit from competitive intelligence include the design and introduction of new products; the evaluation of new market attractiveness; the assessment of a firm's relationship with its suppliers; and the evaluation of salesforce effectiveness.

While projects vary in terms of their information objectives, the functions performed by the competitive intelligence task system remain the same, namely, data collection, analysis, and dissemination. The activities that take place in implementing each of these tasks will be discussed in depth following a review of the nature and scope of project information objectives.

Intelligence Objectives

The establishment of clear and detailed information objectives is perhaps the most critical part of a competitive analysis project. The process of setting information objectives benefits managers in two basic ways. First, it forces them to reflect on the nature and scope of the particular problem. Second, as illustrated in Figure 2, the information objectives guide data collection and analysis which, in turn, determine the ultimate usefulness of the intelligence.

In the absence of meaningful objectives, subsequent steps in the project often fall prey to one or more of the following pitfalls:

1. *The law of diminishing returns.* As with other factor inputs, information is characterized by diminishing returns. In the face of ill-specified objectives, analysts tend to equate effectiveness with the volume of information produced. Consequently, managers spend a great deal of time separating relevant from irrelevant information. This problem is confounded further by the ill-structured nature of

most management decisions that makes it difficult to truly distinguish relevant from irrelevant information.

2. *Managers may not need the information that they request.* Often the process of setting information objectives is one-sided. The analyst "arrives" at the objectives by asking decision makers what types of information they would like to have. The assumption in this process is that managers know what information they need. However, as Mintzberg et al. (1976) have observed, managers are often not able to clearly articulate the true nature and scope of most decisions.

3. *Overconcern with style.* Similar to the problem of providing an excessive amount of information, analysts often prepare reports using analytical techniques and modes of presentation which are (a) completely foreign to the decision maker and/or (b) do not provide intelligence that is relevant to the particular problem.

4. *Overgeneralized reference frames.* Since few decisions are ever completely identical to each other, it follows that competitive intelligence requirements will vary across projects. Unfortunately, in the absence of project information objectives, it is not uncommon to find that both analysts as well as managers perceive the information requirements for "similar" decisions as being more similar than they actually are.

5. *No decision to be made.* A common management response to competitive intelligence reports is that they confirm or are consistent with "what we already know" and, as a result, do not substantively influence the decision. However, confirmation of intuition is more often a reflection of the nature of the decision than the quality of the intelligence report. Specifically, it is not uncommon to find that, when distilled, many problems have only one *truly* viable solution despite the presence of a number of "red herring" alternatives. Under such conditions, there is no decision to be made and, consequently, the perceived value of competitive intelligence is minimal.

Avoidance of these pitfalls mandates ongoing interaction between analysts and end-users. This is particularly true at the objective-setting stage. In setting project intelligence objectives, analysts must not be passive "information order-takers." Rather, they should be prepared to apply their research skills in-house to surface the true information needs of managers. Two interrelated procedures have proved successful for this purpose.

Identification of Decision Makers' Evaluative Criteria. Information objectives should be derived from the criteria utilized by the decision maker to evaluate various alternatives. Managers may, however, experience difficulty articulating their decision criteria. In such cases, decision criteria

Figure 4. An Illustration of How Information Objectives
Are Derived From Project Success Factors and
How They Guide Subsequent Competitive Analysis Processes

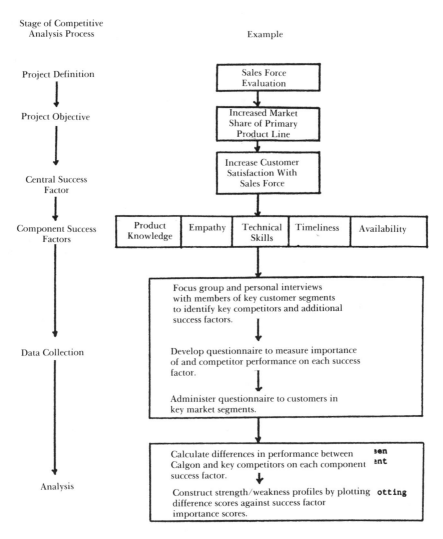

can be inferred from the types of factors that the decision maker believes are pivotal to the success of the project. For example, the national sales manager of Calgon, a leading supplier of water treatment chemicals, wanted to engage in a comprehensive evaluation of his salesforce. The ultimate objective of the project was to improve the market position of its three major products. Upon further questioning, the sales manager indicated that competing products were essentially homogeneous, and consequently, increases in market share relied heavily on customer satisfaction with the salesforce. As illustrated in Figure 4, this global criterion was decomposed into a series of key success factors. The success factors were comprised of salesforce characteristics (frequency of contact, product knowledge, empathy, etc.) judged to be important by customers when selecting a supplier. The subsequent processes of data collection and analysis focused on ascertaining the performance of Calgon's salesforce relative to that of key competitors on each supplier selection criterion. The net result was an array of salesforce profiles that clearly highlighted areas which, if improved, would result in increased customer satisfaction.

Presentation of Simulated Findings. An approach to ascertaining the extent to which viable decision alternatives really exist involves the presentation of simulated research findings to the decision maker. Prior to presentation, the decision maker is asked to specify the course of action he would take if the decision had to be made immediately (i.e., without competitive intelligence). At some point following this disclosure, the analyst provides the decision maker with a set of simulated findings which have been intentionally skewed in several conflicting directions. The decision maker is then asked to indicate: (1) the extent to which the decision would change under the various scenarios, and (2) what additional information would be useful under each scenario. With respect to the first condition, a high degree of stability in the alternative(s) selected provides a signal that, in fact, there is no decision to be made and hence the conduct of competitive analysis would be futile.

Given that competitive intelligence would be of value, the second condition provides yet another stimulus that the analyst can use to surface the true information needs of the project. Specifically, it is not uncommon for managers to raise a series of questions that, if answered, would provide further meaning to the findings of a particular study. In many cases, these additional questions reflect the true competitive intelligence requirements of the project.

Data Collection Process

The data collection phase is the most well known and documented aspect of competitive intelligence. Over the past few years, the information industry has grown considerably due to technological advances in the collection, storage, and distribution of information. Ideally, the types of data that are collected follow naturally from the information objectives. However, knowing which data are needed and identifying the appropriate *sources* of data are two distinct issues.

A source of data can be defined as anything (e.g., person, product, written material) from which information is obtained. Sources of data can be classified into two broad categories: learning curve sources and target sources (Washington Researchers, 1983). Learning curve sources are those with general rather than specific knowledge. They are appropriate when the project is not bounded by severe time constraints and when general insight is necessary prior to tapping target sources which possess more specific data. While learning curve sources typically harbor secondary data (i.e., data from sources such as financial statements and industry studies which were gathered for purposes other than the immediate project), this need not always be the case. For example, Kodak recently undertook a major study to empirically define the competitive boundaries of the entertainment industry. Prior to conducting a national survey of consumers (i.e., target sources), a series of exploratory focus group interviews followed by in-depth personal interviews were conducted to surface the dimension which consumers use to compare dissimilar forms of entertainment (e.g., movies versus the symphony). The qualitative output from these interviews provided the input for structuring the survey questionnaire.

While sources of data abound, ingenuity is often the key ingredient for obtaining the data that are most appropriate for a particular project. Too often, persons involved with data collection become trapped in a methodological "inertia" and, consequently, overlook a variety of potentially rich sources of intelligence. For instance, one of the most underutilized sources of competitive intelligence is a company's own personnel. Salespeople, purchasing agents, controllers, and even custodians and members of the clerical staff often possess valuable insights into competitors' behavior. In an attempt to capture this information, the Market Intelligence Department of a major producer of processed foods has implemented an interesting approach to synthesizing internal knowledge. Periodically, the Director of the Department holds in-house retreats in which a variety of issues concerning the nature of the firm's competition are raised. Typical issues might include:

- What do we know about Competitor X's product quality?
- What do we know about the ways in which Competitor X responds to changes in our prices? Advertising strategies?
- What do we know about Competitor X's recruiting policies?

Members of the group are provided with the issues in advance of the retreat. During the retreat, group members discuss any knowledge they have that is pertinent to a particular issue. This collective body of knowledge is synthesized and made available to interested managers.

The selection of specific data sources should be based, in part, on the quality of data required for a particular decision. Data sources should be evaluated in terms of their reliability and validity. Reliability essentially represents an evaluation of the source itself (Montgomery and Weinberg, 1979) and can be thought of as consistency over time. The fundamental basis for determining reliability is previous experience with the source. For example, many firms conduct periodic interviews with their salespeople to assess the nature of the competitive climate within particular regions or market segments. By tracking a salesperson's responses over time, it is possible to detect biases that would be difficult to observe in one-shot field interviews.

Validity refers to the probable truth of the data itself and is at the foundation of competitive intelligence. Approaches to determining validity typically rely on comparison with other data sources and/or other indicators or proxy measures of the same variable. For example, Calgon's Industrial Water Treatment Chemical Division develops estimates of competitors' market share by geographic region and market segment based upon salesperson records of the firms which they call upon that are served by competing suppliers. These data are converted into dollar values which are summed and compared to estimates of market potential based on input/output analyses for each market. Additionally, periodic telephone interviews of current and potential customers are conducted to identify the names and volume purchased from each of their major chemical suppliers.

While all data collected should be of the highest quality possible, it is critical to recognize that, beyond a certain level, marginal improvements in accuracy often come at considerable expense. In all situations, the cost of data should be evaluated in terms of the benefits of the resulting intelligence. The expenses involved with improving the accuracy of data include not only the cost of accessing multiple sources but also any loss of opportunity that results from the additional time that is typically necessary for validation. The benefits of the intelligence depend upon the size of the investment under consideration and the extent to which decision makers are uncertain as to which alternative is best stated another way. The level of accuracy required depends on both the cost of increased accuracy and the likelihood of making a wrong decision in the absence of more accurate data. Indeed, in cases where the best alternative is readily apparent, managers may only require a level of accuracy which is sufficient to confirm the decision.

Data Analysis

Data analysis involves the conversion of raw factual descriptors into meaningful information. As with data collection, the specific types of

Figure 5. A Parsimonious Approach to Constructing
Competitor Strength-Weakness Profiles

Competitor Evaluated: <u>Competitor A</u>

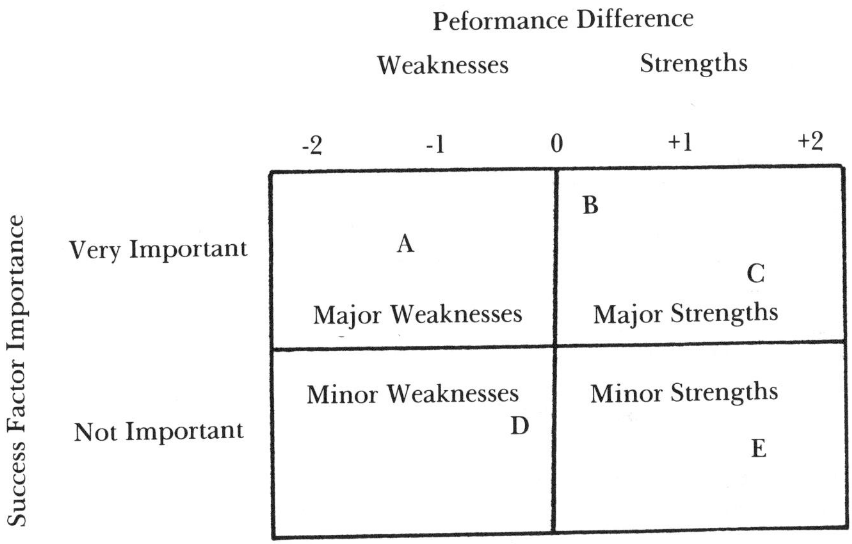

Peformance Difference

Weaknesses   Strengths

| | -2 | -1 | 0 | +1 | +2 |

Success Factor Importance

	Weaknesses	Strengths
Very Important	A Major Weaknesses	B C Major Strengths
Not Important	Minor Weaknesses D	Minor Strengths E

analysis) performance on each success factor and that of Competitor A. Performance was measured on a six-point poor/outstanding scale. The project "success factors" for evaluating salesforce performance were:

A = Product knowledge of salesperson
B = Empathy and awareness of customer needs
C = Timeliness of sales calls
D = Technical knowledge
E = Availability of salesperson

analyses should follow naturally from project information objectives. While many of the techniques commonly used in competitive analysis have their origins in economics and finance (Goldenberg, 1984; Spitalnic, 1984), it is the *logic* behind and the *interpretation* of the output of the techniques, not the techniques themselves, that generate intelligence. Unfortunately, the myth has developed that the quality of intelligence is, in some fashion, related to the level of sophistication of the techniques used. Indeed, many of the frustrations voiced by managers regarding the relevance of competitive intelligence can be traced to analysts' overreliance on sophisticated analytical techniques at the expense of relevance.

The sophistication of analysis should be consistent with the information needs of the project. For example, Smith and Prescott (1987) have developed an approach for identifying a firm's net strengths and weaknesses, a frequent objective of competitive analysis projects, that combines simplicity with effectiveness. The generic technique examines a firm's performance relative to that of its competitors with respect to critical industry or project success factors. Interpretation of differences in performance are further enhanced by including measures of the importance of each success factor. Continuing with the example set forth in Figure 4, Figure 5 illustrates how the combination of relative performance with success factor importance yields a clear definition of a competitor's major and minor strengths and weaknesses.

The quality of analysis can be enhanced further by insuring that persons involved with data analysis are not only technically competent but are also able to clearly translate complex statistics into meaningful information. Ideally, analysts should be aware of industry dynamics and competitor characteristics. Such knowledge is pivotal in extracting meaningful information from seemingly disparate pieces of data. For example, knowledge that a key competitor recently sold a highly profitable manufacturing operation which supplied the firm with a key resource might, at first glance, be interpreted as a signal of financial trouble. However, by combining this piece of data with seemingly unrelated data on the firm's R & D activities, an insightful analyst came to a significantly different conclusion—the company may have in fact developed a technology which made the manufacturing unit obsolete. This hypothesis triggered further investigation that would not have been considered under the former conclusion (Montgomery and Weinberg, 1979).

While generally useful, knowledge of industry dynamics and analytical techniques is a double-edged sword in that it can "color" the interpretation of data. Specifically, such knowledge comprises the perceptual "lens" through which the analyst views data. As Sammon (1984) has observed, this lens may cause certain pieces of data, such as those which appear to confirm deep-seated personal beliefs, to be overestimated in terms of their intelligence value.

To guard against such unintentional and subtle bias in interpretation, the conclusions should be cross-validated. This can be accomplished by having a series of qualified individuals render their impressions of the findings (i.e., the relevant tables, graphs, and charts without any narrative material). In the case of survey-based data, some firms present summary findings to a sample of the survey respondents for interpretation. Convergence across multiple interpretations provides a measure of validity and thus greatly increases the confidence a decision maker can place in the final set of conclusions. Alternatively, the entire analysis may be conducted by an interactive team rather than by a single individual or group of individuals working separately.

Storage and Dissemination

The interaction between the processes used to store and disseminate the output of intelligence projects facilitates decision making by having the right intelligence delivered to the right people at the right time. While on the surface, these processes appear to be almost programmable, they represent a notable problem in the management of competitive intelligence (Prescott, 1987).

Storage. The array of possible storage devices ranges from simple file-drawer systems to complex multiuser micro/mainframe computer networks. The benefits and problems with each have been widely documented (Blair, 1984). The objective of all of these approaches is to catalogue and store intelligence in a manner that is easy to access. In achieving this objective, competitive intelligence system designers must guard against allowing available information technology to dominate in determining the general configuration of the storage-retrieval system. Access can be facilitated greatly by designing the storage-retrieval system in a manner which effectively interfaces current information technology with user (i.e., analysts as well as decision makers) information needs.

Further, most information access systems use completed report titles and specific findings as the main or sole unit of reference (Zaltman and Deshpande, 1979). Such a system is "source" rather than "need" oriented. Often, potential users will not be able to articulate their information needs in terms used in past research. Consequently, information search is broad and inefficient. In contrast, a system which is designed around user needs facilitates focused and efficient search. Such a system is organized around key reserach questions and issues. For example, a report labeled "Market Structure of the Airline Industry" might be more appropriately classified in terms of the research question, "What are the key trends in the structure of the airline industry?" Indeed, management needs are couched in terms of specific intelligence questions. Storage and retrieval systems should reflect this.

Dissemination. As with storage systems, there exist a myriad of approaches to and media for disseminating competitive intelligence (Sammon, 1984; Prescott, 1987). These include newsletters, bulletin boards, presentations, computerized data bases, reports, memos, and personal communications. The frequency of dissemination and the selection of a specific medium are based on the type of intelligence. In this context, intelligence may be of two types: (1) that used to detect discontinuities in the environment, or (2) that used as input to specific projects. For instance, intelligence such as industry capacity utilization and sales of key competitors should be tracked continuously to detect changes in the competitive fabric and thus should be disseminated to managers on an ongoing basis. Other intelligence such as competitor product-quality, executive profiles, employee recruiting practices, and plant locations may be disseminated on a need-to-know (i.e., by request) basis. In general, the medium selected follows naturally from the frequency of dissemination—that is, ongoing intelligence may be distributed in the form of standardized reports which facilitate longitudinal analysis whereas special-request intelligence typically requires a custom-tailored document. One computer firm uses a newsletter approach to distribute new competitive intelligence to its salesforce. Each salesperson has a competitor notebook with specific sections devoted to topics such as new products, technologies, and competitors.

Intelligence Utilization

Effective utilization of competitive intelligence is the ultimate goal of a competitive intelligence system and can be construed as the extent to which intelligence is actually employed by decision makers in evaluating alternatives. Intelligence that has been produced and is made readily available but is either not utilized or underutilized by decision makers, reduces the entire system to a futile intellectual exercise. Unfortunately, the problem of fostering information utilization appears to be acute. As Zaltman and Deshpande (1979) observed, only about a third of the competitor intelligence generated in organizations is used, and only a fraction of that was used successfully.

A number of scholars have explored the problem of intelligence utilization in organizations both conceptually (Ackoff, 1967; Mitroff et al., 1979; Aaker, 1983) and empirically (Deshpande and Zaltman, 1982, 1984, 1987). Following is a summary of the general conclusions which may be drawn from these studies and implications for improving intelligence utilization:

1. Firms which are relatively decentralized and less formalized (i.e., fewer rules define communications, interpersonal roles, and norms) tend to utilize intelligence more (and perhaps better) than their centralized and formalized counterparts.

This finding suggests that in decentralized companies, managers, particularly at lower levels in the organization, may take a more active role in the entire intelligence-gathering process and thus are more committed to using the outputs. Further, less formality may promote greater interaction between analysts and end-users. Consequently, the former are more aware of the information needs and presentation format requirements of the latter.

2. The greater the deviation of research findings from managers' expectations, the less will be the utilization of the findings.

This finding indicates that managers develop "priors" about what they expect intelligence projects to reveal before the research is conducted. Indeed, these priors may serve as "truth tests" by which managers judge the quality of a report—that is, findings that deviate too dramatically from expectations are perceived to be in error. Given these effects, analysts should attempt to identify decision maker expectations in advance or during the conduct of the intelligence project. As findings become available, the analyst, through informal discussions with the decision maker, can gradually begin to sensitize him or her to any contradictory evidence.

3. The greater the perceived ability to take action on the findings in the report, the greater the utilization.

This finding applies to (a) the format of the report, and (b) the extent to which the research objectives were aligned with the true information needs of the project. The latter issue was discussed at length in the section on developing project information objectives. While data do not always "speak for themselves," the use of tables, charts, and figures which capture key relationships in the data can greatly facilitate the acceptance of intelligence. Many managers feel uncomfortable basing decisions strictly on the analyst's interpretation of the data and often prefer to augment the analyst's narrative material with their own interpretation. Decision maker augmentation of intelligence is made considerably less frustrating through the creative use of simple tables and charts. For instance, Figure 5 illustrates a straightforward approach to presenting a series of t-tests which provides substantially more information than would be possible in the traditional tabular form. Note also that the use of " action" or decision-relevant labels further enhances the perceived "actionability" of the findings.

4. (a) The greater the technical quality of the report, the greater the utilization of the intelligence.
    (b) The technical quality of the intelligence report is more salient in the case of findings that are discrepant with expectations than when they confirm expectations.

Given that many managers are not familiar with the strengths, weaknesses, or underlying assumptions associated with many analytical techniques (regression analysis, factor analysis, cluster analysis, discriminant analysis, etc.), analysts should attempt to manage "signals" of technical quality. Quality signals are those characteristics of the research procedure that the decision maker tends to apply as criteria to judge the quality of the intelligence. Through careful probing, the analyst can surface these criteria in informal conversations with the decision maker. For example, a researcher at a large healthcare organization would periodically ask managers what they thought of particular intelligence projects which were conducted in the past. The research projects to which he referred were those whose findings were not utilized extensively in decision making. The responses often revealed the methodological cues that the managers used in evaluating a report. In general, frequently used quality signals include the sample size and its composition; the agency which conducted the research; the inclusion of tables and figures which can be readily comprehended; the cost of the project (if contracted outside); and the time it took for the project to be completed.

In addition to managing quality signals, the perceived technical quality of a report can be enhanced by increasing end-user commitment to the research method itself. This can be accomplished by simply involving the end-user in the design of questionnaires in the case of survey research; the selection of appropriate respondents and the determination of the sample size; and the selection of a data-collection organization if the research is to be subcontracted. Such involvement makes it difficult for the decision maker to dismiss the resulting findings on methodological grounds. Moreover, such a procedure places the manager in a position to defend the research method employed to others involved in the decision.

THE INTELLIGENCE CONTROL SYSTEM

The evaluation and updating of a competitive intelligence system is as challenging as it is important. During our discussions with managers, we have found that intelligence control is not only difficult to manage but it is also the most sensitive of all the issues related to the management of competitive intelligence activities. Therefore, this section deviates somewhat from the previous sections in that there are fewer examples. Given the limited historic treatment of the subject, it is our goal to set forth both the activities that should comprise an intelligence control system and provide specific techniques for implementing these activities.

Intelligence control is concerned with measuring the system's outputs along a set of dimensions, comparing these measures to a set of standards or norms, and generating corrective action if necessary (Neumann, 1982; King, 1983). The intelligence control system operates to evaluate both the effectiveness and efficiency of individual competitive analysis projects as well as the entire competitive intelligence system.

Regardless of the level of evaluation, the intelligence control system is comprised of three key elements: (1) a set of performance indicators and standards on which to base the evaluation of actual performance, (2) procedures for identifying underlying causes of performance deviations, and (3) procedures for incorporating the results of the evaluations into programs for updating and improving the competitive analysis system.

Performance Indicators and Standards

The first and perhaps most critical step in evaluating performance involves the development of evaluation criteria or performance indicators. Performance indicators fall into four general and interrelated categories: (1) those which are related to the quality and usability of the information itself, (2) those which are related to the effectiveness of the system as a whole, (3) those related to the competitive intelligence task system, and (4) those which are related to the efficiency of the system as a whole.

Information Quality. The quality of information may be assessed along a number of dimensions (e.g., Zmud, 1978; Cleland and King, 1975; Neumann, 1982). Among the more frequently applied indicators of information quality are (a) information accuracy and reliability, (b) the extent to which the data analysis is consistent with the research questions, and (c) the extent to which the information is reported in a timely manner and in a format which facilitates use. Information quality indicators essentially measure the performance of the data collection, analysis, and storage/dissemination processes of the competitive intelligence control system. Performance data on each quality indicator are obtained through the use of a post-project review in which the user is requested to render an evaluation of the intelligence generated on each of the indicators. These evaluations are subsequently compared to a standard level of performance to identify potential problem areas.

Aggregate System Effectiveness. An assessment of aggregate system effectiveness is chiefly concerned with the extent to which the system generates intelligence that is aligned with the information needs of a particular business strategy. The evaluation of system effectiveness is essentially a top-down process in that it is concerned primarily with the types of intelligence requests being made by managers. System-level effectiveness evaluation focuses on answering the question, "Is the system generating the right kinds of intelligence?" Stated another way, system effectiveness evaluation attempts to assess the incidence of Type III errors (Mitroff et al., 1979). In statistical jargon, Type I and Type II errors refer to minimizing the chances of making the wrong decision in the presence of the right information . A Type III error, however, refers to the probability of working on solving the wrong problem.

In essence, Type III errors are related to the nature of the inputs to the competitive intelligence task system. As such, the assessment of the prevalence of Type III errors can be thought of as an evaluation of the appropriateness of the system mission statement. Operationally, Type III errors are evaluated in terms of the *types* of intelligence projects requested relative to the types of requests which are best suited for the firm's strategy. The degree of alignment is measured by first examining the ratio of the number of times each type of intelligence (e.g., offensive, defensive, and informational) was requested to the number of total intelligence requests. Each ratio is then compared to a measure of the importance of each type of intelligence to formulating and implementing the firm's competitive strategies. Importance measures may be obtained through managerial consensus and will typically be generated as part of the information audit conducted in developing the system mission statement.

Task System Effectiveness. In contrast to Type III errors, task system errors arise and are best evaluated at the project level. It is valuable to have a "project log" which records the information requested and the information actually obtained. Task system errors may then be measured by the extent to which the intelligence obtained deviates from that which was requested. To facilitate comparison across projects, the number of deviations should be standardized by the number of items of information requested. An aggregate measure of task system errors is obtained by summing across the standardized task system errors per project. In order to allow for longitudinal comparison, this sum should be standardized by the number of intelligence projects conducted during a given time period. Both the project and aggregate error rates may then be compared to predetermined standards.

System Efficiency. System efficiency is evaluated in terms of the net value of the intelligence generated (Zmud, 1978). Net value may be construed as the difference between the estimated economic worth of the intelligence to the user and the actual cost of operating the system. The economic worth of an information system can be estimated by having users assign an economic (dollar) value to each intelligence project which they request. These appraisals are summed across projects and netted against the actual cost associated with operating the system during the time period under consideration.

An alternative approach to measuring efficiency also begins at the project level and is based on the ratio of information utilized to information generated. Extending the project evaluation record, the end user would be requested to estimate the fraction of the intelligence generated that was actually utilized in a particular decision. This fraction is then applied to the cost of obtaining the intelligence to arrive directly at a value of the unused information for a particular project. This value is subsequently compared to an acceptable standard value or range. Summing across projects provides an aggregate measure of the value of unused information.

Setting Standards.   Initially, standards of performance may be somewhat subjective and arbitrary. However, through systematically recording both effectiveness and efficiency measures over time, a body of knowledge will develop about the "expected performance" of the system. To the extent that the performance measures are quantifiable, expected values and the associated variance for each measure may be obtained. Given these two statistics, it is a simple matter to construct intervals of "acceptable" performance of the system. To the extent that the performance measures are quantifiable, expected values and the associated variance for each measure may be obtained. Given these two statistics, it is a simple matter to construct intervals of "acceptable" performance levels. When recorded at the project level, it will not take long until there is a sufficient number of cases to objectively set standards. Further, the usefulness of the standards may be improved considerably by deriving them for particular categories of intelligence projects—for example, strategic group analyses, competitor strength/weakness assessments, and so on.

Identification of Underlying Causes of Performance Deviations

A recurring deviation from a standard performance level on a particular indicator does not constitute a problem per se but only represents a signal or symptom of a problem. Once a symptom has been identified, surfacing the actual problem(s) requires the joint attention of all individuals associated with the symptom. For instance, let us assume that an analysis of task system effectiveness found that most intelligence projects involving the analysis of intraindustry structure had unfavorable deviations in terms of turnaround time and intelligence utilization rate. Individuals involved in surfacing the underlying reasons for such deviations would include the managers and analysts associated with the "deviant" projects. This information may, in turn, be obtained from the project log.

Once the appropriate persons have been identified, their respective appraisals of the underlying problems are obtained. A widely used approach for eliciting such judgments involves the conduct of personal or small-group semistructured interviews by an internal systems auditor or by an individual from outside the organization. The interviews focus on eliciting statements from the analyst(s) and decision maker(s) regarding their perceptions of the source of the problem. Since many of the statements rendered will themselves be symptoms, this task is substantially more challenging than it initially appears. For example, underutilization of intelligence may be explained by the user in terms of more specific symptoms such as the length and complexity of reports. Such a finding suggests lack of awareness of user needs on the part of the analyst. Continued probing may yield more related symptoms such as a relatively low level of interaction between analyst and user. Carried further, it may be found that the low degree of interaction is due to the large number of projects which the analyst manages concurrently, and thus he or she does not have sufficient time to interact with users beyond the initial request for intelligence. Hence, in this example, the symptom of underutilization of intelligence can be traced to the main problem of project scheduling.

It is critical to recognize that all parties involved with evaluation should be briefed extensively in advance of the interviews. Failure to do so often creates the impression that the review process is a "head hunt" in disguise. Such an atmosphere severely reduces the effectiveness of the review process.

Translating Problems into Solutions

The old adage "a problem correctly identified is half solved" may hold considerable merit. The generation and implementation of solutions typically follow naturally from the problem specification. The process of generating alternatives and their associated implementation plans should involve the persons interviewed in the problem identification phase in addition to anyone directly engaged in executing any system changes. Such a practice reinforces the value of the review process and increases commitment to any changes which are implemented.

Many organizations have found that brainstorming sessions, or similar informal yet focused discussions, provide a valuable forum for generating alternative solutions to a particular competitive intelligence system problem. Participants are provided with definitions of the key problems in advance of the session. During the session, participants are requested to offer as many alternatives as possible. The session moderator should be fair and impartial to encourage equal participation. It is not uncommon to use the person who conducted the interviews in the previous stage to moderate the brainstorming session.

It is vital to realize that changes in a component of the system (e.g., the number of projects that one analyst is expected to manage in a given period of time) cannot be made in isolation. For example, increasing the number of analysts in an attempt to reduce the project load per analyst can be expected to raise the average cost per project and thus require a corresponding adjustment in any cost-based performance standards. The complex web of component interrelationships may not be apparent to any single individual. Therefore, following the generation of alternatives, it is generally advisable that participants in the brainstorming session be asked to enumerate which and how other system components would be affected by each alternative.

DIRECTIONS FOR FUTURE RESEARCH

This chapter has presented a broad conceptual overview of the components and processes that comprise a competitive intelligence system. It essentially takes a cross-sectional perspective of a competitive intelligence system as it might exist at a point of advanced development. While this perspective is based upon an extensive integration of existing literature in both competitive intelligence and management information systems, a number of questions remain to be answered.

One of the first areas that needs to be addressed is the level of sophistication that firms currently possess regarding the gathering, analysis, and management of industry and competitor intelligence. The formation of the Society of Competitive Intelligence Professionals attests to the growth in formal approaches to competitive analysis. However, as noted earlier, most of the writing in the area of competitive intelligence has focused on techniques of gathering information and to a limited extent on data analysis. Although there is some literature on the management of competitive intelligence systems, it is based primarily on case studies and anecdotal evidence. With the exception of the work by Zinkham and Gelb (1985) in industrial marketing, there has been no systematic attempt to describe current practice in competitive intelligence. What is needed is a comprehensive survey of firms that conduct competitive intelligence focused on questions such as: What types of data are gathered and by whom? Who are the major users and why? What are the most commonly used techniques for analyzing data? How is intelligence disseminated and with what effects? What are the emerging problems in each aspect of the project-based system (i.e., collection, analysis, dissemination, storage), and what solutions have been developed?

While a state-of-the-art study would provide needed demographics, in-depth case studies that explore the processes of intelligence acquisition, analysis, dissemination, and utilization, as well as system development and change, would provide valuable insights for starting or enhancing the competitive intelligence function. Key research questions include: How do firms share internal charges across departments for intelligence services? How is cross-functional cooperation obtained and managed? How are budgets of competitive intelligence departments determined? How are managers informed of the availability and uses of competitive intelligence services? How are competitive intelligence personnel selected and trained? How are the competitive intelligence needs of various projects determined? What are the forces that drive evolution of competitive intelligence systems?

A related area of research involves the construction of a typology of competitive intelligence systems. Organizational and environmental constructs such as the structural and intelligence system conditioners described in this chapter represent contingency factors that are expected to have a significant impact on system design as well as effectiveness. Data for developing a typology may be obtained from case studies and then tested by survey research.

A fourth area for future research concerns competitive intelligence system control and measurement of aggregate system effectiveness. It is time to broaden the perspective from user satisfaction studies and analysis of utilization rates (which reflect the performance of various system components) to a systemwide analysis. In a normative sense, overall system effectiveness should be measured in terms of system-level goals, namely, the extent to which uncertainty about the competitive environment is reduced. At a project level, such objectives may be measured in terms of managers' certainty or confidence in a particular decision. King's (1983) work in strategic planning system evaluation could serve as a model for this research. Key research questions in this area include: What is the role of user feedback in updating report formats, the types of intelligence obtained, and the frequency with which it is gathered? How are various sources of information evaluated in terms of their validity and reliability? How do firms evaluate the effectiveness of their competitive intelligence system? To what extent does perceived confidence in a decision vary across different information sources? Relative to other forms of information used in making a decision, what is the role of competitive intelligence and how does it vary across types of decisions?

Finally, research needs to be done in the area of competitive intelligence utilization. Research should focus on the ways in which various information and presentation formats affect decisions. For example, there may be certain presentation formats that promote risk taking among managers. We have observed increased risk taking in a number of cases where managers have viewed videotaped "focus groups" of their customers and suppliers discussing the company's strengths and weaknesses vis-a-vis competitors. Invariably, videotape presentations seemed to give managers a great deal of confidence in their chosen course of action. Considerably different reactions were found when data from focus groups were presented in the form of a written report.

CONCLUSIONS

The wide acceptance of competitive intelligence programs as a legitimate function in organizations requires managers to explicitly address a series of issues related to the design and implementation of systems to administer these programs. To date, there has been little guidance for managers who often struggle to implement intelligence programs. The framework developed in this chapter is an attempt to assist managers by identifying the key design components of competitive intelligence systems. To conclude, we would like to provide a set of guidelines that managers have found useful in facilitating the implementation of competitive intelligence systems.

1. *Nurture clients.* As a staff function, competitive intelligence programs need to pay attention to their clients. One approach is to provide clients with additional benefits in the form of support, interpretation assistance, or additional intelligence which extends beyond what is requested.
2. *Integrate with other units.* A competitive intelligence program contained within another unit has the advantage of being associated with an established structure, set of personnel, operating budget, and so forth. An independent unit, on the other hand, must establish legitimacy as well as build a structure to support its activities.
3. *Remain small.* Once a competitive intelligence program becomes established, it can be run with a small set of personnel. In most organizations, competitive intelligence activities are run on a project basis. Therefore, rather than increase the size of the staff in the competitive intelligence program, an alternative is to develop a list of individuals throughout the organization who can assist in various projects. It is also our belief that a small, but effective and efficient program, will be less affected during budget crises.
4. *Pay your own way.* Several companies have established their competitive intelligence operations in their internal consulting group. As a result, they become a profit center. While this is not possible in many organizations, competitive intelligence units which are perceived as providing value to their clients will be more likely to receive support during budgeting and planning periods.
5. *Provide tangible outputs.* There is a wide variety of products that a competitive intelligence program can provide. It is critical that intelligence professionals identify those products that are most needed by the program's clients and focus on their advancement. One approach for a new program is to conduct an industry analysis for a client and present both the process of the analysis as well as the results of the study to a diverse group of potential clients. This process

shows initiative, demonstrates the types of activities and capabilities of the program, and helps to stimulate managers' ideas concerning the value of competitive intelligence.

6. *Require feedback from clients.*   While several managers have voiced the concern that feedback from clients opens a can of worms, it is our experience that documented feedback is valuable to the viability of a program. Feedback helps to identify strengths and weaknesses, suggests new courses of action, and serves as another way to nurture clients.

7. *Maintain visibility.*   Above all, a competitive intelligence group must be visible. Addressing the guidelines presented above will help in this regard. In addition, a competitive intelligence program should have a strategic plan which includes tactics for the development of visibility and credibility.

REFERENCES

Aaker, David A. (1983). "Organizing a Strategic Information Scanning System." *California Management Review* 25:76-83.

Ackoff, Russell L. (1967). "Management Misinformation Systems." *Management Science* 14:B147-B156.

Adler, Lee (1967). "Systems Approach to Marketing." *Harvard Business Review* 45:105-118.

Aguilar, Francis Joseph (1967). *Scanning the Business Environment.* New York: Macmillan.

Allison, Graham T. (1971). *The Essence of Decision: Explaining the Cuban Missile Crisis.* Boston: Little, Brown.

Blair, David C. (1984). "The Management of Information: Basic Distinctions." *Sloan Management Review* 25:13-23.

Blake, Robert R., and Jane S. Mouton (1969). *Building a Dynamic Corporation Through Grid Organization.* Reading, MA: Addison-Wesley.

Boulton, William R., William M. Lindsay, Stephen G. Franklin, and Leslie W. Rue (1982). "Strategic Planning: Determining the Impact of Environmental Characteristics and Uncertainty." *Academy of Management Journal* 25:500-509.

Bower, Joseph L. (1972). *Managing the Resource Allocation Process.* Homewood, IL: Irwin.

Camillus, John C. (1986). *Strategic Planning and Management Control.* Lexington, MA: Lexington Books.

Cleland, David I., and William R. King (1975). "Competitive Business Intelligence Systems." *Business Horizons* 18:21-29.

Cowan, David A. (1986). "Developing a Process Model of Problem Recognition." *Academy of Management Review* 11:763-776.

Day, George S. (1984). "Marketing Theory With a Strategic Orientation." *Journal of Marketing* 48:79-89.

Deshpande, Rohit, and Gerald Zaltman (1982). "Factors Affecting the Use of Market Research Information: A Path Analysis." *Journal of Marketing Research* 19:14-31.

————— (1984). "A Comparison of Factors Affecting Researcher and Manager Perceptions of Market Research Use." *Journal of Marketing Research* 21:32-38.

————— (1987). "A Comparison of Factors Affecting Use of Marketing Information in Consumer and Industrial Firms." *Journal of Marketing Research* 24:114-118.

Donaldson, Gordon and Jay W. Lorsch (1983). *Decision Making at The Top*. New York: Basic Books.

Fahey, Liam, and William R. King (1977). "Environmental Scanning for Corporate Planning." *Business Horizons* 20:61-71.

Freeman, Edward R. (1984). *Strategic Management: A Stakeholder Approach*. Marshfield, MA: Pitman Publishing.

Fredrickson, James W. (1985). "Effects of Decision Motive and Organization Performance on Strategic Decision Processes." *Academy of Management Journal* 28:821-843.

Fredrickson, James W., and Terence R. Mitchell (1984). "Strategic Decision Processes: Comprehensiveness and Performance in an Industry with an Unstable Environment." *Academy of Management Journal* 27:399-423.

Fuld, Leonard M. (1985). *Competitor Intelligence: How to Get It; How to Use It*. New York: Wiley.

Goldenberg, David I. (1984). "Economics' Contributions to Competitor Intelligence in Business." In William L. Sammon, Mark A. Kurland, and Robert Spitalnic (eds.), *Business Competitor Intelligence: Methods for Collecting, Organizing, and Using Information*. New York: Wiley, pp. 240-267.

Grant, John H., and William R. King (1982). *The Logic of Strategic Planning*. Boston, MA: Little, Brown.

Gupta, Anil K., S. P. Raj, and David Wileman (1986). "A Model For the Study of R&D—Marketing Interface in the Product Innovation Process." *Journal of Marketing* 50:7-17.

Hambrick, Donald C. (1981). "Environment, Strategy, and Power Within Top Management Teams." *Administrative Science Quarterly* 26:253-275.

————— (1982). "Environmental Scanning and Organizational Strategy." *Strategic Management Journal* 3:159-174.

Hax, Arnoldo C., and N. S. Majluf (1984). *Strategic Management*. Englewood Cliffs, NJ: Prentice-Hall.

Hellriegel, Don, and John W. Slocum, Jr. (1986). *Management*, 4th Edition. Reading, MA: Addison-Wesley.

Jain, Subhash. (1984). "Environmental Scanning in U.S. Corporations." *Long Range Planning* 17:117-128.

Janis, Irving L., and L. Mann (1977). *Decision Making*. New York: Free Press.

Jung, Carl (1953). *Collected Works*. Vols. 7,8, and 9. Read H. Dart, M. Fordham, and G. Adler (eds.). Princeton, NJ: Princeton University Press.

Kefalas, A. G., and P. P. Schoderbeck (1973). "Scanning the Business Environment: Some Empirical Results." *Decision Sciences* 4:63-74.

King, William R. (1978). "Information for Strategic Planning: An Analysis." *Information and Management* 5:59-66.

————— (1983). "Evaluating Strategic Planning Systems." *Strategic Management Journal* 4:236-277.

Lawrence, Paul R., and Jay W. Lorsch (1967). *Organization and Environment: Managing Differentiation and Integration*. Homewood, IL: Irwin.

Lenz, R. Thomas, and Jack L. Engledow (1986). "Environmental Analysis Units and Strategic Decision-Making: A Field Study of Selected 'Leading Edge' Corporations." *Strategic Management Journal* 7:69-89.

Miles, Raymond E., and Charles C. Snow (1978). *Organizational Strategy, Structure, and Process*. New York: McGraw-Hill.

Miller, Danny, and Peter Friesen (1983). "Strategy-making and Environment: The Third Link." *Strategic Management Journal* 4:221-235.

Mintzberg, Henry (1973). *The Nature of Managerial Work*. New York: Harper and Row.

Mintzberg, Henry, Duru Raisinghani, and Andre Theoret (1976). "The Structure of 'Unstructured' Decision Processes." *Administrative Science Quarterly* 21:246-275.

Mitroff, Ian I., Ralph C. Kilmann, and Vincent P. Barabba (1979). "Management Information Versus Management Misinformation Systems." In Gerald Zaltman (ed.), *Management Principles for Nonprofit Agencies and Organizations*. New York: American Management Association, pp. 401-429.

Montgomery, David B., and Charles B. Weinberg (1979). "Toward Strategic Intelligence Systems." *Journal of Marketing* 43:41-52.

Neumann, Ahituv (1982). *Principles of Information Systems For Management*. New York: W. C. Brown.

Porter, Michael E. (1980). *Competitive Strategy*. New York: Free Press.

————— (1985). *Competitive Advantage*. New York: Free Press.

Prescott, John E. (1987). "A Process for Applying Analytical Models in Competitive Analysis." In William R. King and David I. Cleland (eds.), *Strategic Planning and Management Handbook*. New York: Van Nostrand and Reinhold, pp. 222-251.

Prescott, John E., and John H. Grant (1988). "Managers' Guide to Competitive Analysis Techniques." *Interfaces* 18:10-22.

Prescott, John E., and Daniel C. Smith (1987). "A Project-Based Approach to Competitive Analysis." *Strategic Management Journal* 8:411-423.

Quinn, James Brian (1980). *Strategies for Change: Logical Incrementalism*. Homewood, IL: Irwin.

Rodriquez, Jaime I., and William R. King (1977). "Competitive Information Systems." *Long Range Planning* 10:45-50.

Rogers, Everett M., and Rekha Agarwala-Rogers (1976). *Communications in Organizations*. New York: Free Press.

Ruekart, Robert W., and Orville C. Walker, Jr. (1987). "Marketing's Interaction With Other Functional Units: Conceptual Framework and Empirical Evidence." *Journal of Marketing* 51:1-19.

Sammon, William L. (1984). "Competitor Intelligence: An Analytical Approach." In William L. Sammon, Mark A. Kurland, and Robert Spitalnic (eds.), *Business Competitor Intelligence: Methods for Collecting, Organizing, and Using Information*. New York: Wiley, pp. 90-146.

Sammon, William L., Mark A. Kurland, and Robert Spitalnic (eds.) (1984). *Business Competitor Intelligence: Methods for Collecting, Organizing, and Using Information*. New York: Wiley.

Shrivastava, Paul, and John H. Grant (1985). "Empirically Derived Models of Strategic Decision Making Processes." *Strategic Management Journal* 6:97-114.

Smith, Daniel C., and John E. Prescott (1987). "Couple Competitive Analysis With Sales Management Decisions." *Industrial Marketing Management* 16:45-52.

Spitalnic, Robert (1984). "The Financial Dimension: Penetrating Financial Statements." In William L. Sammon, Mark A. Kurland, and Robert Spitalnic (eds.), *Business Competitor Intelligence: Methods for Collecting, Organizing, and Using Information*. New York: Wiley, pp. 215-239.

Steiner, George (1979). *Strategic Planning*. New York: Macmillan.

Tucker, Frances G., Seymour M. Zivan, and Robert C. Camp (1987). "How to Measure Yourself Against the Best." *Harvard Business Review* 65:8-10.

Thompson, James D. (1967). *Organizations in Action*. New York: McGraw-Hill.

Wall, Jerry (1974). "Probing Opinions: A Survey of Executive Attitudes, Practices, and Ethics Vis-à-Vis Espionage and Other Forms of Information Gathering." *Harvard Business Review* 52:23-25.

Washington Researchers (1983). *Company Information: A Model Investigation*. Washington, D.C.: Washington Researchers, Ltd.

Weber, Edward C. (1986). Tracking Strategy's Continued Viability: Profile of the Executive Curriculum and Their Companies. Working Paper, School of Business Administration, University of Wisconsin, Milwaukee.

Weick, Karl (1979). *The Social Psychology of Organizing*, 2nd Edition. Reading, MA: Addison-Wesley.

Woodward, Joan (1965). *Industrial Organization: Theory and Practice*. London: Oxford University Press.

Zaltman, Gerald, and Rohit Deshpande (1979). "Increasing the Utilization of Scientific and Technical Information." In William R. King and Gerald Zaltman (eds.), *Marketing Scientific and Technical Information*. Boulder, CO: Westview Press, pp. 93-109.

Zinkham, George M., and Betsy D. Gelb (1985). "Competitive Intelligence Practices of Industrial Marketers." *Industrial Marketing Management* 14:269-275.

Zmud, Robert W. (1978). "An Empirical Investigation of the Dimensionality of the Concept of Information." *Decision Sciences* 9:187-195.

INTERPRETING ENVIRONMENTS AND TAKING ACTION:
TYPES AND CHARACTERISTICS
OF STRATEGIC ISSUE
MANAGEMENT SYSTEMS

Edward J. Ottensmeyer and Jane E. Dutton

Top managers devote substantial time and energy to figuring out what is happening of strategic importance in and around their organizations. Subsequently, they attempt to fashion responses appropriate to those issues interpreted as strategic. These two fundamental top management activities—interpretation and action—are the focus of this chapter. More specifically, we describe the systems employed by top managers to handle those issues deemed most critical to an organization's success.

Traditional models of strategic management (Andrews, 1971; Schendel and Hofer 1979) have treated strategic issues as obvious, unambiguous starting points for organizational decisions and actions. However, more recently, organizational scholars have modified this picture with the research findings from cognitive psychology (Weick, 1979; Lyles and Mitroff, 1980; Kiesler and Sproull, 1982; Srivastva, 1984). In so doing, they have reminded us of the often-problematic nature of discovering, interpreting, and responding to strategic issues.

Coinciding with these refinements, there has been a renewed interest in the systems devised by organizations to manage strategic issues (Ansoff, 1980). A strategic issue management system (SIMS) is defined as that cluster of organizational structures, processes, and personnel devoted to identifying, analyzing, and responding to strategic issues (Wartick and Rude, 1986; Dutton and Ottensmeyer, 1987). Strategic issue management systems refer to both formal and informal activities and processes of organizations. In the academic and practitioner literatures, these activities have been given various labels (e.g., environmental scanning, social issues management, strategic planning). All of these activities, considered individually, refer to specific forms or components of strategic issue management systems as defined here.

Strategic issues are developments or trends emerging from an organization's internal or external environment that are perceived to have the potential to significantly affect the organization's strategy, performance, or survival (Ansoff, 1980; King, 1982). The term *strategic* underscores the notion that the issues must be perceived to be of major consequence to the organization. While most research has been done on the process of managing external social and political issues (Chase, 1984), strategic issue management also includes issues that emanate from the organization's internal environment (Brown, 1981).

The term *issue* is used as an umbrella concept for trends, developments, events, or other types of data suggesting a change in the internal or external environment. The term is meant to include problems, threats, and opportunities. Thus, the process of strategic issue management includes what others have called problem sensing (Kiesler and Sproull, 1982), problem formulation (Lyles and Mitroff, 1980), and issue diagnosis and interpretation (Dutton et al., 1983; Daft and Weick, 1984). However, rather than looking at these processes in isolation, the broader-gauged perspective developed in this chapter encourages scholars and practitioners alike to focus on the *management system* in which sensing, interpreting, analyzing, and responding all take place.

These generic activities are conducted, and specific forms of SIMS develop, within the bounds of an internal political economy defined as the combination of political and economic structures and processes at work inside an organization (Zald, 1970). A political economy functions not only in accord with economic rationality but is also affected by the realities of power relationships among key executives (Cyert and March, 1963; Pfeffer and Salancik, 1978).

Building on our earlier work, this chapter has three major purposes. First, we provide background on strategic issue management systems and the context in which they take shape and operate. Second, we develop a typology of SIMS forms based on organizational propensities for interpretation and action. Third, we elaborate on this typology by profiling four basic SIMS forms in much greater detail, putting forth a set of *implicit* propositions that serve as *explicit* invitations for further research. We extend our earlier work in two significant ways—first, by examining in more depth the contexts of SIMS and, secondly, by bringing SIMS more to life through a set of profiles of the four basic types briefly sketched in Dutton and Ottensmeyer (1987). The former contribution is more theoretical, while the latter draws on several business examples and has a more practical focus.

STRATEGIC ISSUE MANAGEMENT: AN OVERVIEW

Assumptions

Three fundamental assumptions underlie the analysis of systems for managing strategic issues. First, organizations are systems that process and interpret information from both their external and internal environments. Recent theoretical treatments of organizations as interpretation systems (Daft and Weick, 1984) appear to neglect the internal environment of organizations, focusing instead on the problems of interpreting and responding to the external environment's uncertainties, dependencies, and equivocalities. However, Morgan (1986) points out that organizations of even moderate complexity are faced with problems of self-discovery and self-interpretation. Thus, we assume that decision makers must contend with multiple sources of strategic issues. Under certain conditions, an organization's internal environment may be the dominant source of strategic issues (for example, human resource concerns) while under other conditions the external environment may prevail as the major generator of strategic issues.

The second assumption is that all organizations have strategic issue management systems, in the same way that all organizations have control systems or reward systems. That is, SIMS are inherent to organizations but manifest themselves in a variety of shapes or forms. At one end of the spectrum are informal and rudimentary systems, relying on the intuition of one executive to define what issues merit attention and what actions to take. At the opposite extreme are systems that rely on large corporate staffs to "track" a set of issues chosen in advance by top executives through a carefully prescribed process, with potential responses debated widely, and with actions shared by several operating units. For example, Sperry Corporation and Connecticut General Insurance Company house formal SIMS involving both staff and line personnel in identifying and responding to strategic issues (Brown, 1981).

A major implication of this assumption is that identifying SIMS by title or location may not be easy. In some organizations, the SIMS may be identical to environmental scanning units; in others, it may fall within the realm of public affairs, strategic planning, marketing, or human resource management units. Further, a SIMS may cut across internal structural boundaries. It might include in its inner circle representatives of major functional units (like marketing or production), staff offices (like planning or government relations), or outside consultants. But no matter where the strategic issue management process takes place, it is distinct in that it focuses on identifying, analyzing, and responding to strategic issues.

The third assumption is that strategic issue management systems may serve symbolic as well as instrumental functions (Pfeffer, 1981). By putting such systems into place, top managers, in addition to actually dealing with critical issues, create symbols and images in the eyes of powerful internal or external constituents (Feldman and March, 1981; Meyer, 1984). (For a complete discussion of the symbolic function of SIMS, see Dutton and Ottensmeyer, 1987).

Strategic Issues

Organizational choices about operating domains and about competitive strategies within those domains play a central role in defining an organization's array of external strategic issues. However, what becomes defined and treated as a strategic issue may vary among firms operating in the same industry. These varying issue interpretations may be the result of different competitive positions selected by firms in the same industry (Porter, 1980); the actual or sought-after position then provides a ready-made decision frame for defining what sort of issues are perceived as strategic in a firm. For example, a firm that considers itself an industry leader in pharmaceuticals will see innovative bio-engineering techniques as more strategic to it than will the firm adopting a product-market strategy of making and selling generic drugs.

Differing interpretations of the same issue, event, or data may also arise in organizations with very similar strategies operating in the same environment (Kiesler and Sproull, 1982; Daft and Weick, 1984). More visible examples of this situation might involve two similar firms, one that perceives an issue as strategic earlier than the other and that subsequently takes action based on this perception, achieving a substantial benefit because of the action's timeliness (Miles and Snow, 1984). Examples abound: Sears and the development of flameproof children's pajamas, Timex and the low-priced wristwatch, and Turner Broadcasting and the "Superstation" concept.

Similar points can be made regarding internal issues. Certainly a firm's product-market strategy makes a difference in the array of potentially strategic internal issues. For example, firms relying on state-of-the-art research and development are more likely to find human resource issues, such as managing scientists and engineers, taking on strategic importance than will firms that are followers in innovation. Additionally, firms may differ in their abilities to perceive internal issues as critical.

Those adopting a traditional view of strategic management might see these simply as examples of firms developing and implementing new or distinct competitive postures. However, left unattended by this traditional perspective is the variation in the systems through which organizations interpret and respond to the *same* information or events. We know very little about these system differences. Learning more about such systems is critical to a more informed understanding of the strategic choices made by organizations.

Whatever their origins, strategic issues do not arrive at top management's doorstep neatly labeled (Dutton et al., 1983). Instead, data on new technologies, market trends, competitors, employee morale, or government policy need to be interpreted and treated as "strategic issues" by organizational leaders. Given a situation in which interpretation and judgment are central, one can see ample room for competition to develop among executives seeking to enhance their individual power and influence. For example, an executive who identifies an issue as strategic (and achieves a consensus among top executives that it *is* strategic) earlier than his or her colleagues/competitors stands to gain both credibility and power. This sort of credibility is sought not only by junior executives hoping to get promoted but by CEOs attempting to bring about needed strategic change (Quinn, 1980).

Formal Units for Strategic Issue Management

As a structural and process innovation for organizations, formal strategic issue management is gaining in popularity. Over 400 managers are currently members of the Issues Management Association, an association founded to promote communication and professional affiliation among managers directly involved in these activities. Aside from this formal affiliation, there are countless other managers whose implicit or explicit roles involve them in identifying, interpreting, or responding to strategic issues. In a 1983 tabulation of the formal positions of IMA members, for example, the most common affiliation was public affairs (n = 35), followed by corporate planning (n = 33), corporate communications (n = 21), government affairs (n = 20), and policy analysis (n = 16) (Wartick and Rude, 1986).

Whatever these processes are called, they are seen to confer certain instrumental benefits upon organizations that employ them. These are

Table 1.   Examples and Benefits of Strategic Issue Management Systems

Sample of Organizations Using Formal Strategic Issue Management Systems	*Benefits Cited by Users**
Monsanto	More lead time for coordinating responses
Dow Chemical	
	Better anticipation of critical changes
DuPont	
Shell Oil	Reduced vulnerability to changes in internal or
Sperry	external environment
PPG	Improved integration of strategic planning and
Allied Chemical	research on public policy issues
Sears, Roebuck	
	Greater internal and
General Electric	external credibility
Citicorp	Greater competitive advantage
Port Authority of New York and New Jersey	Improved top management confidence in strategic
State of Colorado	decision making

*Adapted from Brown (1981) and Wartick and Rude (1986).

summarized in Table 1. As the table suggests, the major role of strategic issue management is in facilitating the organization's adaptive capability by increasing the lead time, speed, and ease of responding to changes in both internal and external environments (Chakravarthy, 1982).

Context of Strategic Issue Management Systems

Strategic issue management systems take their original form and then change over time as a result of a complex interplay of identified strategic issues and an internal political economy that encompasses interpreting and acting on those issues. Making up this internal environment is a set of formal and informal structures, power configurations among key managers, prior issue interpretations, and shared critical assumptions, all of which help to mold a SIMS. Once in place, this system becomes critical to the enactment of future environments (Weick, 1979). This duality underscores a fundamental point that organizations not only adapt to environmental

Figure 1. Fundamental Relationship between Organizational
Environments and Strategic Issue Management Systems

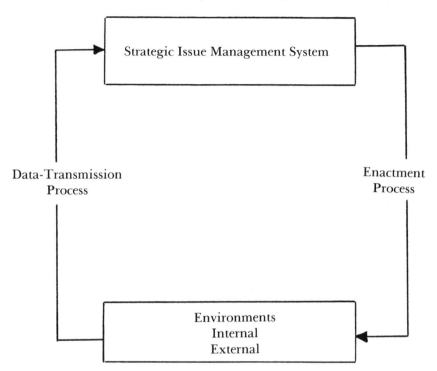

forces, they also play a role in creating, both through their actions and their
interpretations, the environments to which they adapt (Weick, 1979;
Hrebiniak and Joyce, 1985). Figure 1 displays the mutually-causal relationship between environments and forms of SIMS.

Determinants of SIMS Forms. Specific forms of SIMS are shaped by
several intertwined factors. The most critical of these are:

1. Strategic choice of domain (Child, 1972; Miles and Snow, 1978; Miles,
   1982).
2. Amount of information available in these chosen domains or
   environments (Galbraith, 1977).
3. Equivocality or ambiguity of information (Daft and Weick, 1984).
4. Accountability pressures (Hannan and Freeman, 1984; Tetlock, 1985).
5. Levels of internal structural differentiation (Lawrence and Lorsch,
   1967).

Figure 2.   Contextual Factors and Strategic Issue Management Systems

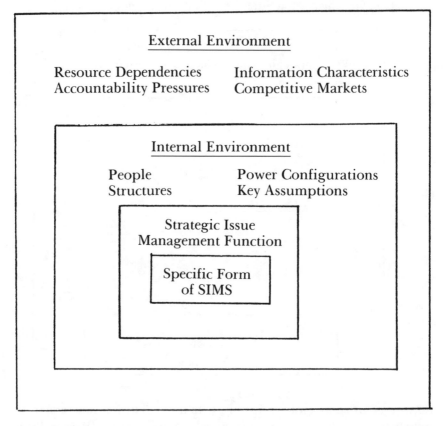

6.   Instrumental or symbolic functions served (Dutton and Ottensmeyer, 1987).
7.   Prior organizational learning (Duncan and Weiss, 1979).
8.   Dynamic workings of an internal political economy (Zald, 1970).

Figure 2 portrays a specific form of strategic issue management system residing within the generic function of managing strategic issues. Along with other management systems (e.g., planning, reward, control), the SIMS is embedded in an internal environment. External environments provide an additional set of forces and are shown as the outermost layer of the figure.

The environments of a firm or organization are determined by prior strategic choices of domain (e.g., industries or segments of industries) and by prior organization-environment interactions or exchanges (e.g., hostility, passivity). Thus, an organization, through its choices, selects or changes the set of issues associated with its external environments. For example, tobacco companies have recently become major players in the food and beverage industry, in their efforts to limit the risk associated with operating in an increasingly hostile environment (Miles, 1982). In the extreme case, some firms have changed domains (and their strategic issue set) completely. For example, American Can moved recently from the low-growth packaging industry into the rapidly-changing financial services sector.

Organizations may be seen as residing in an interorganizational network whose prior workings provide data for intraorganizational interpretation, response, and learning. For example, a traditional pattern of interaction between old firms in a regulated industry and the regulatory agency provide data for firms new to the industry. So, too, interaction patterns among competitors in an industry can be important signals to astute observers.

From scanning to interpreting to acting to learning, there is ample opportunity to examine the role of people at work in the SIMS. People compete for power that comes from identifying and handling strategic contingencies (Hickson et al., 1971), from controlling critical resources (Pfeffer and Salancik, 1978), from achieving centrality in major intraorganizational networks (Tichy and Fombrun, 1979), and from achieving a prominent position in the organization's formal hierarchy (Astley and Sachdeva, 1984). To this internal competition, individual managers bring bounded rationality (Simon, 1957); cognitive biases (March and Simon, 1958); functional perspectives, values, and assumptions about external environments (Daft and Weick, 1984); and face-to-face interaction styles (Donnellon, 1987). Additionally, internal market demand may be generated by top executives for a set of elusive products such as feelings of greater efficacy, greater certainty on issues, confirmation of past interpretations or actions, or rationalizations for past mishandling of strategic issues. Taken together, these facets of the organization add idiosyncracy to the SIM process and keep it from being a highly determinate one.

Strategic Issue Arrays. From the universe of all internal and external issues, an array of strategic issues receives attention inside an organization (Dutton, 1986). Any element in this array takes on meaning as it moves through a SIMS—that is, as data or events are transformed into strategic issues, as issues are analyzed, as responses are fashioned, and as followup data on responses and outcomes are gathered and interpreted.

Outcomes of organizational action are also interpreted—some as successes, some as failures, some as mixtures of the two. Here, too, power positions of key players may be affected by these second-order interpretations. For example, some players in the SIMS may fall from favor because their actions in attempting to handle an issue are interpreted as failures. Likewise, credibility and trust accrue to those players uncovering issues previously ignored, integrating issues previously considered separate, adding to the interpretive process through their interpersonal or technical skills, or handling a response successfully.

At any given point in an organization's development, specific SIMS forms can be viewed as structural embodiments of the generic process of interpreting and acting on strategic issues. Specific shapes or forms develop from interaction of numerous internal and external forces. In the following section, we develop a typology of SIMS forms.

A TYPOLOGY OF STRATEGIC ISSUE MANAGEMENT SYSTEMS

Specific forms of strategic issue management systems develop as a result of two major forces: an organization's interpretive focus (reflecting the primary source of strategic issues) and its tendency toward action (reflecting the intensity of activity devoted to issue interpretation and response) (Dutton and Ottensmeyer, 1987). These two forces are shaped, in turn, by the various environmental factors previously discussed. The first dimension, interpretive focus, distinguishes SIMS in terms of the issues most likely to be detected and legitimated. The second dimension, action intensity, encompasses how aggressively organizations respond to strategic issues (Ottensmeyer, 1982) as well as the level of intrusiveness (Daft and Weick, 1984) displayed by organizations in attempting to decipher their environments. Thus, the types of issues organizations focus on and their action tendencies together form the basis for a simple typology of specific SIMS forms.

Types of Issues (Focus of an Organization's Interpretive Effort)

Organizations face two distinct types of strategic issues distinguished by whether or not they originate inside or outside the organization's boundaries. Issues such as a decline in employee morale or the development of a new technology by an organization's R & D group represent *internal* strategic issues. Such issues are strategic since they could alter the organization's performance if left unnoticed or unaddressed. Internal issues may take on strategic importance because of their linkage to external forces and prior strategic choices. For example, a new technology may represent a strategic issue not only on its own merits but also because of its importance to the external competitive positioning of the firm.

Some forms of SIMS are designed exclusively to monitor and respond to internal issues. Organizations that treat SIM as part of the budgeting process come closest to this internal view. In this form of SIMS, internal issues are often triggered by deviations in the organization's or a subunit's performance from targeted performance goals. For example, in one study of a SIMS in a large diversified organization, where the SIMS was closely aligned with the organization's budgeting process, the majority of the issues detected were of the internal type (Dutton, 1986). In this case issues such as declining subunit performance dominated the strategic issue agenda.

In contrast, *external* strategic issues are the ones that emanate unambiguously from outside the organization's boundaries. For example, a competitor's new product offerings, changes in international monetary conditions, or changes in governmental tax or regulatory policies represent external strategic issues.

A SIMS that focuses primarily on external issues is consistent with the view of managers who see SIMS as environmental scanning or political issues management. A SIMS, when seen to include the public affairs function, may play a major role in identifying significant public policy issues and responding to these issues before legislative action (Arcellus and Schaeffer, 1982).

Action Tendencies of Organizations (Search and Response Patterns)

Specific forms of SIMS can also be distinguished by the intensity or aggressiveness with which organizations (1) seek out potentially-strategic issues, and (2) act on issues interpreted as strategic. On one hand, a firm's SIMS may be depicted as *passive*, involving little if any direct effort to identify or alter internal processes or external forces. On the other hand, SIMS may be quite *active*, designed to seek out issues and either to aggressively adapt or to take action to reshape the internal or external environmental forces themselves (Pfeffer and Salancik, 1978; Ottensmeyer, 1982).

Relatively passive forms of SIMS include processes for the collection and dissemination of information. In some cases, this process is formalized. For example, some firms like Citicorp utilize an internal polling process to collect information on top decision makers' perceptions of strategic issues so that monitoring activities can be better focused (Moore, 1979). In other cases, managers utilize informal discussions or the intuition or "gut feel" of key managers to identify issues requiring attention.

Boundary spanners and other participants in a SIMS, because they filter and evaluate information, construct the meaning of issues and label them in particular ways. For example, a technological development in an industry may be interpreted as a major threat by one firm while in another the same development may be construed as a major opportunity (Dutton and Jackson, 1987). Thus, SIMS participants act as interpreters and packagers of strategic

Figure 3.   Basic Forms of Strategic Issue Management Systems

	Interpretive Focus	
	Internal	External
Passive	Collector	Antenna
Active	Activator	Intervener

(Action Intensity)

issues. They focus attention on particular aspects of an issue that, in turn, have particular meanings to key decision makers (Daft and Weick, 1984).

A SIMS may encompass activities more extensive than those described thus far. These activities might include direct attempts to alter environments such as personal contact with public officials to modify the speed and direction of unwelcome legislation (Arrington and Sawaya, 1984) or very active attempts to discourage union organizing efforts. Shell Oil, for example, employs eight policy development specialists charged with developing alternative actions for strategic issues in the oil industry (*Chemical Week*, 1981).

By simultaneously considering the action tendencies and interpretive focus of organizations, four specific SIMS forms can be identified (see Figure 3). A *Collector* is a form that focuses on internal strategic issues and is relatively passive with regard to those issues. An active SIMS designed primarily to monitor and handle internal issues is termed an *Activator*. An *Antenna* form refers to a passive system that focuses on external issues. Finally, a system that aggressively tackles external issues is termed an *Intervener*.

These four basic forms encompass alternative views of the generic strategic issue management function described in the management literature. Collector and Activator forms of SIMS most closely resemble those information and budgeting systems that focus on the identification of internal issues, often as means of corporate control (e.g., Lorange and Vancil, 1977; Rhyne, 1985). Antenna systems represent a form of SIMS that approximates traditional environmental scanning activities focused on the identification of external threats and opportunities (Fahey and King, 1977). When the identification of external issues also involves active attempts to respond, then a SIMS becomes an instrument for an organization's use in seeking greater control of its environment, an Intervener. Finally, when the SIMS involves the full spectrum of possible activities in the identification, interpretation, and response to issues, it most clearly resembles what Ansoff (1980) has called strategic issue management. Thus, strategic issue management systems may emerge in a variety of forms. Some major forms are profiled below.

PROFILES

Having developed a typology of strategic issue management systems, we now move to a more detailed consideration of the specific forms (see Table 2 for a summary). In the discussion below, we make tentative predictions about the emergence and operation of specific SIMS forms. These profiles embody propositions about SIMS and thus serve as invitations for further research. Within each section below, we consider:

1. The environments in which each form is most likely to evolve
2. Examples of organizations likely to house each form
3. Internal structural and process characteristics of each form
4. Products likely to be generated within each form
5. Problems endemic to each form.

This effort is intentionally descriptive with the aim of developing a logic for the emergence of some forms of SIMS instead of others. Prescriptions for the effective design of SIMS (e.g., Ansoff, 1980) have not treated the dimensions along which SIMS can vary nor are they based on theoretical rationales that explain why some forms are more likely to develop than others. By developing profiles of specific forms of SIMS, we hope to improve understanding of the full range of activities SIMS can incorporate and to suggest factors important to their emergence, operation, and persistence.

In the following profiles, we sketch a set of likely behaviors and characteristics associated with the four basic forms of strategic issue management systems introduced above. It is possible to complicate this analysis considerably by examining the workings of hybrid forms that, for example, exhibit active external/active internal behavior or those that are active external/passive internal. Further gradations of "active" and "passive" also might be considered in a more finely-grained typology. Clearly, organizational reality is more complex than simple typologies can fully capture. We hope, however, that our efforts will stimulate further theorizing and research into this critical management process.

Table 2. Summary of SIMS Profiles

	Collector	Activator	Antenna	Intervener
1. Environments	External (interpreted) as "under control" or "out of control"	External (similar to Collector)	External (interpreted as "under control" or "out of control")	External (interpreted as "controllable")
	Internal (interpreted as "under control")	Internal (focus on responsive adaptation and harmonious functioning)	Internal (interpreted as "under control")	Internal (interpreted as "under control")
2. Examples	Monopolies/oligopolies	Professional organizations	Industry followers	Industry leaders
	Prestigious universities	Firms with highly secure market niches	Government agencies	Market-driven adapters
	Small business firms		Highly regulated utilities	Aggressive diversifiers
				Small colleges
				Alliance shapers
				"Gladiators"

	SIM processes in traditional units	SIM processes diffused	SIM processes in a few externally focused units	SIM processes in a separate unit
3. Internal Characteristics	Focus on internal budgeting and policy planning	Focus on human resource management, production, and efficiency	Possible internal rivalry	Focus on action
	Politicized process		Focus on scanning and tracking	Focus on strategic issue agenda-setting
				Possible internal rivalry
4. Products	Budgets	Efficiency reports	Research reports	Action plans
	Reports	Climate surveys	Clipping files	Issue reports
				Surveys
5. Problems	External and internal "shocks"	External "shocks"	The "free-rider" problem	Over-interpretation
	"Sleeping Giant" syndrome		Executive efficacy	Hyperactivity
	"Helpless Dwarf" syndrome			Cost
				Credibility loss

Collector (Passive/Internal Focus)

Environments. This form is likely to appear in environments that are interpreted as either being highly controllable or highly uncontrollable. The Collector would thus be more likely to appear in either monopolistic/ oligopolistic or highly competitive industries. In the former situation, uncertainties and accountability pressures are virtually eliminated because of sheer dominance of the environment by the firm. In the latter case, individual firms have little power, and the possibility of reducing uncertainty is so small that firms simply do not pay much attention to external sources of strategic issues. Decision makers look inward, if they look anywhere, for strategic issues, and they search and respond passively when issues are located. Internal issues typically revolve around the factors of production (i.e., labor and capital) and the efficiency with which they are employed.

Examples. Local monopolies/oligopolies, regulated enterprises that have captured their regulators (Stigler, 1971), nationalized industries, or powerful institutionalized organizations (e.g., universities) represent candidates for the Collector form of SIMS. These organizations are in environments which are relatively stable and predictable and in which accountability pressures are few. Having the luxury of few external pressures, managers focus their attention on internal operations.

At the opposite end of this spectrum is the great multitude of small firms for which environmental uncertainties are so strong and overwhelming that they are simply not attended to. For such organizations, uncertainties posed by this sort of environment are, like the sun, simply too powerful to spend much time looking at.

Internal Characteristics. The Collector form is likely to resemble budgeting or internally-focused planning and be based primarily on resource allocation activities. In the powerful Collector, internal rivalry for resources among key players may be politicized because of few external accountability pressures or vaguely defined effectiveness measures (e.g., large state universities). In the Collector form, SIM activities are likely to be incorporated into regular organizational units such as budgeting or personnel departments. In one study of eight firms using formal SIMS, half of the firms could be described as using Collector forms (Wartick and Rude 1986). In these firms, there was an emphasis in the SIMS on education and information as opposed to advising; internally-focused "issues managers" had only occasional contact with their managers.

Products. Products generated by this type of SIMS would tend to be budgets and internal reports about problems that had risen to a fairly high threshold of visibility. These reports tend to have tactical instead of strategic relevance.

Problems.   Problems arising in passive, internally-focused systems are often associated with significant changes in the external environment. That is, forces that managers assume to be predictable and certain may shift dramatically. Examples here might include U.S. airlines prior to deregulation, or U.S. Steel at the peak of its market power. The Collector SIMS form thus tends to develop in "sleeping giants" that are subsequently surprised due to their neglect of external strategic issues. Having gotten out of the habit of attending to external forces, and having developed a passive-internal approach to managing strategic issues, managers simply lose their ability to interpret external data effectively. And, the form of SIMS that evolves in a setting like this proves ineffective in saving top managers from themselves!

Relatively weak organizations, or "helpless dwarfs," are simply unable to do anything but look internally for ways to survive in the face of overwhelming external forces. When external forces take a turn in the "wrong" direction, these organizations simply go out of existence. Recent examples include the small independent travel agencies that folded during a period of intense price cutting by major airlines. Just as small firms operating in competitive markets are considered price-takers by economists, they also can be seen as "environment-takers"—their environments are largely "given."

Collector problems, therefore, often revolve around interpretations of organizational power vis-à-vis external forces. In one instance, organizations may see themselves as too powerful and their environments as too stable or predictable. In the other instance, organizations may view themselves as essentially powerless with respect to their environments. Thus, the Collector form is more likely to appear in organizations that have mainly closed themselves off from their external environments.

Adopting a Collector form may be hazardous to long-run survival. Organizations, operating with a sense of either too much or too little power, may fail to act on issues that indeed could be acted on. Large, powerful organizations may be surprised by external issues previously interpreted as insignificant and reflected as such in their SIMS. Witness the surprise on the part of many utility officials over the public furor surrounding the nuclear power issue.

Likewise, organizations viewing themselves as powerless may overlook opportunities to improve their bargaining positions by forming coalitions with other firms to improve their power bases. For example, small hospitals have been known to form purchasing associations, making them more powerful in their bargaining with large hospital supply firms. The movement toward regional banking firms reflects a similar networking trend.

Activator (Active/Internal Focus)

Environments. The Activator differs from the Collector in its activity levels on internal issues. That is, it is both more intrusive in searching out potentially serious *internal* issues and more aggressive in developing solutions once issues are interpreted as strategic.

Activator forms arise in organizations that expend considerable energy trying to understand their internal workings. The Activator is designed to have many inwardly-turned ears and eyes to detect and respond to potentially strategic issues. It is meant to identify, for example, new processes and product technologies early so that they might be moved along expeditiously toward implementation through internal networks.

The Activator and the Collector may operate in quite similar external environments—interpreted, in general, as either being largely under control or out of control. The primary difference is that the Activator views its internal environment as more critical to interpret and act upon.

Activator forms develop when organizations enact stable, slow-to-change external environments. Effective adaptation is achieved by being able to respond to external changes when they infrequently occur; staying in touch with the internal environment helps assure a quick response when needed. Top managers are likely here to design systems by saying, in effect, "We can succeed by understanding and controlling our internal processes and by improving these as best we can." It is of course possible to imagine Activator forms emerging as mostly symbolic gestures intended to convey to internal audiences enlightenment, sensitivity, or accountability on the part of top decision makers (Dutton and Ottensmeyer, 1987).

Examples. Activator forms of SIMS will be more likely to develop in those organizations that rely heavily on human resources, and that operate in external environments that are enacted as safe. Thus, an internal focus of organizational attention becomes feasible.

We would expect to see Activator forms emerge in organizations of professionals (e.g., accounting firms, HMOs, architectural firms) or in firms operating in secure market niches. In general, such forms will arise in organizations that rely heavily on people skills or on the people/technology mix for their long-run success. Organizations having the resources and the desire to be viewed as "enlightened," as well as firms fighting off employee unionization, may also exhibit Activator characteristics. Smooth, harmonious internal functioning, because it supports the quick response capability important to the Activator, is seen as critical to effective adaptation and to maintaining limited power vis-à-vis external environmental forces. Rivalry among managers in this setting will tend to be based less on political concerns than on norms of rationality (Thompson, 1967). Thus, internal rivalry among key SIMS participants likely will be based more on disagreements over which methods, techniques, or responses yield greater efficiencies or improvements, which internal department or unit is best situated to deliver desired results, and so on.

Lincoln Electric, the Ohio-based producer of arc welding equipment and supplies, provides an excellent setting in which this form of SIMS can be observed (Lincoln Electric, 1983). Secure in its very strong market position, and recognizing the importance of achieving production efficiencies that can be translated into lower prices for its customers, this firm has developed an internally-focused strategic issue management system that, over time, has brought into being generous wages and bonuses, a high level of job security, internal promotions, and accessible top managers all in the service of the primary internal strategic issue, manufacturing efficiency.

Internal Characteristics. Activator SIMS forms are likely to be structurally diffuse, with identification, interpretation, and response efforts shared widely throughout the organization. Key units in such systems are likely to be those most attuned to the organization's core technologies and its people: human resource management, process engineering, and manufacturing, with budgeting and planning units providing formal mechanisms for the assembly of potential strategic issues. Thus, in this form of SIMS, there is widespread involvement of organizational units and managers in the management of internal strategic issues.

Products. Primary products of this SIMS form revolve around improved understanding of an organization's internal processes, culture, quirks, strengths, weaknesses, or neuroses. Reports about internal problems and possibilities, comparisons with similar organizations, internal "climate" surveys, employee participation programs, or reports by efficiency experts would typify efforts generated by this type of SIMS.

Problems. The Activator form has much the same set of problems as the Collector. That is, its predominantly internal focus makes it vulnerable to major external shocks or surprises. The Activator, however, is likely to be able to respond more quickly to external issues. Once external issues rise to the threshold of attention in firms with Activator systems, their pattern of internal responsiveness puts them in a stronger positon to act in an effective and timely manner, if an internal response is called for. In this way, Activator SIMS are likely to be effective forms in environments characterized by lower rates of change and interpreted as such by key managers.

Antenna (Passive/External Focus)

Environments. The Antenna form approximates traditional environmental scanning activities, including the identification of external threats and opportunities (Fahey and King, 1977). Antenna forms indicate a primary sensitivity to external issues but relatively passive efforts at both analysis and action. Organizations enacting relatively stable external and highly stable internal environments are the likeliest candidates for this form of SIMS.

The Antenna form might track a set of external issues but not in a particularly aggressive way. In the event that a regulatory issue became a major threat, for example, firms with the Antenna form might respond actively, but they are more likely to take the familiar "free rider" role (if it is available). Thus, these firms are more likely to watch from the sidelines on issues that affect an industry as a whole. Some have argued that such free-rider organizations often focus their external scanning or tracking efforts on other similar organizations (e.g., competitors, industry leaders) that respond more aggressively to the same issue (Ottensmeyer, 1982). Also, the Antenna form may emerge for symbolic reasons so that organizations using this type of SIMS might convey an appearance of accountability to powerful constituencies (Ranson et al., 1980).

In general, the Antenna form is similar to the Collector form. It crops up in firms either with environments enacted as stable and predictable, low in equivocality, and with few accountability pressures (that is, environments enacted as being "under control") or in firms with less stable, highly equivocal environments and with little power to make much of an impact (i.e., environments enacted as being "out of control"). A larger external issue array seems likely to emerge from the Antenna form, possibly because of operating domains of greater complexity than that of the Collector. This difference reflects the increased external focus of SIMS activity.

The lack of attention to internal issues suggests relative stability on that front also. Manufacturing technologies would tend to be slow to change. Other internal issues might be viewed as of nonstrategic importance or simply "under control." The primary concern of managers of such SIMS is having sufficient internal response capacity to make changes if required.

Examples. Organizations likely to develop Antenna forms might include large firms in stable industries with few "life-threatening" external issues, or government agencies. In short, one is likely to find Antenna SIMS in those organizations whose internal issues are perceived to be of little strategic consequence and whose external environments are either relatively stable or inhabited by other organizations willing and able to respond aggressively (thus sparing organizations with Antenna SIMS the trouble). Organizations that have had many of their external issues taken over by external actors—Rhenman's (1973) "appendix organizations"—may be likely candidates for this SIMS form. Examples here might include state-controlled community colleges or certain regulated utilities.

Internal Characteristics. The Antenna form is likely to be inhabited by scanners, trackers, and boundary spanners with research rather than action orientations. Especially in larger organizations, with greater numbers of issues and more specialized, formal monitoring processes, there is room for considerable internal competition among major players vying for the attention of top decision makers. The SIMS would likely be embodied in those functions closest to external issues such as marketing, market research, government relations, legal affairs, or fundraising.

Internal rivalry might have a decidedly political tenor in organizations with this SIMS form. This occurs for two reasons. First, there is a greater degree of unstructured decision making involved in managing external issues, issues that often do not lend themselves to programmed responses. Unstructured decisions about external issues may often carry high degrees of uncertainty about appropriate action choices and eventual outcomes. Secondly, there may be "turf" rivalry among units involved in external scanning. Especially if a special unit had been formed for scanning, then one would expect rivalry between it and other, more traditional units with an external focus (e.g., marketing or public affairs). Thus, the Antenna form has high potential for internal rivalry and conflict. In a large organization with an Antenna form, it is possible to have several boundary-spanning or issue-tracking units vying for attention and interpretation "rights."

Products. Products generated by this form of SIMS reflect the organization's predisposition for scanning and tracking. Larger organizations with the Antenna form may have specialized departments to perform this function. Further, these units would likely be designed to generate routine reports on a set of predetermined issues, to monitor industry associations, to scan newsletters and other publications, to maintain clipping files on selected issues, or to develop a collection of materials on external issues or key players for research purposes. In conjunction with other units, scanning or tracking units would attend to external issues in a manner reflecting a research orientation. Smaller, less powerful organizations would be more likely to carry out this function informally, relying on established units and roles to carry out the monitoring and scanning and to report findings. The informal external networks in which top managers participate would be potentially useful sources of information (Kotter, 1982).

Problems. Key problems associated with the Antenna form are likely to revolve around generic difficulties in adopting free rider and follower approaches to managing external issues. The interests of free riders may not be well represented by powerful industry "gladiators," borrowing Milbrath's (1965) colorful metaphor. That is, followers may be surprised or harmed by the actions of industry leaders. However, many small organizations with this type of SIMS have few options. The more effective of this group protect themselves as best they can from the impact of these problems by judicious choice of market niche, domain shifting, or through cooperative strategies (Astley, 1984).

SIMS that are passive and focused externally may reflect less the nature of the environment than the beliefs or assumptions of top executives. Because of prior experiences with external issues, managers may feel more or less efficacious about their ability to handle them well (Ottensmeyer, 1982). Thus, one would expect to find Antenna forms in those organizations operating in unstable, unpredictable, complex environments whose executives rate low in executive efficacy.

Intervener (Active/External Focus)

Environments.   Some organizations develop a SIMS that is highly active in seeking out and responding to external strategic issues. We label this the Intervener. One would expect that organizations with this form of SIMS interpret their environments as having substantial levels of uncertainty, equivocality, and accountability pressure but, in contrast to the Antenna form, as "controllable." That is, the external environment enacted by Interveners is one that is far from being "out of control." Interveners often have a history of successful action so that they come to believe in their ability to influence the environment.

Examples.   The Intervener is active in external affairs, not hesitating to take action to shape the texture of its external environment (Pfeffer and Salancik, 1978). Unlike the other three SIMS forms, organizations with Intervener forms are more likely to appear in the headlines of the business and popular press. Examples are seen in business firms that are market-driven: aggressively seeking new markets for their products, new products for existing markets, entirely new markets, better market positions, new acquisitions, more favorable relations with government agencies, and so on. Government agencies may also house Intervener forms (e.g., by building powerful coalitions with the legislative branch or by redefining their original mandates). Local economic development groups may aggressively promote their regions to carefully selected industries. Organized religions may choose to send missionaries to far off places to spread their messages. All of these organizations share an aggressive approach toward monitoring and responding to strategic issues with the ultimate purpose of transforming their environments.

On public policy issues, Interveners are most likely to enter the fray, Mobil Oil being a well-known example. On issues of strategy domain, they are the most likely to make dramatic moves to improve their long-range adaptiveness, such as competitors in the tobacco industry in recent years

(Miles, 1982). On issues of survival, they are the ones that go down fighting or scramble the hardest to stay alive (e.g., Chrysler). If small and weak, they are the organizations most likely to form strategic alliances or coalitions, cooperative strategies, or industry associations to improve their chances for survival. In industry associations, they are the ones most likely to take the lead (e.g., MIT or the University of California in matters involving government policy for basic research). In short, entities with Intervener forms are externally focused activists or gladiators—monitoring their environments, interpreting them as subject to influence or control, and ready for action.

Internal Characteristics.   Intervener forms are likely to be inhabited by much the same cast of characters as that of Antenna forms: scanners, trackers, and boundary spanners. However, instead of a passive research orientation, the Intervener is more likely to combine research with action. In order to house this expanded set of activities, Intervener forms are likely to emerge as separately constituted structural units. In an eight-company study, half of the firms established separate units. In these firms issues managers maintained high internal visibility by playing a more pronounced role in determining the strategic issues agenda for top management, viewing themselves as "leaders, coordinators, and consensus builders" (Wartick and Rude, 1986, p. 12). This more prominent role in setting the agenda was made possible by having managers report frequently, and on a routine basis, directly to the chief executive or indirectly through a high-level committee.

Any internal rivalry in the Intervener resembles that of the Antenna form, having a political tone resulting from the less structured nature of decisions and the possibility of turf disputes among key players. Its action orientation increases the possible arenas of internal political conflict; that is, not only might there be conflict over who tracks or monitors which issues (the primary source of conflict in Antenna forms), there is also room for substantial rivalry over what action to take, who takes it, and which criteria to use in evaluating action.

Products.   Products of Intervener SIMS resemble those of the Antenna (due to their external focus) and those of the Activator (due to their action orientation). In addition to doing research on external issues, Intervener SIMS are geared for action. Thus, contingency or action plans are more likely to appear along with the raw data gathered, and issue task forces are likely to be formed with the explicit task of devising and monitoring plans. One would expect this form of SIMS to act more intrusively in seeking out potential issues, to exert considerable organizational effort in researching and sorting issues by importance, and in designing issue responses. In short, organizations in which the Intervener emerge expend large amounts of resources on interpretation and action and, by so doing, convey an image of responsiveness and adaptability.

Problems. Problems attendant specifically to Intervener forms revolve around over-interpretation of external events or issues, an excessive propensity for action, ineffective actions (i.e., responses that fail to alleviate or that make worse the issues facing them), and problematic interpretation of outcomes (both successes and failures) that result in managers viewing their efficacy as too high or too low.

Just as organizations may be unpleasantly surprised by not attending to important internal or external issues, they may also waste resources by responding aggressively to too many external issues. In addition, they may lose credibility and effectiveness in certain of their external arenas (e.g., regulatory agencies) if they choose to respond with a high degree of predictability to a wide variety of issues emanating from that source (i.e., their responses may be discounted over time by those receiving them).

Organizations housing Intervener forms run the risk of being hyperactive, viewing actions and responses as good for their own sake. Such organizations may be prone to errors of aggressiveness—diversifying too hastily, attacking regulatory bodies too predictably, or responding too quickly to competitors' actions. An exclusively external focus also runs a risk of neglecting internal issues.

The external environments enacted by Intervener SIMS are likely to be "subject to control." Thus, organizations see themselves as able to take aggressive, externally-focused action that will yield stronger positions vis-à-vis other forces in those environments. Because the Intervener form reflects such an action orientation, there is a strong possibility that a "social desirability" effect may be at work in some organizations displaying such forms. In general, a SIMS facade is more likely to be present in the Intervener or the Activator than in the Collector or the Antenna. In response to accountability pressures from both outside and inside, top decision makers may treat the SIMS as a symbolic gesture, creating an impression of a vigorous action orientation where none truly exists.

FUTURE RESEARCH DIRECTIONS

As evidenced by the speculative nature of the previous profiles, little systematic empirical research has been done to explore qualitatively or quantitatively this critical organizational activity. However, embedded in the discussion of the types and profiles of SIMS are a number of theoretical propositions that invite further research.

First, the profiles suggest a relationship between the forms of SIMS and the environments an organization inhabits. This relationship is hypothesized to be mutually causal. On the one hand, beliefs about environments are hypothesized to affect the form of SIM activity. At the same time, the SIMS form that evolves in an organization is hypothesized to affect the nature of the environments that are enacted.

Key to this mutual process are managerial assumptions about levels of control over environments. Where an environment is seen as either highly controllable or highly uncontrollable, the scope of SIM activities is hypothesized to be limited. However, as the scope of activities for SIM increases, level of perceived efficacy may be affected, modifying decision makers' views of the environment. Thus, it is striking how SIMS have appeared most frequently in maturing industries that experienced excessive turbulence during the 1960s and 1970s (Wartick and Rude, 1986). The systematic appearance of these adaptive structures in mature organizations and industries is not coincidental. Future research needs to examine how organizational environments determine the form of SIMS that emerges in an organization, and, in turn, how the creation of a certain type of SIMS affects the way environments are enacted.

Future research should also examine how SIMS forms relate to different internal processes of organizations. One assumption of this chapter has been that, inside organizations, there is a market for strategic issues. Which issues are identified, how they are interpreted, and how these interpretations are linked to action have important implications for the content and process of strategic management (Lyles and Mitroff, 1980; Kiesler and Sproull, 1982; Dutton and Duncan, 1987a, b). Given the high stakes associated with the recognition of, interpretation of, and response to issues critical to effectiveness, the political motives and behaviors of individuals party to these processes are activated. How these political activities influence or shape the processes of recognition, interpretation, and response, and ultimately organizational adaptation, remains a mystery. Others have pointed out that little empirical work has been done on the political dimension of strategy formulation (MacMillan, 1978; MacMillan and Guth, 1985). Since a SIMS includes activities critical to strategy formulation, formal SIM units and activities would seem fruitful focal points for studying political processes. Just as political scientists study the process of agenda building in the halls of Congress (Cobb and Elder, 1972; Walker, 1977), organizational scholars need to study the political processes of agenda building by examining the processes of and activities embedded in strategic issue management systems.

Finally, future research needs to consider the relationship between the different forms of SIM and organizational effectiveness. As explained more fully in Dutton and Ottensmeyer (1987), systems for strategic issue management have symbolic as well as instrumental value to organizations. This perspective helps to identify a variety of approaches for evaluating the effectiveness of a particular strategic issue management system. These approaches range from efficiency criteria such as the speed and accuracy of issue identification to more externally focused criteria such as the image of legitimacy, accountability, or power that the existence of a formal SIM unit (or a systematic SIM process) may convey to important stakeholders.

However, organizational scholars lack empirical findings to solidly ground definitions of SIMS effectiveness or link SIMS effectiveness to overall organizational survival and performance. At a basic level, the questions are: Do strategic issue management systems make a difference? If so, how? Simply stated, the "value-added" of strategic issue management systems has not been systematically studied. Separately-standing SIM units represent an innovation in organization structure (Ehling and Hesse, 1982). The emergence or formation of these units per se is of interest to scholars, as are their links to other, more traditional internal units, their perceived effectiveness, and their persistence or transformation.

CONCLUSION

Once organization theorists realized that strategic issues do not always arrive at the executive suite prepackaged and neatly labeled, strategic management became a considerably more complex process to describe and explain. It became necessary to explain how internal and external stimuli, data, or events became translated into occasions for executive choice and action. Theories based generally on the concept of organizations as vehicles of enactment have emerged to help both scholars and practicing managers explain these realities.

In this chapter, we have attempted to refine this general conceptualization by: (a) elaborating the notion of strategic issue management systems (SIMS) as a *process* associated with the basic *problems* of interpretation and action, (b) specifying contextual factors that shape SIMS, (c) developing a typology of specific SIMS forms based on the interpretive focus and the action tendencies of organizations, and (d) fashioning profiles of SIMS forms focusing both on environmental interpretations likely to spawn them and on internal functioning.

There remains the rather gnarly problem of actually studying the complex structure and process of a SIMS with all its intertwined linkages. However, we believe that scholarly efforts to study such elusive processes and systems are absolutely critical to advancing knowledge about organizational functioning.

It is said that William de Koonig's paintings attempt to capture slipping glimpses of reality. In like manner, students of organizations strive to capture glimpses of organizational realities—strategies, the leaders who manage them, and the internal grindings of structures and processes. The slipping glimpse metaphor seems an especially apt one to characterize what strategic management scholars know about how top managers identify and handle the issues most critical to their organizations. The glimpses that we do have of these organizational systems—from a few case studies, the autobiographies of top managers, and the like—serve only to whet our appetites for a more complete picture of how strategic issue management really works, in all its variety, complexity, and richness.

ACKNOWLEDGMENT

This research was supported by a grant from the Tenneco Fund Program at the Graduate School of Business Administration, New York University.

REFERENCES

Andrews, Kenneth (1971). *The Concept of Corporate Strategy*. Homewood, IL: Irwin.

Ansoff, H. Igor (1980). "Strategic Issue Management." *Strategic Management Journal* 1:131-148.

Arcellus, F., and Schaeffer, N.W. (1982). "Social Demands as Strategic Issues: Some Conceptual Problems." *Strategic Management Journal* 3:347-357.

Arrington, Charles, and Richard Sawaya (1984). "Managing Public Affairs: Issue Management in an Uncertain Environment." *California Management Review* 16:148-160.

Astley, W. Graham (1984). "Toward an Appreciation of Collective Strategy." *Academy of Management Review* 9:526-535.

Astley, W. Graham, and Paramjit Sachdeva (1984). "Structural Sources of Intraorganizational Power: A Theoretical Synthesis." *Academy of Management Review* 9:104-113.

Brown, James (1981). *Guidelines for Managing Corporate Issues Programs*. New York: The Conference Board.

Chakravarthy, Balaji (1982). "Adaptation: A Promising Metaphor for Strategic Management." *Academy of Management Review* 7:35-44.

Chase, W. Howard (1984). *Issue Management: Origins of the Future*. Stamford, CT: IAP.

Chemical Week (1981). "Issue Management: Preparing for Social Change." October 28:46-51.

Child, John (1982). "Organizational Structure, Environment, and Performance: The Role of Strategic Choice." *Sociology* 16:1-22.

Cobb, R., and C. Elder (1972). *Participation in American Politics: The Dynamics of Agenda Building*. Boston: Allyn and Bacon.

Cyert, Richard, and James G. March (1963). *A Behavioral Theory of the Firm*. Englewood Cliffs, NJ: Prentice-Hall.

Daft, Richard L., and Karl E. Weick (1984). "Toward a Model of Organizations as Interpretation Systems." *Academy of Management Review* 9:284-296.

Diffenbach, John (1982). "Influence Diagrams for Complex Strategic Issues." *Strategic Management Journal* 3:133-146.

Donnellon, Anne (1987). Management as a Conversational Process. Ph.D. Dissertation, The Pennsylvania State University.

Duncan, Robert, and Andrew Weiss (1979). "Organizational Learning: Implications for Organizational Design." In Barry Staw (ed.), *Research in Organizational Behavior*, Vol. 1. Greenwich, CT: JAI Press, pp. 75-124.

Dutton, Jane E. (1986). "Understanding Strategic Agenda Building in Organizations and Its Implications for Managing Change." *Scandinavian Journal of Management Studies* 3:3-24.

Dutton, Jane E. (1988). "Perspectives on Strategic Issues Processing: Insights from a Case Study." In Robert Lamb and Paul Shrivastava (eds.), *Advances in Strategic Management*, Vol. 5. Greenwich, CT: JAI Press.

Dutton, Jane E., Liam Fahey, and V.K. Narayanan (1983). "Toward Understanding Strategic Issue Diagnosis." *Strategic Management Journal* 4:307-323.

Dutton, Jane E., and Susan E. Jackson (1987). "Categorizing Strategic Issues: Links to Organizational Action." *Academy of Management Review* 12:76-90.

Dutton, Jane E., and Robert B. Duncan (1987a). "The Influence of the Strategic Planning Process on Strategic Change." *Strategic Management Journal* 8:103-116.

Dutton, Jane E., and Robert B. Duncan (1987b). "Strategic Issue Diagnosis and the Creation of Momentum for Change." *Strategic Management Journal* 8:279-295.

Dutton, Jane E., and Edward J. Ottensmeyer (1987). "Strategic Issue Management Systems: Forms, Functions, and Contexts." *Academy of Management Review* 12:355-365.

Edelman, Murray (1964). *The Symbolic Uses of Politics*. Champaign, IL: University of Illinois Press.

Ehling, William, and Michael Hesse (1982). "The Use of 'Issue Management' in Public Relations." *Public Relations Review* 6:18-35.

Fahey, Liam, and William King (1977). "Environmental Scanning in Corporate Planning." *Business Horizons* 20:61-71.

Feldman, Martha, and James G. March (1981). "Information in Organizations as Signal and Symbol." *Administrative Science Quarterly* 26:171-187.

Galbraith, Jay (1977). *Organization Design*. Reading, MA: Addison-Wesley.

Hannan, Michael T., and John H. Freeman (1984). "Structural Inertia and Organizational Change." *American Sociological Review* 49:149-164.

Hickson, David, C. Robert Hinings, C. Lee, Rodney Schneck, and Johannes Pennings (1971). "A Strategic Contingencies Theory of Intraorganizational Power." *Administrative Science Quarterly* 16:216-222.

Hrebiniak, Lawrence G., and William F. Joyce (1985). "Organizational Adaptation: Strategic Choice and Environmental Determinism." *Administrative Science Quarterly* 30:336-349.

Kiesler, Sara and Lee Sproull(1982). "Managerial Response to Changing Environments: Perspectives on Problem Sensing from Social Cognition." *Administrative Science Quarterly* 27:548-570.

Kotter, John (1982). *The General Managers*. New York: Free Press.

Lawrence, Paul, and Jay Lorsch (1967). *Organization and Environment: Managing Differentiation and Integration*. Boston: Division of Research, Harvard University Graduate School of Business Administration.

Lincoln Electric Co. (1983). Case #9-376-028. Boston: Harvard Business School Case Services.

Lorange, Peter, and Richard Vancil (1977). *Strategic Planning Systems*. Englewood Cliffs, NJ: Prentice-Hall.

Lyles, Marjorie, and Ian Mitroff (1980). "Organizational Problem Formulation: An Empirical Study." *Administrative Science Quarterly* 25:102-119.

MacMillan, Ian (1978). *Strategy Formulation: Political Concepts*. St. Paul: West Publishing.

MacMillan, Ian, and William Guth (1985). "Strategy Implementation and Middle Management Coalitions." In Robert Lamb (ed.), *Advances in Strategic Management*, Vol. 3. Greenwich, CT: JAI Press, pp. 233-254.

March, James G., and Herbert A. Simon (1958). *Organizations*. New York: Wiley.

Meyer, Alan D. (1984). "Mingling Decision-Making Metaphors." *Academy of Management Review* 9:6-17.

Milbrath, Lester (1965). *Political Participation.* Chicago: Rand-McNally.

Miles, Raymond E., and Charles C. Snow (1978). *Organizational Strategy, Structure, and Process.* New York: McGraw-Hill.

————— (1984), "Fit, Failure, and the Hall of Fame." *California Management Review* 26:10-28.

Miles, Robert H. (1982). *Coffin Nails and Corporate Strategies.* Englewood Cliffs, NJ: Prentice-Hall.

Morgan, Gareth (1986). *Images of Organization.* Beverly Hills, CA: Sage.

Moore, B. (1979). "Planning for Emerging Issues." *Public Relations Journal,* 35:42-46.

Ottensmeyer, Edward J. (1982). Strategic Organizational Adaptation and the Regulatory Environment. Ph.D. Dissertation, Indiana University.

Pfeffer, Jeffrey (1981). "Management as Symbolic Action: The Creation and Maintenance of Organizational Paradigms." In Larry Cummings and Barry Staw (eds.), *Research in Organizational Behavior,* Vol. 3. Greenwich, CT: JAI Press, pp. 1-52.

Pfeffer, Jeffrey, and Gerald Salancik (1978). *The External Control of Organizations: A Resource Dependence Perspective.* New York: Harper & Row.

Porter, Michael E. (1980). *Competitive Strategy.* New York: Free Press.

Quinn, James Brian (1980). *Strategies for Change.* Homewood, IL: Irwin.

Ranson, Stuart, C. Robert Hinings, and Roy Greenwood (1980). "The Structuring of Organizational Structures." *Administrative Science Quarterly* 25:1-17.

Rhenman, Eric (1973). *Organization Theory for Long Range Planning.* London: Wiley.

Rhyne, Lawrence (1985). "The Relationship of Information Usage Characteristics to Planning System Sophistication: An Empirical Examination." *Strategic Management Journal* 6:319-337.

Schendel, Dan, and Charles Hofer (1979). *Strategic Management: A New View of Business and Planning.* Boston: Little, Brown.

Simon, Herbert A. (1957). *Administrative Behavior.* Second Edition. New York: Free Press.

Srivastva, Suresh and Associates (1984). *The Executive Mind.* San Francisco: Jossey-Bass.

Stigler, George (1971). "The Theory of Economic Regulation." *Bell Journal of Economics and Management Science* 2:3-21.

Tetlock, Philip (1985). "Accountability: The Neglected Social Context of Judgment and Choice." In Larry Cummings and Barry Staw (eds.), *Research in Organizational Behavior,* Vol. 7. Greenwich, CT: JAI Press, pp. 297-332.

Thompson, James D. (1967). *Organizations in Action.* New York: McGraw-Hill.

Tichy, Noel, and Charles Fombrun (1979). "Network Analysis in Organizational Settings." *Human Relations* 32:923-965.

Walker, Jack (1977). "Seeing the Agenda in the U.S. Senate: A Theory of Problem Selection." *British Journal of Political Science* 7:423-445.

Wartick, Steven L., and Robert E. Rude (1986). "Issues Management: Corporate Fad or Function?" *California Management Review* 29:124-140.

Weick, Karl E. (1979). *The Social Psychology of Organizing.* Second Edition. Reading, MA: Addison-Wesley.

Zald, Mayer (1970). "Political Economy: A Framework for Analysis," in Mayer Zald (ed.), *Power in Organizations.* Nashville, TN: Vanderbilt University Press, pp. 221-261.

ORGANIZATIONAL DESIGNS FOR POST-INDUSTRIAL STRATEGIES:

THE ROLE OF INTERORGANIZATIONAL

COLLABORATION

W. Graham Astley and Richard A. Brahm

Around the turn of the twentieth century, American industry began to perfect a new system of production geared to manufacturing large quantities of relatively simple, standardized products. The key to this system was long production runs with each step along the way made simple and routine. The objective was to move materials through the manufacturing process at great velocity. By utilizing productive assets more intensively, high-speed, high-volume flows of goods and services permitted fixed costs to be spread over a greater volume of production, thus dramatically reducing unit costs. Chandler (1977) referred to this new organization of production as a "managerial revolution" whose timing depended on the advent of new technologies and expanding markets. Emerging mass-production technologies fostered an unprecedented output of goods, while rapidly growing markets were essential to absorb such output.

The new system of production also required the introduction of a new organizational form. Lower costs were attained by coordinating and integrating activities within hierarchical, multiunit business enterprises rather than through traditional market processes. Such enterprises permitted more effective production scheduling and fuller employment of facilities and personnel. Innovation in organizational design thus came as a direct response to the unique historical conditions provided by changing technologies and markets.

Whereas this characteristic form of industrial production has persisted throughout most of the twentieth century, several factors indicate that the U.S. economy has entered the "postindustrial" era (Bell, 1973). The arrival of this new era was, again, fundamentally related to shifting technologies and markets. First, radically different kinds of technology have emerged, especially in information-based sectors of the economy. As technological lifecycles grow shorter, and as different technologies converge in terms of functional capability, industrial structure becomes more and more fluid. Not only do economic sectors rise and fall with greater rapidity, the boundaries between formerly distinct branches of industry become increasingly blurred. Second, markets have also changed as global competition affects a rising number of U.S. industries. Firms can no longer view the domestic and foreign spheres as separate competitive domains: to compete effectively at home often requires that firms coordinate and systematize their activities on a worldwide basis. Increasingly, investments in plants and facilities abroad are not equivalent to stand-alone investments in a financial portfolio, they must be managed within the context of a single, integrated plan. Decisions taken in one country can significantly help or undermine a firm's competitive position in other countries throughout the world.

Together, new technologies and markets call for new, and sometimes radically different, corporate strategies. Firms must enhance their adaptive capability for responding to new technological developments and, at the same time, closely coordinate their activities in worldwide markets. Such postindustrial strategies call, in turn, for new organizational designs that will simultaneously promote flexibility and the coordination of diverse activities. This need has been met, in part, by modifications to the hierarchical, multiunit business enterprise of the industrial era. Such modifications include "self-designing" (Hedberg et al., 1976), "ambidextrous" (Duncan, 1976), "matrix" (David and Lawrence, 1977), "innovating" (Galbraith, 1982), and "postindustrial" (Huber, 1984) organizational designs. By limiting attention to the internal restructuring of organizations, however, all of these designs represent only variations of the basic form described by Chandler (1962). This chapter, in contrast, focuses on a much different organizational design: interorganizational arrangements for coordinating business activity. Interorganizational collaboration is a phenomenon of increasing importance, with strategic implications potentially as significant as those of Chandler's managerial revolution.

In the first section of the chapter, the historical development of the strategies and structures of U.S. firms is described. This is followed by a discussion of similar developments in multinational corporations. In the second section, the determinants and alternative modes of interorganizational collaboration are examined. Essentially, this section describes how the twin forces of technology and globalization have challenged organizations to simultaneously be more flexible while coordinating increasingly diverse activities. The final section presents some concluding comments.

THE HISTORICAL EVOLUTION OF STRATEGY AND STRUCTURE

Domestic Strategies and Structures

Discussions of organizational evolution fall into two types, depending on whether observers view organizations as capable of substantially changing their forms as they develop and grow over time or whether they retain essentially the same forms that were established at the time of their origin. The first of these views has received far greater attention than the second. For example, Galbraith and Kazanjian (1986) summarized several models of organizational growth based on Chandler's (1962) stagewise developmental sequence for the strategies and structures of U.S. enterprises. Chandler argued that the structure of an organization follows from its growth strategy. Specifically, as organizations change their strategies to employ resources more profitably in the face of shifting environments, the new strategy poses new administrative problems which are solved through structural reorganizations. This produces a series of growth stages consisting of new strategy creation, emergence of new administrative problems, decline in economic performance, adoption of a new structure, and subsequent recovery to profitable levels.

The second, less prevalent, view of organizational evolution derives from the work of Stinchcombe (1965). Stinchcombe observed a correlation between the structures of different types of organization and the social conditions existing at the time when those particular organizational types originated. Stinchcombe concluded that, both because such organizations can function effectively with those forms, and because the forms tend to become institutionalized, their basic structure, once introduced, tends to remain relatively stable and to reflect the environmental and task conditions existing at the time of their founding. For example, the urban construction industry, which was developed in European cities before the Industrial Revolution, continues to function today with specialized craft workers, craft-specialized subcontractors, craft trade unions, and contractual relations between the

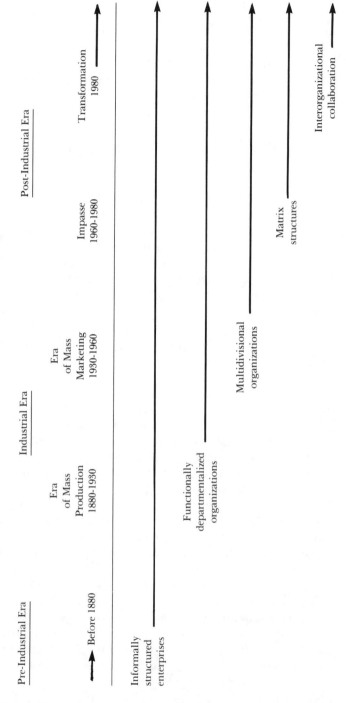

Figure 1. Historical Development of Organizational Design in the United States

construction enterprise and the consumer. Similarly, with only a few exceptions, extensive "staff" departments made up of professionals trained in colleges and universities do not appear in industries founded before the twentieth century, while virtually all industries whose organizational forms were developed within this century have extensive staff departments.

It seems clear that both of these views have empirical support. Historical accounts such as Chandler's show that many organizations, especially the large ones that dominate core U.S. industries, do undertake structural transformations as they pursue different growth strategies over time. On the other hand, the vast majority of organizations—especially small, owner-managed, entrepreneurial organizations—neither grow much during their life spans nor change their forms appreciably from the time of their founding. Therefore, to accommodate both views of organizational evolution, Figure 1 simply indicates which historical period is associated with the introduction of a specific organizational form. This leaves open the possibility that any particular organization may, through structural transformations, assume different forms over time, and yet it does not assume that historically-specific forms represent consecutive stages of development through which all organizations must inevitably pass.

A useful place to start the discussion of evolving strategies and structures is Ansoff's (1979) account of the historical transformation of the firm's strategic environment. Ansoff divided the history of American business into four distinct eras. The first era extended from 1830 to 1900 and included the basic technological inventions of the Industrial Revolution and the construction of the nation's industrial infrastructure of canals, railroads, telegraph, and telephone. The second era, extending from 1900 to 1930, was the era of mass production wherein management attention shifted from the creation of new production systems to the refinement of current systems to achieve high-volume, low-cost output. Ansoff labeled the third era that of "mass-marketing." This period extended from 1930 to 1960 and was a response to the growing saturation of consumer goods markets which began to demand differentiated products rather than standardized low-cost goods. Finally, Ansoff labeled the period extending from 1960 to the present as the "postindustrial era," a period in which the stable industrial structure existing since 1900 became subject to increasing environmental turbulence.

This section of the chapter draws heavily on Ansoff's classification of industrial eras, though two modifications to his scheme seem appropriate. First, it appears useful to demarcate the period extending from 1880 to 1930 as a single era. These dates were selected by Chandler (1977) to identify the period during which hierarchical, multiunit enterprises first appeared. Chandler presented evidence to show that "traditional" entrepreneurial organizations began to give way to mass production organizations by 1880. Consequently, this date is chosen as the end of the "preindustrial era" and the beginning of the "mass production era" (Figure 1). Second, it is useful to divide the "postindustrial era" into two separate periods. The first, which corresponds to the strategic and environmental conditions described by Ansoff, extends from 1960 to 1980. Reich (1983) has described this period as one in which U.S. industry experienced an "impasse": though placed under increasing pressure to adapt to shifting competitive and environmental conditions, industrial leaders resisted the need for change and (inappropriately) retained the same basic structure that was fashioned during the previous "industrial" era. There are clear signs, however, that since 1980 a structural transformation of the U.S. economy is now taking place. Thus, the postindustrial era can usefully be segmented into a period of "impasse" (1960-1980) and a period of "transformation" (1980 onwards). The characteristics of each of these eras, and the organizational forms historically associated with them, are discussed below.

The Preindustrial Era (Before 1880). Prior to 1880, American business relied almost entirely on commercial practices and procedures invented and perfected centuries earlier in Europe. Even though the U.S. economy grew rapidly during the nineteenth century, the size and nature of business enterprises changed very little. From 1800-1880, the population more than quadrupled, and the total volume of goods produced and distributed increased enormously. Nevertheless, the business organizations responsible for the increased output continued to be traditional "single-unit enterprises" perfected by British and Dutch merchants as early as the twelfth and thirteenth centuries (Chandler, 1977, p. 14).

Mintzberg (1979: 242) identified two variants of the single-unit business firm, the "craft structure" and the "entrepreneurial structure." Craft organizations were comprised of a single, informally structured group of workers. A natural division of labor was found in these organizations, but specialization was not rigidly defined nor jobs easily interchanged. There was little need for direct supervision since activities were coordinated through mutual adjustments between workers. Often there was no recognized leader, or if there was one, he or she worked alongside the others on tasks similar to theirs. Craft organizations persist to the present day and are typical of the small proprietorships commonly found in retailing, construction, agriculture, and so on.

The entrepreneurial structure resembled the craft form in that the performance of work was still conducted within an informally structured, single-unit enterprise. However, these organizations were dominated by an entrepreneur who personally supervised subordinates. This created a vertical division of labor, with the entrepreneur making all important decisions. Despite being centralized, the entrepreneurial firm lacked formalization, sophisticated controls, or an elaborate structure. This preserved operating flexibility and made the firm completely responsive to the entrepreneur's directives. Being more common than the craft form, this was the dominant type of organization until late in the nineteenth century (Edwards, 1979, p. 23). The entrepreneurial structure remains typical of small, present-day firms that focus their efforts on a single market and emphasize a single function such as marketing or manufacturing.

The Era of Mass Production (1880-1930).   From 1880 onwards, the focus of industrial activity shifted from custom-made products sold in regional markets to mass-produced goods sold in national markets. Along with expanding markets, new technologies permitted an unprecedented output of goods at ever-decreasing unit costs. Because most industries provided ample growth opportunities, managerial attention was not directed toward developing new markets and products but was focused inwardly on the efficiency of production techniques and organization. This fostered an economic expansion in the U.S. that was unparalleled in world history. In 1860, the annual value of manufactured goods totaled $1.8 billion; by 1900, it had grown to $11 billion (in constant dollars). The annual increase in productivity, which had hovered around three-tenths of one percent for most of the nineteenth century, suddenly surged in the last two decades to nearly six times that rate. These productivity increases were the direct result of the introduction of mass-production techniques.

The new system of mass production required a new form of organization. The growth of national markets demanded that firms expand their operations geographically and create multiunit enterprises. A growing volume of output also required increases in plant size. Simultaneously, vertical integration was necessary to ensure an uninterrupted flow of goods to the market. Manufacturing plants created their own warehouses and wholesaling operations, and often their own salesforces. Integration permitted better control of the supplies flowing into, and the products flowing out of, the enlarged plant facilities. To integrate specialized activities across geographically dispersed units, firms developed functionally departmentalized structures. Functional interdependence, in turn, required the creation of elaborate hierarchies of authority to effect interunit coordination. Then, as firms grew too large to be managed through direct supervision, managers introduced formal rules, standard operating procedures, and other bureaucratic devices. The result was that informally organized, traditional firms were replaced as the dominant organizational form by hierarchical, functionally departmentalized, vertically integrated, mass-production enterprises.

The Era of Mass Marketing (1930-1960).   For the first 30 years of the twentieth century, commercial success went to firms that offered the lowest-priced products. Products were largely undifferentiated, and the ability to produce at the lowest unit cost was the key to creating competitive advantage. But, by 1930, the demand for basic consumer goods was beginning to reach saturation. Increasing affluence led consumers to become more sophisticated and to look for more than the basic performance offered by standardized goods. This meant that, in contrast to the earlier emphasis on mass production, competitive success began to depend increasingly on a firms' marketing skills. Differentiating products to create new markets became a priority of management. Moreover, increasing market saturation encouraged firms to diversify in search of new growth opportunities. Firms moved into new sectors of industry to keep managerial and organizational resources fully employed as primary markets matured or declined.

The increasing diversity of organizational activity, resulting from the differentiation of products and markets and the entry of firms into new industrial sectors, encouraged the development of new organizational structures. Diversification into several lines increased administrative complexity and led to the creation of decentralized, divisionalized organizations. For example, among the largest 500 U.S. companies, the percentage of functionally organized firms declined from 76% in 1949 to 49% in 1959, while the number of divisionalized firms increased from 24% to 51% in the same period (Rumelt, 1974, p. 65). By assigning operating autonomy and responsibility to divisional managers, the new structure was designed to achieve maximum penetration of markets along product or geographical lines. The shift from functional to divisional managers diverted attention away from an internal focus on production efficiency toward an external focus on consumer needs within specific market segments. As Mintzberg (1979, p. 114) noted, the divisional structure is inherently marketing oriented in that it makes managers directly accountable for the specific niches the organization serves—the customers it supplies, the places where it supplies them, and so on.

The Postindustrial Era: Impasse (1960-1980). Before 1960, domestic markets provided a base for the U.S. economy's continued growth and prosperity. The strategy of product differentiation enabled U.S. firms to increase sales penetration by offering a "full line," while growth opportunities farther afield were provided through diversification. By the 1960s, however, possibilities for additional domestic expansion had begun to reach their limits. Consumer goods markets for differentiated, as well as standardized products, had become largely saturated, and demand leveled off sharply in core sectors of the economy such as steel, automobiles, textiles, and chemicals. Much of this market saturation was due to competition from abroad. Prior to 1960, foreign trade did not figure significantly in the U.S. economy. This situation had changed dramatically by 1980, when 70% of all the goods produced in the U.S. were actively competing with foreign-made goods. By 1980, America was importing 25% of its cars, 25% of its steel, 60% of its calculators, 27% of its metal-forming machine tools, 35% of its textile machinery, and 53% of its numerically-controlled machine tools. Twenty years earlier, imports had accounted for less than 10% of the U.S. market for each of these products.

Clearly, foreign competition had a major impact on the nation's economic prosperity. Measured in constant 1981 dollars, the Dow Jones industrial average declined from 2,624 in 1965 to around 1,000 in 1980. The profit rate of America's nonfinancial corporations dropped steadily from 12.7% in the 1960s to around 9% by 1980. Productivity growth slowed from an average yearly increase of 3.2% between 1948 and 1965 to an average of 2.4% between 1965 and 1973. In spite of the threat posed by foreign competition and the marked deterioration of the economy's health, however, U.S. industry did little to restructure its industrial base or to reorganize its systems of production. Rather than treating the changed economic conditions as signs of a new, postindustrial era, managers reacted to them as a temporary recession, to be endured until prosperity again returned. Because of industry's stake in productive arrangements that were based on the logic of mass production and mass marketing, radical change was resisted. Thus, for the most part, organizational forms invented in the industrial era persisted, creating an impasse in organizational development.

Consequently, the vast majority of medium and large-sized organizations continued to utilize functional or divisional structures. Some changes in strategy and structure were, however, necessary. Many firms could no longer operate successfully where foreign producers possessed a systematic competitive edge deriving, for example, from lower labor or capital costs, or from a system of industrial organization that could not be readily adopted in the U.S. economic and regulatory environment. Faced with relatively intractable disadvantages, many firms attempted to avoid head-on competition from abroad by moving "up-market" into more limited-volume but higher value-added niches. The two major ways to achieve this were, first, to increase the technological sophistication of manufacturing processes, and, second, to offer customized products and services. Since the main challenge from foreign competition lay in sectors producing standardized, mass-produced goods, it was possible for many firms to survive in such relatively protected niches. Thus, the adoption of niche-oriented strategies gradually increased in importance between 1960 and 1980 but without radically altering the basic organizational structures established in earlier eras.

The niche strategy was largely responsible for the development of a new organizational form, the matrix structure, although this form was adopted by a relatively small number of firms compared to the continued widespread use of functional and divisional structures. According to Kingdon (1973), the initial appearance of matrix structures in the 1960s came when the U.S. government required research and development contractors to use a project management system. This allowed government agencies to deal with one individual—the project manager—who had full responsibility for meeting costs and deadlines, rather than having to negotiate with a number of functional heads each having only partial responsibility. In many cases, this led to the development of matrix structures since firms superimposed project management on top of the existing functional structure that was retained to ensure specialized expertise essential for work of high technical quality. Matrix organization thus emerged as a response to the government's requirements for technologically sophisticated, customized projects (e.g., in aerospace). The new form was equally useful in non-project settings where, as in the defense industry, firms carved out niches by delivering up-market products and services. Prestigious companies such as GTE, Hughes Aircraft, 3M, ITT, Lockheed, TRW, NCR, and Texas Instruments, among others, adopted matrix structures in the 1960s and 1970s (Knight, 1976).

The Postindustrial Era: Transformation (1980 Onwards). The impact of foreign competition hit hardest in the capital-intensive, high-volume industries that the U.S. had depended upon most throughout the twentieth century. By 1980, the core industries of the industrial era—steel, automobiles, petrochemicals, textiles, consumer electronics, electrical machinery, metal-forming machinery—were in trouble. These were the sectors in which mature, standardized technologies could be transferred abroad and operated mostly by unskilled or semiskilled labor. Developing countries were able to purchase the world's most modern steel-rolling mills, computer-controlled machine tools, chemical plants, and so on. They could also get training and technical supervision to accompany the production facilities. This flow of technical know-how across international boundaries undermined the traditional strength of U.S. industry—its technological leadership in devising standardized mass-production systems for delivering goods and services at low unit cost.

Throughout the 1960s and 1970s, the U.S. faced increasing challenges to transform its economic structure to meet the new realities of global competition, but a variety of protectionist policies sought to preserve its old industrial base (Reich, 1983). High-volume, standardized production had been the engine of prosperity for so long that fundamental change threatened the well-being of numerous vested interests. So the nation acted as if the industrial era had not really ended. Where adaptive actions were taken, they tended to be piecemeal, essentially short-term measures. Even extensive rationalization and cost-cutting in the 1970s failed to rejuvenate the economy sufficiently to restore America's former position of dominance in world markets. Such revamping of traditional production methods could only forestall the onset of industrial transformation. Basic structural changes were needed in the mix of industries that constituted the economy's core. The fact that U.S. industry resisted such change for so long simply meant that structural transformation would be all the more dramatic when it eventually came.

By 1980, it had become clear that the U.S. could no longer simply fight a rearguard action against foreign incursions into its traditional industrial base. This realization was reflected in the increasing proportion of industrial activity being established in communications, information processing, and other high-technology sectors. Rather than attempt to rescue ailing sunset industries, it had become obvious that realistic prospects of renewed economic growth lay in these emerging sectors. This encouraged a large-scale transfer of the nation's productive assets from aging mass-production facilities to the new areas of technological growth. One indicator of this structural transformation of the economy in the 1980s was the sharp increase in spinoffs, mergers and acquisitions, divestitures, leveraged buyouts, and recapitalizations. In size and scope, this activity exceeded anything witnessed in U.S. history: between 1983 and 1986 nearly a fifth of the current value of all traded stocks changed hands. If this were to continue at the 1986 rate, every public company could be turned over to new owners by the year 2000. The potential for economic benefit of this reshuffling of corporate assets was reflected in the fact that the stock market value of divested corporate units consistently exceeded their value before divestment (as reflected in their relative asset share of the total corporation).

This reshuffling is permitting a redeployment of economic resources to more productive uses in emerging branches of industry. Moreover, the shift of assets to new, increasingly high-technology, industries represents more than just a transfer of investments from low-growth to high-growth sectors of the economy. It also represents a fundamental reorientation in the way that organizations operate. Traditionally, U.S. firms have pursued a strategy of price-based competition undergirded by large market share and low unit costs derived from scale economies and rapid movement down the experience curve. But this strategy is no longer suited to the new conditions in high-technology industries and must be replaced by what can be referred to as "flexible-system production." In contrast to mass production, flexible-system production requires an increased emphasis on new product development to prevent the transformation of competition into a commodity game. This involves the development of flexible, general-purpose production facilities rather than highly specialized equipment dedicated to manufacturing single-purpose products. Competition thus revolves around product performance, quality, and innovation rather than price. Flexible-system production has an advantage over mass production whenever profitability can be increased more sharply by solving new problems than by improving solutions to old problems.

This new strategy suggests the appropriateness of organizational forms that are based on *interorganizational* rather than intraorganizational modes of coordination. In the past, most major U.S. firms have attempted to develop almost all their own product technology internally (although process technology is commonly purchased from capital goods producers). However, with the increased diffusion of know-how across industrial and international boundaries, and the consequent shortening of product and technological lifecycles, this situation has changed dramatically. Firms find it increasingly difficult to keep abreast of the latest technological developments without help from the outside, and, because of the increased cost and development time needed for high-technology products, internally developed products may be prohibitively expensive or run the risk of being obsolete by the time they reach the market. Thus, in high-technology sectors, firms are engaging in a variety of equity and nonequity collaborative arrangements with other organizations. For example, there has been an "explosion" of joint venture activity since 1978, especially in sectors based on information-related technologies (Harrigan, 1985, p. 7). In 1983 alone, the number of domestic joint ventures announced in some industries, like communications systems and services, exceeded the sum of all previously announced joint ventures in those sectors. The forces underlying the growth of joint ventures, as well as other modes of interorganizational collaboration, are discussed in greater detail later in the chapter.

Multinational Strategies and Structures

As the discussion above indicates, global competition has had a profound impact on the historical evolution of domestic strategies and structures. The discussion was limited, however, to the impact of global competition on the structure of industries and markets within the U.S. We now turn to the structural transformation of world industries and markets. For the increasing proportion of U.S. companies operating on an international scale, the global competitive environment has undergone a series of radical changes during the twentieth century. The changing structure of world markets and global competition has, consequently, produced distinct evolutionary phases in the strategies and structures of these multinational corporations.

A useful point of departure in distinguishing between such phases is Perlmutter's (1969) contention that managers may adopt one of three basic orientations toward international competition. These may be described as "ethnocentric" (home-country oriented), "polycentric" (host-country oriented), or "geocentric" (world-oriented). Ethnocentrically-oriented multinationals centralize authority in their headquarters and apply similar management processes, operating procedures, and performance criteria to

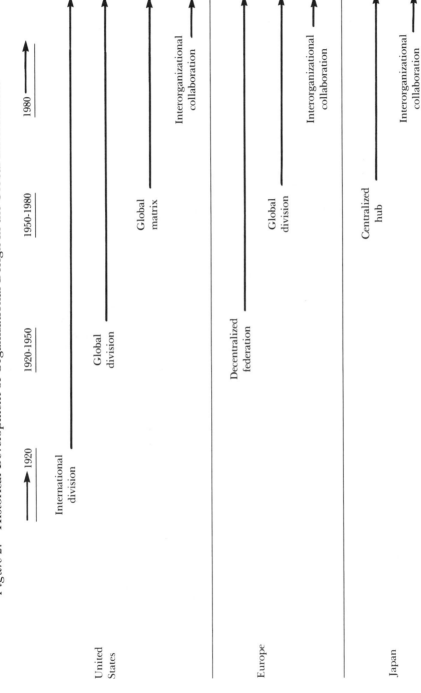

Figure 2. Historical Development of Organizational Design in the Global Environment

their foreign operations. Polycentric multinationals, in contrast, begin with the assumption that since host-country cultures and competitive environments are fundamentally idiosyncratic, local managers must be given considerable autonomy to operate their subsidiaries. Finally, geocentric multinationals adopt a worldwide approach in both headquarters and subsidiaries. The firm's subsidiaries are thus neither dependent satellites nor independent operating units but collaborative partners attempting to integrate local with worldwide objectives as part of a coherent global strategy.

Perlmutter (1969) postulated an evolutionary movement from ethnocentrism to polycentrism to geocentrism. He argued that firms tend to be ethnocentric when they first venture abroad, but their highly standardized approach creates social and political repercussions and inhibits competitive innovations. This often leads to the adoption of a polycentric approach designed to achieve a more intensive penetration of local markets, the acquisition of better information about customers, and more host-government support. Finally, firms become geocentric as they realize the need to mobilize resources on a worldwide scale to take advantage of interdependencies among national markets and to retaliate against rivals who use different competitive tactics in different markets to create a global strategic advantage. Though the present discussion follows Perlmutter's in broad outline, it also distinguishes between the rather different evolutionary paths followed by multinationals located, respectively, in the U.S., Europe, and Japan—the world's major regional bases of multinational headquarters. A simple stagewise evolutionary development cannot adequately account for the diverse approaches taken to international competition by organizations founded in these three major regions of economic activity. Consequently, Figure 2 portrays the alternative strategies and structures adopted by U.S., European, and Japanese corporations.

American Multinationals.   Prior to 1880, U.S. international trade was conducted entirely through merchants who acted as middlemen between domestic producers of goods and independent distributors scattered around the world. The volume of trade was small since U.S. markets were expanding with rapid population growth and provided ample outlets for available manufactured goods. Domestic consumption continued to absorb most of U.S. industrial output until new manufacturing technologies and new methods of high-volume distribution were invented around the turn of the century. When it became obvious that industrial giants located in Eastern states could supply foreign markets, sometimes as easily as those in California, they quickly extended their marketing organizations overseas. Soon afterwards, most of these large firms became multinational by investing in production facilities abroad. By 1914, the value of direct foreign investment by U.S. multinationals equaled 7% of the gross national product, a figure that was still the same in 1966 (Chandler, 1986, p. 424).

The early entry of U.S. firms into foreign markets conformed to what has generally become known as the "waterfall model," according to which expansion abroad occurs as domestic markets begin to reach saturation, and business activity "spills over" into countries offering greater potential for market growth. This is indicated by the fact that the first U.S. multinationals appeared in the same mass-production industries—food, tobacco, chemicals, oil, rubber, machinery, transportation equipment, and so on—that were responsible for the birth of the industrial era in the domestic economy. Foreign activity represented a simple extension of the production and distribution methods established at home. Firms initially managed foreign operations through the creation of a separate export unit in a marketing division. As international markets grew, however, new operating units were established abroad. Typically, these units were coordinated by the manager of an international division who reported directly to the highest levels of management. Though the international division was an independent unit not directly integrated with domestic operations, its activities were watched very closely by the CEO and the Board of Directors. And, because responsibility for all international operations was given to a single division manager, foreign operations tended to be more or less standardized throughout the world, with little accommodation of activities to the peculiarities of national markets.

From these basically ethnocentric origins, U.S. corporations proceeded more or less directly to the adoption of geocentric strategies and structures. On the whole, American multinationals skipped over the polycentric phase described by Perlmutter (1969). Though foreign activities became, over time, increasingly differentiated and tailored to the competitive conditions associated with diverse countries, they did so only within a framework of policies designed to integrate those activities with domestic operations. Stopford and Wells (1972) thus observed that the international division was a transitory form that gave way to another, more global form. Which global form a company moved to depended on the firm's international growth strategy. Most firms, especially those that took their entire diversified domestic product line abroad, eventually adopted worldwide product divisions. On the other hand, those firms that expanded internationally with only their dominant business adopted geographic divisions, though the latter were in the minority. Regardless of the number of different countries served through diverse divisions, however, foreign operations remained highly integrated with those at home. Though strategies and policies varied, to some extent, between national markets, activities were coordinated through managerial methods and procedures invented at corporate headquarters.

European Multinationals.   The initial period of expansion of European multinationals came after World War I. It occurred primarily in the chemical and electrical products industries, in contrast to American multinationals which were also common in the food, fabricated metals products, and nonelectrical machinery industries. The spread of European multinationals was distinctive not only in terms of industry distribution but also in terms of geographical distribution. European firms located their foreign operations primarily in other developed European countries. This contrasted with the tendency of American multinationals to produce anywhere that national markets grew rapidly. According to Franko (1976), the location in which European multinationals established foreign subsidiaries was determined not by the size of the market but almost entirely by the attempt to circumvent trade barriers in the neighboring countries of Europe. Historically, European markets were highly fragmented by trade barriers, and this protection against imports meant that foreign firms needed to establish local production facilities in order to compete effectively as insiders.

The Balkanization of European markets, and the reduction of competitive pressures within nation states, led to the establishment of a distinctive organizational form within European multinationals. The vast majority of such firms were, until the mid 1970s, organized as international holding companies with subsidiaries that were highly autonomous in their respective national markets—what have been described as "decentralized federations" (Chandler, 1986). The relationship between headquarters and subsidiaries was informal rather than governed by written rules and procedures and a formal organization structure. Personal relationships based on career, social, friendship, and family ties characterized links between countries. The most powerful forces producing this form of organization were the barriers to trade which kept national markets separate from one another and thus limited the need for cross-border communication. For example, a distinctive feature of European multinationals was the absence of any managers with strictly supranational responsibilities. This organizational structure was the logical counterpart to the economic structure of Europe. The tariff, nontariff, and cartel barriers to trade which kept national markets economically separated from one another removed the need or opportunity for a supranational strategy.

In consequence, European multinationals were, throughout most of the twentieth century, highly polycentric in orientation. Success depended primarily on the subsidiaries' abilities to negotiate a favorable environment with host-country governments and to manage their relationships with local competitors. All of this changed in the 1970s, however, with the elimination of tariff barriers within the E.E.C. and with the entrance of both American and Japanese firms into local markets. The intensification of competitive pressures then forced European firms to switch increasingly to multidivisional structures for coordinating global product or area divisions. This switch was not, as in the American case, simply a matter of structure following strategy (Franko, 1974). Many of the European multinationals had long been highly diversified without experiencing the need to adopt multidivisional structures. Changes in the competitive environment, rather than changes in strategy, were the primary forces underlying reorganization. As competition increased, firms found the need to increase intercountry communication in order to mobilize resources worldwide to provide an effective response to rivals who were competing not on a national but on a global basis. In the 1970s and 1980s, European multinationals have thus gradually abandoned their polycentric orientations to adopt geocentric, or truly global, strategies.

Japanese Multinationals. Japanese multinationals originated much later than both U.S. and European multinationals; they appeared mainly after World War II but then grew rapidly in importance and by 1970 had emerged as major global competitors. Because of their late entry into world markets, the Japanese chose not to match the well-established local marketing capabilities and facilities that U.S. and European firms had built up. The Japanese challenge came, instead, from exports; Japan's competitive advantage lay in the "upstream" end of the value chain. Primarily because of the existence of a large, homogeneous market at home, the Japanese developed efficient, scale-intensive plants, which, in a global environment of declining tariffs, could also be directed toward expansion abroad. This expansion came not in the skilled, labor-intensive technologically sophisticated industries dominated by American and European firms but in relatively competitive industries producing standardized or traditional goods. The Japanese strategy emphasized manufacturing, cost advantages, and quality assurance, rather than product innovation and strong marketing skills (Franko, 1983).

Because of the Japanese competitive advantage in manufacturing at home, there was little need for extensive direct investment in production facilities in Europe and the U.S. The investments that were made took the form of sales companies rather than manufacturing plants. These enterprises were established primarily as a means of promoting Japanese exports—as a beachhead for developing marketing channels and networks of local distributors. In addition, direct investment served as a means of getting behind real or threatened barriers to trade. The Japanese traditionally had little motivation to establish production facilities in Europe and the U.S. since the cost of labor and materials was much more expensive than at home. Thus, Japanese investments in these countries remained, with rare exceptions, adjuncts to production systems based in

Japan rather than acting as substitutes for them. This concentration of production facilities at home, moreover, permitted tight central control of product development, procurement, and manufacturing. For this reason, the organizational structure and management system adopted by Japanese multinationals has been described as a "centralized hub" (Bartlett, 1986).

Japanese multinationals have, thus, adopted a primarily ethnocentric orientation to competing in world markets. Lately, however, there are signs that Japan is moving toward the adoption of more geocentric strategies. In part, this is because growing protectionist sentiments are forcing the Japanese to establish production facilities in major markets abroad in order to jump trade barriers. But a much more important force behind recent increases in foreign direct investment is the increasing need for Japan to bolster its export-based strategy by taking advantage of lower factor costs in lesser developed countries. In this regard, the expansion abroad of Japanese multinationals is taking place for quite opposite reasons than the expansion abroad of U.S. multinationals. Whereas U.S. multinationals have traditionally moved abroad to reinforce a product or technological edge in industries in which they possessed a strong worldwide lead, Japanese firms are moving production abroad in those industries in which they are losing their competitive edge. Because Japanese exports have been concentrated largely in commodity products, Asian and Latin American countries providing highly productive, low-cost labor have been able to compete with the Japanese at their own game. For this reason, Japanese multinationals have found it necessary to move production to lesser developed countries in order to sustain their traditional strategy of exporting inexpensive,high-quality goods to the world's advanced economies.

Competition in a Geocentric World.   By the 1980s, the differing paths of historical development of American, European, and Japanese multinationals were beginning to converge. The adoption of a geocentric orientation grew increasingly necessary for rivals on every continent as it became obvious that neither a completely centralized, ethnocentric approach nor a completely decentralized, polycentric approach was sufficient to compete effectively abroad. Forces of centralization and decentralization were both growing stronger simultaneously. On the one hand, the need for worldwide coordination and integration of activity increased at the upstream end of the value chain, and, on the other hand, the need for a greater degree of national differentiation and responsiveness increased at the downstream end. Multinationals were thus faced with the task of devising organizational systems for achieving both local and worldwide objectives as part of a coherent global strategy.

Two major forces called for more centralized decision making and greater strategic coordination on a global level. First, global industries became increasingly capital-intensive. Between 1960 and 1980, the labor content of traditional manufacturing and assembly operations in chemicals, textiles, steel, and so on, dropped from 25% to somewhere between 5 and 10% of the total cost of the product. The trend was even more prevalent in new global industries, such as semiconductors, whose direct labor content dropped to below 5%. The most important strategic implication of this trend was that it required firms to penetrate markets throughout the world to attain the volume necessary to defray heavy initial investment. Domestic markets, even those as large as Japan or the U.S., proved to be too small for world-class automated plants in industries such as semiconductors and machine tools. Second, R & D costs escalated sharply. As technological life cycles grew shorter, less time was available to recoup fixed R & D costs. This also demanded that companies achieve a deep and quick penetration of markets worldwide. Firms were required to sell simultaneously to the entire world in order to amortize front-end investment. This meant that companies could no longer be content to develop domestic markets first before moving on to overseas markets; a global approach was needed from the outset.

At the same time, there was increasing pressure to decentralize downstream activities at the local level. Perhaps the most important consequence of rising capital and R & D costs was the increased burden placed on firms to create effective global distribution systems. To avoid being preempted, and thereby failing to attain the sales volume necessary to remain competitive, companies had to enter markets much more quickly. Speed became a critical element of global strategy. This required firms to develop organizational arrangements for exploiting local markets through flexible distribution capabilities. The task was made even more critical by the rising tide of protectionism. The postwar trend toward free trade was, especially in the 1980s, curtailed by an awareness on the part of national governments that their home markets were increasingly susceptible to invasion by foreign competitors operating on a global scale. The new wave of protectionism extended not just to tariff barriers but to requirements for local content and local ownership. Even Japanese firms were forced to supplement their export-based strategies with an increasing amount of direct investment in Europe and the U.S. Thus, at the same time that centralized planning and coordination on a worldwide basis became essential, pressures increased to decentralize operations to accommodate national differences and maintain responsiveness to local conditions.

The forces encouraging the adoption of geocentric strategies also encouraged the development of new organizational designs. Stopford and Wells (1972), for example, foresaw the eventual replacement of worldwide product divisions and area divisions by global matrix or "grid" structures. The latter were seen as a way to coordinate areas and products simultaneously when foreign market penetration and production diversity reached critical levels requiring an integrated managerial effort worldwide. The main problem with global matrix structures, however, is that they can overcentralize decision-making authority in headquarters' offices without encouraging sufficient autonomy at the subsidiary level to ensure a truly geocentric orientation. In the attempt to build a consistent global strategy, there is a tendency to use matrix organization to coordinate key decisions and control global resources in a way that imposes too much uniformity on subsidiaries.

Bartlett and Ghoshal (1986) have, consequently, drawn attention to a new model of global organization based on the assumption that dispersed responsibility among subsidiaries is necessary to exploit the latter's exposure to diverse environmental conditions. While this model emphasizes the need for subsidiaries to be locally responsive, it also emphasizes the need to integrate activities across subsidiaries worldwide. This can be achieved by intersubsidiary cooperation to offset the problems caused by the company's dispersed and decentralized operations. Relationships among managers are thus built not on dependence, as in the ethnocentric model, nor on independence, as in the polycentric model, but on interdependence and collaboration. In contrast to matrix organization, which essentially superimposes one hierarchy on another, this model resembles a global network of decentralized subsidiaries whose activities are nevertheless integrated through collaborative mechanisms into a coherent global strategy.

Another increasingly important adaptation to the unique demands placed upon organizations that pursue geocentric, or global, strategies is the formation of interorganizational coalitions. Such coalitions are similar to networks of subsidiaries in that they rely upon collaboration as a mechanism for achieving strategic integration though, of course, they represent a radical departure from the traditional model of the wholly-owned multinational corporation. International coalitions are not new, but the pattern of liaisons now taking shape is unprecedented, and the strategic significance of such arrangements is increasing dramatically as a geocentric approach to global strategy becomes more widespread (Porter and Fuller, 1986). Coalitions are appropriate mechanisms for dealing with global competition because they can accommodate opposing pressures for both local responsiveness and worldwide integration of activities. On the one hand, where growing protectionism requires that firms establish marketing channels in countries they traditionally served through exports, coalitions can provide immediate access to local distribution networks. On the other hand, coalitions facilitate a coordinated global response in situations requiring preemptive action and rapid simultaneous entry into markets worldwide (Ohmae, 1985). Thus, in the 1980s and beyond, interorganizational collaboration is and will be of growing importance in international as well as in domestic environments.

ORGANIZATIONAL DESIGN IN CONTEMPORARY ENVIRONMENTS

Growing Importance of Interorganizational Collaboration

The twin forces of technology and globalization are placing new demands on organizations in both domestic and international spheres. This changing strategic environment calls for organizational designs that are radically different from their historical predecessors. Prior to 1980, organizational designs generally evolved in a way that produced greater intraorganizational structural complexity. However, as the economy shifts toward a high-technology base, and as global competition grows increasingly intense, one major trend is apparent: a move toward the use of *interorganizational* modes of coordination. In some sectors of the domestic economy, especially in high-technology areas, the number of such arrangements has recently increased rapidly. In the international domain, where such ventures have long been employed, their strategic significance has grown markedly even though their numbers have remained generally constant.

As a mechanism for organizing economic activity, interorganizational collaboration represents an intermediate form of coordination falling between "markets" and "hierarchies" (Williamson, 1975). While this mechanism involves the purposeful regulation of activity within a managerially administered framework, it also involves an exchange of resources between organizations, as in market relationships. Some forms of collaboration are based on equity-sharing arrangements and thus come closer to hierarchies than to markets, while other forms of collaboration do not involve equity sharing and so approximate market coordination to a greater degree. The increasing importance of interorganizational collaboration is the result of two forces that are encouraging a departure both from pure hierarchical and from pure market forms of coordination. On the one hand, the need for greater flexibility is requiring organizations to disaggregate their activities and externalize certain functions to be performed by collaborating partners, domestically or internationally. On the other hand, the need for greater integration and coordination of activities across interdependent markets, industries, and countries is requiring organizations to manage their exchange relationships through negotiated arrangements designed to stabilize operations. Figure 3 illustrates how these two forces are leading to the adoption of both equity-based and nonequity-based modes of collaboration.

Figure 3. Interorganizational Collaboration as an Intermediate Form of Coordination

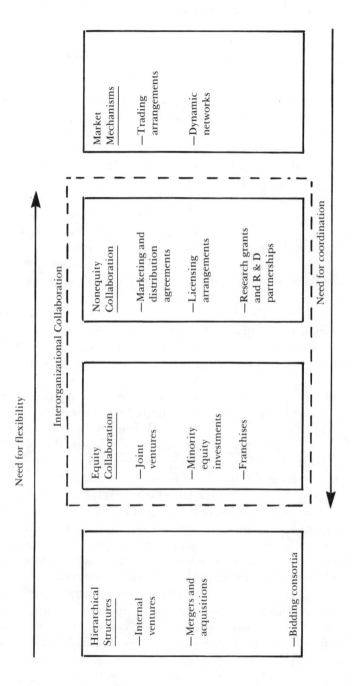

Need for Flexibility. The conventional means by which firms have responded to potential profit and growth opportunities offered by emerging technologies has been to develop internally new technical capabilities. Though internal development remains a major way of entering into new ventures, contemporary environments increasingly call for more responsive ways of exploiting growth opportunities. Research indicates that internally developed ventures typically take 8 years before breaking even and 12 years before matching the returns of established lines of business (Biggadike, 1979). The decreasing revenue-generating life of product-markets and technologies in information-based sectors of the economy thus makes internal development less and less economically feasible.

One alternative means of entering into new product-market niches, often employed by firms in the past, has been merger and acquisition. By providing immediate access to new opportunities, this method is favored where speed is a necessary part of a firm's growth strategy. Even acquisitions, however, appear to have important limitations in contemporary environments. Increasingly, potential synergies derive not from capital assets and technological hardware but from the skills and know-how of employees in the acquired firm. Unfortunately, perhaps the major reason underlying the failure of many recent high-technology acquisitions has been the difficulty of merging different corporate cultures and power structures without triggering an exodus of managers from the acquired firm. The solution to this problem is to adopt a "hands off" policy by granting operating autonomy to acquired firms (Shanley, 1986). This policy, however, also presents acquiring firms with a dilemma since it precludes the potential for synergy to develop through interaction between employees of the respective firms.

This latter problem may sometimes be overcome by the use of equity joint ventures. Because joint ventures can be established relatively quickly, like acquisitions, they avoid the delays associated with internally developed ventures and can provide an immediate presence in new markets. At the same time, since they imply a more equal commitment from participating companies, joint ventures can overcome many of the operating control problems associated with the merging of different corporate cultures and power structures. Such problems may also be circumvented by the establishment of joint ventures as autonomous operating units—separate entities that are unencumbered by the parent's potentially stifling controls. In this way, joint ventures can exploit technological synergies through a merging of expertise while, at the same time, offering flexibility and speed in seizing new technological opportunities.

In addition to emerging technologies, the dynamics of global competition are making interorganizational collaboration important as a means of enhancing operational flexibility. One reason for this is that firms must constantly migrate around the globe in search of the lowest available factor costs. Labor cost advantages, for example, shift from country to country in relatively short periods of time. Once a particular country has been identified as having low-cost labor, companies from all over the globe move in, and since they can only recruit labor by means of money, labor costs inevitably rise. Experience shows that, after the initial discovery of a pool of low-cost labor, a country will typically retain its cost advantage for little more than a five-year period. Thus, the initial advantage held by Japan shifted over time to Korea, Taiwan, and Singapore, and later to Thailand, Malaysia, Hong Kong, and the Philippines. Currently, India, Sri Lanka, and Indonesia are gaining a competitive edge, and firms are beginning to turn their attention to China where one billion people exist in a low-wage labor market. The situation is made even more fluid by fluctuating exchange rates which can dramatically alter a country's factor costs within months. The recent rise of the Japanese yen, for example, has encouraged many Japanese companies to move production offshore.

Because cost advantages are increasingly short-lived, the traditional means of setting up production facilities abroad through wholly owned subsidiaries has become less and less attractive. Permanent investments in plant and other facilities reduce a firm's global mobility and its capacity to take advantage of new competitive opportunities available elsewhere. In this situation, joint ventures provide a mechanism for the sharing of costs with others. This is particularly the case in capital-intensive industries where the minimum efficient scale is large and the burden of cost is too high for a single firm to bear. As Davidson (1982, p. 31) noted, the frequency of entry by means of joint ventures into foreign production is determined largely by the fixed costs associated with foreign investment decisions; the higher such costs, the greater the likelihood that joint ventures will be used. High research and development costs, for example, encourage firms to seek help in attaining sufficient volume worldwide to cover their initial investments. By participating in several such ventures around the globe, a firm can both reduce exit costs when a country's factor advantages disappear and hedge its bets in anticipating the relative economic benefits associated with producing in different countries. In this way, sufficient flexibility is maintained to enable firms to compete effectively on a global basis by taking advantage of opportunities whenever and wherever they arise.

Need for Coordination. In an attempt to achieve greater flexibility in utilizing the best of available technologies, many firms have started to uncouple the basic elements of their production process by purchasing components in the marketplace rather than making them in-house. IBM's well-known strategy for entering the personal computer market, with its flexible policy regarding the sourcing of components, provides a good example. IBM used Intel processors (which originated from Hitachi), an Epson printer, a TDK power supply, Tanden Shugart disk drives, IBM-designed keyboards from Keytronics and AMP, a motherboard from SCI Systems, and a monitor from Atlas. This trend toward less integrated production processes and greater outsourcing is developing in high-technology industries throughout the economy. Such a strategy is becoming more feasible as firms adopt common technical standards that permit them to design technological systems on the basis of nonproprietary open architectures. Because open architecture allows a wide variety of technologies to be linked together, a large number of diverse organizations must closely coordinate their activities with each other.

Miles and Snow (1986) refer to such systems of organization as "dynamic networks." The characteristics of a dynamic network as a means of coordinating interorganizational activity are: (a) the "vertical disaggregation" of functions (manufacturing, marketing, distribution, etc.) typically conducted within the boundaries of a single enterprise into performance by independent organizations within a network; (b) the use of "brokers" to link together the different organizations into business groups for the performance of specific tasks; (c) the governance of relationships between organizations by "market mechanisms" rather than by plans and controls; and (d) the substitution of "full-disclosure information systems" for lengthy trust-building processes based on experience (individual participants in the network agree on a general structure of payment for value-added and then hook themselves together in a continuously updated information system so that contributions can be mutually and instantaneously verified).

There is considerable support for Miles and Snow's contention that vertically disaggregated functions will promote flexibility by acting as autonomous building blocks to be assembled, reassembled, and redeployed within and across organizational and national boundaries. Increasing rate of technological obsolescence and the greater incidence of technological substitutions demand such flexibility. On the other hand, there is less reason to believe that market mechanisms will be the primary mode through which the redeployment of these organizational building blocks will be achieved. For one thing, the assumption that firms will be willing to fully disclose information regarding all of their value-added activities, especially details pertaining to how their technologies function, may not always be realistic since it implies that firms will abandon a traditional source of competitive advantage—the possession of proprietary information. Some degree of "information impactedness," as Williamson (1975) describes market imperfection, is to be expected wherever firms seek positions of strategic superiority. As Killing (1980, p. 43) noted, it is because the market for technology is a "small, fragmented, inconsistent market in which both buyers and sellers operate with little information" that joint ventures, licensing, and other forms of interorganizational collaboration replace pure market processes. Miles and Snow (1986, p. 64) seem to view the increased use of joint ventures, subcontracting, and licensing activities as evidence of the growing importance of dynamic network structures, but such long-term agreements cannot be regarded as equivalent to the one-time transactions that constitute market processes.

What the notion of a dynamic network leaves unspecified are the interfirm coordinating mechanisms through which organizations manage and stabilize their operating environments. Toffler (1985, p. 113), for example, while agreeing that traditional hierarchies should be disaggregated into "constellations" of interdependent organizations, argued that those hierarchies should be replaced not by market mechanisms but by intermediate forms of coordination "somewhere between the hands-off relationship of buyer and seller and the hands-on relationship of franchiser and franchisee." To enhance flexibility in high-technology industries such as telecommunications, Toffler recommended the vertical disintegration of operations into "modules" to form an interorganizational system whose elements could be easily reconfigured in response to environmental change. At the same time, however, to ensure the functional integration of such modules as part of a coherent system, an overarching "framework" of planning and coordination would be necessary. The construction of this framework would be a collective effort on the part of a network of related organizations none of which individually would be indispensable to the functioning of the network. Thus, while the modularization of the system would make it highly adaptive to external contingencies, overall consistency of action would be maintained by an overarching structure of plans and policies implemented through various mechanisms of interorganizational collaboration.

The need to compete on a global scale also sharply increases requirements for coordination across the full range of a company's activities. One particularly clear example of this is the need for global competitors to manage cash flow on a worldwide basis. The coordination of global cash flow lies at the heart of a pattern of strategic interaction involving the cross-subsidization of activities across world markets (Hout et al., 1982; Watson, 1982; Hamel and Prahalad, 1985). This occurs when an aggressive competitor decides to use the cash flow generated in its home market to subsidize an attack on the markets of domestically oriented foreign competitors. If a targeted firm does not compete in the market where the aggressor generates most of its subsidizing profits, its ability to respond competitively is usually limited to cutting costs and prices. The problem with this response, however, is that the entire battle gets fought in the targeted company's market. If a targeted company generates most of its profits in the domestic market, it will be far more susceptible than an attacker that exposes only a small fraction of its revenues to margin pressure. The only effective action that can be taken in this situation is for the targeted company to retaliate by competing in the attacker's profit sanctuary. In other words, the company must expand operations to international markets and begin to manage cash flow on a global basis in a way that counters the attacker's strategic moves.

The demands on a firm's capacity to coordinate activities on a worldwide basis are made even greater when this pattern of international cross-subsidization and retaliation is conducted not just within a particular market segment but across a full product line. If firms cross-subsidize between product lines, as well as between national markets, the advantage goes to those firms with the most extensive international reach and the broadest portfolio of products, since this will provide greater scope and flexibility both in targeting vulnerable competitors and in responding strategically to attacks from abroad. In this situation, and especially in an increasingly protectionist environment, access to a worldwide distribution system becomes the critical factor underlying global competitive success. Taken to its extreme, this argument implies that, in order to maximize the potential for coordinating global cash flow, competitors should strive to establish distribution channels for as many product lines, and in as many international markets, as possible.

In reality, of course, a single firm cannot do everything. No firm can maintain a competitive advantage across an unlimited range of activities or justify the massive investment in a distribution system that extends throughout the far reaches of the globe. To establish such a distribution system would also inhibit a firm's flexibility to enter only those competitive arenas around the world where it possessed a strategic advantage and to strategically exit those where it did not. To achieve this balance between the need for coordination and the need for flexibility, interorganizational collaboration is often the only feasible alternative. Through semipermanent strategic alliances firms can enter distant markets in a relatively short time and preempt the opportunities of both local and global competitors while minimizing the costs of future exit. Thus, flexibility is assured at the same time that access to distribution channels is guaranteed. This dual capability allows a firm to reallocate its global cash flow at will and to achieve a competitive advantage over firms that are not similarly hooked into a network of cooperative relationships extending throughout the globe.

Determinants of the Mode of Collaboration

Implied in Figure 3 is the notion that the form of interorganizational collaboration employed by a firm, equity or nonequity, will vary depending upon the firm's needs for flexibility and coordination. This section of the chapter develops this idea by specifying how the forces of technology and globalization determine such needs. The analysis also specifies some of the circumstances under which a particular type of equity or nonequity arrangement will be used.

Technology and the Mode of Collaboration. Contemporary industrial environments are characterized by two prominent features: an increasing pace of technological change and an increasing amount of technological interdependence. Rapid technological change is evidenced by the shortening of technological life cycles, while technological interdependence has produced a blurring of boundaries between formerly distinct industrial sectors. Because the pace of technological change varies with the stage of the life cycle, and because there are different types of technological interdependence, it is important to examine these aspects of the industrial environment more closely. Both factors have implications for the growth of interorganizational collaboration and for the particular modes of collaboration that are adopted in different situations.

First, the mechanisms through which technological strategies are implemented vary depending on the stage of development of an industry's technological life cycle. Hamilton (1985) associated three different strategies with three stages of an industry's technological development. In the early stages of scientific and technical development, firms typically pursue a "window strategy" for identifying and monitoring leading-edge technologies. Then, as the focus of technical activity narrows in scope, firms pursue an "options strategy" in which they define opportunities for future active participation by concentrating on particular market areas or commercial applications. Finally, at the later stages of technical development, firms adopt a "positioning strategy" in which they stake out their competitive positions in selected technologies and markets. Hamilton (1985) found that these strategies were implemented through differing organizational modes: (a) research grants and contracts with other organizations were most often used for the information-gathering activities characterizing the window strategy; (b) the more defined focus of the options strategy usually required licensing and joint venture agreements; and (c) positioning strategies relied on a combination of joint ventures and internally developed programs. In other words, as an industry develops toward greater technological maturity, nonequity forms of collaboration gradually give way to equity forms of collaboration and, subsequently, to noncollaborative in-house developments.

Harrigan (1985, p. 325) reached a similar conclusion regarding the occurrence of equity and nonequity-based alliances. In embryonic industries where great uncertainty existed concerning which technological standards would be adopted, and which technologies would emerge as the dominant

Figure 4. Technology and Modes of Interorganizational Collaboration

Stage of Technological Life Cycle

		Embryonic	Mature
	X Interdependence	Marketing/ distribution agreements Supply agreements	Minority equity holdings Licensing agreements
	Y Interdependence	Research consortia	Equity joint ventures

Form of Technological Interdependence

ones, partners kept their collaborative activities informal and brief, and they engaged in a large number of liaisons of short duration. Typically, such arrangements did not involve equity sharing; they were loose partnerships, often combined with licensing agreements and other ways of disseminating and exploiting technical information. These informal alliances saved time and kept firms from being preempted by competitors. On the other hand, equity-based joint ventures typically emerged as the industry entered maturity, when technology changed less rapidly and technical standards became established. At this stage of technological development, firms entered into a fewer number of relationships with other organizations, though each venture normally encompassed a larger investment and scope than those characteristic of embryonic industries. In contrast to nonequity-based arrangements, which were designed to enhance strategic flexibility, these equity-based joint ventures were typically used to create scale economies or to reduce risk by pooling capital and other resources.

Second, the type of technological interdependence existing between firms seems to make a difference in the kind of relationships they forge with each other. Porter and Fuller (1986) distinguished between two types of coalitions: "X coalitions" that span across the borders of different activities and "Y coalitions" that are confined to a particular group of activities. In X coalitions, firms specialize in a subset of the activities within an industry, as, for example, in vertical divisions of labor where one partner manufactures and the other markets. In Y coalitions, the firms share the performance of the same activity, as, for example, with horizontally related firms that jointly manufacture a product. X coalitions imply that firms have asymmetric strengths which they combine in a symbiotic relationship, whereas Y coalitions result when partners have similar strengths. In other words, the two types of coalition reflect different forms of organizational interdependence, and often this is due directly to technological factors (Mariti and Smiley, 1983). Ghemawat et al. (1986) found that Y coalitions tend, disproportionately, to be organized as equity joint ventures, while X coalitions are usually structured as nonequity licensing, marketing, or supply agreements. This seems to confirm Porter and Fuller's (1986) contention that it is generally harder to switch partners in Y coalitions than it is in X coalitions. In Y coalitions, the alternative to the coalition is often complete integration through a buyout, whereas in X coalitions the alternative is more likely to be that of replacing one partner with a new one.

These findings suggest a classification of collaborative arrangements whose occurence varies by the particular technological conditions existing in a firm's operating environment. Figure 4 cross-classifies two stages of the technological life cycle (embryonic and mature) with two types of technological interdependence (X interdependence and Y interdependence). According to the research summarized above, equity joint ventures would appear to be the preferred mode of collaboration between firms performing similar activities in industries characterized by mature technologies. Such ventures typically permit firms to achieve scale economies, to reduce excess capacity, to transfer knowledge, or to pool risks. The opposite case, involving collaboration between firms performing symbiotically related activities in embryonic industries, calls for arrangements that permit a maximum of flexibility such as marketing, distribution, and supply agreements that allow firms in uncertain, emerging industries to keep their options open with regard to the selection of future exchange partners.

The intermediate conditions between these two extreme cases typically call for some mixture of limited equity involvement along with the use of nonequity collaboration. For example, in the upper right-hand quadrant of Figure 4, vertically linked firms operating in mature industries where technological standards are well established might cooperate through licensing agreements, which are often accompanied by minority equity holdings, as in the case of IBM's relationship with Intel. In the lower left-hand quadrant of Figure 4, on the other hand, firms involved in similar activities within embryonic industries might participate in research consortia such as the Microelectronics and Computer Technology Corporation which is funded by membership fees from over 20 firms that collaborate in a variety of ways to develop advanced semiconductor, computer, and software technology.

Globalization and the Mode of Collaboration. Modes of collaboration also vary between firms whose activities are linked across international

Figure 5. Globalization and Modes of
Interorganizational Collaboration

Configuration of Activities

		Geographically Dispersed	Geographically Concentrated
Coordination of Activities	High	Equity joint ventures	Export franchises
	Low	Minority equity investments	Nonequity marketing and distribution agreements

boundaries. A useful starting point for conceptualizing the various mechanisms through which firms cooperate internationally is Porter's (1986) classification of the different ways in which firms can compete globally. Porter's classification is based on two major dimensions. The first is the *configuration* of a firm's activities worldwide, or the location in the world where each activity in the value chain is performed, including how many places. Configuration options range from geographically concentrated (performing an activity, such as manufacturing, in one location and serving the world through exports) to geographically dispersed (performing the activity in every country). The second dimension is the degree of *coordination* effected between a firm's activities worldwide. Coordination options range from none to many. For example, a firm producing in three plants could at one extreme allow each plant to operate with full autonomy. At the other extreme, the plants could be tightly coordinated by employing the same integrated information system, the same production process, the same parts, specifications, and so forth.

Porter's scheme has direct implications for the design of a multinational's internal operating structure, such as the choice between centralizing all operations at headquarters, decentralizing completely within autonomous subsidiaries, or closely coordinating and integrating activities across subsidiaries scattered throughout the world. However, the scheme also suggests that a global strategy can be implemented through a different set of mechanisms involving interorganizational collaboration rather than internal hierarchical relationships. Figure 5 summarizes various forms of collaboration that might correspond to Porter's types of international strategy.

The upper right-hand quadrant of Figure 5 represents the situation in which firms pursue what Porter (1986) calls a "simple global strategy." This strategy concentrates as many activities as possible in one country, serves the world from this home base, and tightly coordinates through standardization those activities that must inherently be performed near the buyer. This is the strategy adopted by many Japanese firms in the 1960s and 1970s. Traditionally, this strategy has involved distributing goods abroad through local sales offices. An alternative to this method of distribution, however, is to use an export franchising system. Franchises constitute a form of interorganizational collaboration affording a high degree of centralized control over distribution and sales, usually through a detailed set of procedures specifying closely how brand marketing, customer relations, and so on, should be conducted. Through this mechanism, firms can concentrate most of their decision making and activities at headquarters and also tightly coordinate the performance of downstream functions abroad.

In the upper left-hand quadrant of Figure 5, firms geographically disperse their activities by engaging in considerable investment abroad but nevertheless coordinate the activities of their foreign operations to maintain a high degree of centralized control over global strategy. For example, a firm may disperse its manufacturing facilities throughout the world and yet centralize R & D at home while also maintaining a consistent approach to marketing and servicing worldwide. Ordinarily, this strategy would imply the existence of wholly-owned subsidiaries abroad but, alternatively, could be implemented through equity joint ventures with foreign partners. Often this alternative is necessary in order to circumvent a host government's protectionist policies for local content and local ownership. In this way, firms can maintain a coherent global strategy, utilizing home-country personnel abroad in manufacturing and sales operations, even where full ownership of offshore facilities is not possible.

The bottom right-hand quadrant of Figure 5 represents a situation where a firm pursues an export-based strategy but relinquishes control over downstream functions such as marketing and distribution. In many service industries, for example, downstream activities are tied to buyer location since they must be tailored to the unique conditions found within national markets. One way to implement this strategy is by using a highly decentralized marketing organization and local sales offices overseas. Increasingly, however, especially in the case of Japanese companies exporting to the U.S., firms are turning to strategic alliances with overseas partners who perform the downstream activities (Reich and Mankin, 1986). Such alliances take the form of nonequity agreements for the assembly, distribution, or marketing of exported goods. A typical arrangement is for foreign producers to supply products to a partner abroad which sells them in the home market under its own brand name and using its own distribution channels.

Finally, in the bottom left-hand quadrant of Figure 5, firms pursue a completely country-centered strategy in which foreign investment is highly dispersed throughout the world, and the firm retains little or no centralized control over foreign operations. In effect, such firms do not have a coherent global strategy since they make no attempt to coordinate or integrate their activities across national boundaries. Managers of foreign operations are given complete autonomy over all aspects of the business so that a unique strategy emerges within each foreign market. Ties to the headquarters office are based primarily on transfers of financial resources. This so-called portfolio approach to international competition has historically been implemented through wholly owned subsidiaries abroad. Increasingly, however, as multinationals have attempted to extend their reach to every corner of the world, they have created minority equity holdings and other financial ties to companies abroad that act on their behalf. Because the companies entering such arrangements have no direct involvement in foreign operations, they retain considerable flexibility to reallocate their investments as changing conditions demand. In this way, they gain a foothold in international markets and gain quick access to foreign distribution channels without possessing any prior experience in those countries. A good example is AT&T's attempt to expand internationally through minority equity investments in firms such as Olivetti which sells AT&T's technology in European markets.

CONCLUSION: TOWARD AN APPRECIATION OF THE NEW ORGANIZATIONAL DESIGNS

The second half of the nineteenth century witnessed an unprecedented transformation of economic activity as fundamental changes in industrial environments reconfigured the possibilities for competitive behavior. In the U.S., rapidly expanding markets provided the stimulus for development of a new transportation and communications infrastructure which in turn set in motion the competitive dynamics of growth strategies. In industries where technological innovations created the possibilities for scale economies, firms could gain production cost advantages through centralized growth. However, growth could not be effectively managed within the framework of traditional organizational designs; it necessitated administrative innovations consistent with the emerging logic of mass production. The mechanisms of bureaucratic coordination and control were developed and institutionalized (Weber, 1947), and the vertically integrated, hierarchically controlled organization became the dominant vehicle for successful pursuit of the strategy of growth. Thus, environmental change necessitated strategic adaptation which in turn required structural reorganization (Chandler, 1962, 1977).

With the proliferation of basic new technologies and the globalization of industrial competition, industrial environments are again undergoing a fundamental transformation. The information revolution is creating a new infrastructure for economic conduct, markets have shifted from national to global in scope, and globalization has revived aggressive technology competition as a norm for industrial behavior. The result of this environmental metamorphosis is that firms are confronted by the need to move beyond traditional strategies based on the low cost/high share logic of mass production of standardized goods. To remain adaptive in the post-industrial era, firms must develop radically new strategies to cope with escalating pressures to become both more flexible and better coordinated. Greater flexibility is necessitated both by the reinvigoration of technology competition, which has shortened technological life cycles and sparked an explosion of potentially lucrative new technologies, and by the expansion of global markets which has elevated the importance of local responsiveness and intensified the urgency of rapid transitions to exploit migrating factor cost advantages. Greater coordination, on the other hand, is necessitated by increasing interdependence among formerly distinct technologies, by advances in information technologies which are revolutionizing the possibilities for productivity improvements, and by the transition from a domestic to a global competitive arena, requiring the exploitation of cross-subsidization, new potential scale economies, and simultaneous entry into geographically dispersed markets.

However, the environmental pressures for greater flexibility and coordina-tion which have short-circuited the logic of traditional mass production strategies have also overburdened the capacity of traditional organizational designs. These designs, such as the functional, multidivisional, and matrix, are not suited to the new strategies precisely because they evolved in response to different competitive pressures. Just as the new, postindustrial strategies are a radical departure from the mass production logic of the previous era, so too are the emerging designs radically different from the self-contained atomism of previous organizational forms. The distinctive feature of the new designs is the essential role accorded within them to systematic interorganizational collaboration. As argued in this chapter, utilization of alternative forms of interorganizational collaboration within the framework of a geocentric strategic management approach provides the firm with new capacities in flexibility and coordination to adapt to the mounting pressures created by environmental changes in technology and markets.

As yet, however, there is little awareness among managers and organization theorists that the increasingly widespread use of these collaborative mechanisms is creating fundamentally new organizational designs. In addition to the fact that the transformation process began very recently, two factors help to explain the general failure to recognize this phenomenon.

First, collaborative mechanisms such as cooperative R & D projects, co-marketing agreements, and equity joint ventures have been in use for a long time, so that it is not obvious that their newfound strategic importance is a change in kind rather than simply degree. The fact that the recent escalation in both their frequency and significance has tended to occur within any particular firm through an approximately five-to-ten year process of accretion, and not through a single dramatic transformation, also has helped to obscure their revolutionary impact. While a few scholars such as Miles and Snow (1986) and Perlmutter (1986) have called attention to the radical nature of the process, there is still a tendency to view the "strategic alliance phenomenon" as just one more managerial fad which will run its course and then largely disappear.

Second, neither managers, consultants, nor academicians have come to grips as yet with the implications of systematic reliance upon interorganizational collaboration for the management of the firm. Because many firms have formed these linkages largely on an ad hoc basis, often below the corporate level, there has been a general tendency to treat the management of collaboration as somehow isolated from the regular business of managing the firm. This is, however, rapidly changing. Firms such as Kodak, with its recent wave of biotechnology joint ventures, AT&T, with its utilization of collaboration as a means to penetrate global markets, and IBM, with its attempts to cooperate its way into the telecommunications arena, are vivid examples of how organizations can fully integrate alternative mechanisms of interorganizational collaboration into their managerial routines.

Nonetheless, achieving integration poses a difficult managerial challenge, since interorganizational collaboration often necessitates both the relinquishment of some degree of control over the cooperative activities and the development of "interfacing" systems that are compatible with the operating systems of different collaborating partners. Thus, as firms systematize their planning, reporting, and control of collaborative arrangements, they are compelled to learn how to vary selectively both the decision-making autonomy and managerial systems of their organizational subunits while simultaneously achieving desired coordination with other organizations.

Our expectation, therefore, is that the new organizational structures, with their reliance upon various forms of interorganizational collaboration, will become widely recognized as new design forms only as a number of firms succeed in systematizing this structural balancing act between extended differentiation and innovative coordination. The administrative innovations that arise to accomplish these tasks will succeed in diffusing the transformational impact of collaboration throughout the firm's managerial systems and thereby enable it to fully exploit the new designs' potential for simultaneously improving flexibility and coordination.

Systematizing interorganizational collaboration within a coherent global strategy presents top managers with both enticing opportunities and formidable challenges. Firms that successfully meet the challenges of the new designs should be able to establish entrenched positions of international prominence; firms that hesitate or stumble along the way face the risk of becoming inflexible technology laggards whose survival depends upon government protection and subsidization. In the competitive conditions of the postindustrial era, knowing when and how to collaborate has become a critical determinant of organizational success.

REFERENCES

Ansoff, H. Igor (1979). "The Changing Shape of the Strategic Problem." In Dan E. Schendel and Charles W. Hofer (eds.), *Strategic Management: A New View of Business Policy and Planning.* Boston: Little, Brown, pp. 30-44.

Bartlett, Christopher A. (1986). "Building and Managing the Transnational: The New Organizational Challenge." In Michael E. Porter (ed.), *Competition in Global Industries.* Boston, MA: Harvard Business School Press, pp. 367-401.

Bartlett, Christopher A., and Sumantra Ghoshal (1986). "Tap Your Subsidiaries for Global Reach." *Harvard Business Review* 86:87-94.

Biggadike, Ralph (1979). "The Risky Business of Diversification." *Harvard Business Review* 57:32-477.

Bell, Daniel (1973). *The Coming of Post-Industrial Society.* New York: Basic Books.

Chandler, Alfred D. (1962). *Strategy and Structure.* Cambridge, MA: MIT Press.

———— (1977). *The Visible Hand: The Managerial Revolution in American Business.* Cambridge, MA: Harvard University Press.

———— (1986). "The Evolution of Modern Global Competition." In Michael E. Porter (ed.), *Competition in Global Industries.* Boston, MA: Harvard Business School Press, pp. 405-448.

Davidson, William H. (1982). *Global Strategic Management.* New York: Wiley.

Davis, Stanley M., and Paul R. Lawrence (1977). *Matrix.* Reading, MA: Addison-Wesley.

Duncan, Robert B. (1976). "The Ambidextrous Organization: Designing Dual Structures for Innovation." In Ralph H. Kilmann, Louis R. Pondy, and Dennis P. Slevin (eds.), *The Management of Organization Design: Strategies and Implementation.* New York: Wiley, pp. 132-151.

Edwards, Richard (1979). *Contested Terrain: The Transformation of the Workplace in the Twentieth Century.* New York: Basic Books.

Franko, Lawrence G. (1974). "The Move Toward a Multidivisional Structure in European Organizations." *Administrative Science Quarterly* 19:493-506.

_____ (1976). *The European Multinationals: A Renewed Challenge to American and British Big Business.* New York: Harper & Row.

_____ (1983). *The Threat of Japanese Multinationals—How the West Can Respond.* New York: Wiley.

Galbraith, Jay R. (1982). "Designing the Innovating Organization." *Organizational Dynamics* 10:5-25.

Galbraith, Jay R., and Robert K. Kazanjian (1986). *Strategy Implementation: Structure, Systems, and Process.* St. Paul: West.

Ghemawhat, Pankaj, Michael E. Porter, and Richard A. Rawlinson (1986). "Patterns of International Coalition Activity." In Michael E. Porter (ed.), *Competition in Global Industries.* Boston, MA: Harvard Business School Press, pp. 345-365.

Hamel, Gary, and C. K. Prahalad (1985). "Do You Really Have a Global Strategy?" *Harvard Business Review* 63:139-148.

Hamilton, William F. (1985). "Corporate Strategies for Managing Emerging Technologies." *Technology in Society* 7:197-212.

Harrigan, Kathryn R. (1985). *Strategies for Joint Ventures.* Lexington, MA: Lexington.

Hedberg, Bo, Paul C. Nystrom, and William H. Starbuck (1976). "Camping on Seesaws: Prescriptions for a Self-Designing Organization." *Administrative Science Quarterly* 21:41-65.

Hout, Thomas, Michael E. Porter, and Elaine Rudden (1982). "How Global Companies Win Out." *Harvard Business Review* 60:98-108.

Huber, George P. (1984). "The Nature and Design of Post-Industrial Organizations." *Management Science* 30:928-951.

Killing, Peter (1980). "Technology Acquisition: License Agreement or Joint Venture." *Columbia Journal of World Business* 15:38-46.

Kingdon, Donald R. (1973). *Matrix Organization.* London: Tavistock.

Knight, Kenneth (1976). "Matrix Organization: A Review." *Journal of Management Studies* 13:111-130.

Mariti, Paul, and Richard H. Smiley (1983). "Cooperative Agreements and the Organization of Industry." *The Journal of Industrial Economics* 31:437-451.

Miles, Raymond E., and Charles C. Snow (1986). "Organizations: New Concepts for New Forms." *California Management Review* 28:62-73.

Mintzberg, Henry (1979). *The Structuring of Organizations.* Englewood Cliffs, NJ: Prentice-Hall.

Ohmae, Kenichi (1985). *Triad Power: The Coming Shape of Global Competition.* New York: Free Press.

Perlmutter, Howard V. (1969). "The Tortuous Evolution of the Multinational Corporation." *Columbia Journal of World Business* 4:9-18.

Porter, Michael E. (1986). "Competition in Global Industries: A Conceptual Framework." In Michael E. Porter (ed.), *Competition In Global Industries.* Boston, MA: Harvard Business School Press, pp. 15-60.

Porter, Michael E., and Mark B. Fuller (1986). "Coalitions and Global Strategy." In Michael E. Porter (ed.), *Competition In Global Industries.* Boston, MA: Harvard Business School Press, pp. 315-343.

Reich, Robert E. (1983). *The Next American Frontier: A Provocative Program for Economic Renewal.* New York: Penguin.

Reich, Robert E., and Edward D. Mankin (1986). "Joint Ventures with Japan: Give Away Our Future?" *Harvard Business Review* 64:78-86.

Rumelt, Richard (1974). *Strategy, Structure, and Economic Performance.* Cambridge, MA: Harvard University Press.

Shanley, Mark (1986). "Post-Acquisition Management Approaches: An Exploratory Study. Ph.D. Dissertation, The Wharton School, University of Pennsylvania.

Stinchcombe, Arthur L. (1965). "Organizations and Social Structure." In James G. March (ed.), *Handbook of Organizations*. Chicago: Rand-McNally, pp. 153-193.

Stopford, John, and Louis Wells (1972). *Managing the Multinational Enterprise*. London: Longman.

Toffler, Alvin (1985). *The Adaptive Corporation*. New York: Bantam.

Watson, Craig (1982). "Counter Competition Abroad to Protect Home Markets." *Harvard Business Review* 60:40-45.

Weber, Max (1947). *The Theory of Social and Economic Organization,* translated by A. M. Henderson and Talcott Parsons, edited by Talcott Parsons. New York: Free Press.

Williamson, Oliver E. (1975). *Markets and Hierarchies: Analysis and Antitrust Implications*. New York: Free Press.

PART III

HUMAN RESOURCE MANAGEMENT

INTEGRATING OPERATIONS AND HUMAN RESOURCE MANAGEMENT IN THE SERVICE SECTOR

Richard B. Chase and David E. Bowen

Most services tend to be "operations" dominated. Although advertising and promotions may bring people to the service system, once the customer enters the facility (bank, hospital, restaurant, airline terminal, and so forth) marketing typically has little say in how the service is delivered. The obvious cause of this sometimes unfortunate condition is the classic separation of functions in organizations: marketing promotes the product to the potential customer, and operations makes the product. However, while this functional separation may be logical for manufacturing firms where production and marketing take place independently, it is questionable for service businesses which are characterized by simultaneous marketing and production. The practical effect of this separation is a tendency to try to improve productivity via operations management techniques and to overlook possible sales opportunities that might arise from applying a balanced operations and marketing perspective.

273

In this chapter, we will describe how this balance of operations and marketing perspectives translates, in many ways, into a need to integrate operations *and* human resource management (HRM) in the design, production, and delivery of services. Service employees run the service operation, market the service, and are even viewed as the service itself by many customers (Lovelock, 1981). Consequently, the way these employees are selected, trained, rewarded, and so on, has a pervasive effect on system productivity and customer perceptions of service quality. Furthermore, since customers frequently help co-produce the service they receive, it becomes critical to manage them as human resources as well (Bowen, 1986).

Clearly, operations and human resources in the service sector need to be managed in different ways than in the manufacturing sector. In the first section of this chapter, we describe some of the unique attributes of service businesses, highlighting their implications for operations and human resource management. In the second section, we present a service design matrix, developed by Chase and his colleagues (Chase et al., 1984; Chase, 1986), that indicates how these service attributes vary across alternative delivery options. The matrix also describes the human resource requirements of each service delivery option. A case study of the design matrix's application to a savings and loan firm is then offered. In the final section, we discuss directions for further research on operations and human resource management in the service sector.

DEFINING ATTRIBUTES OF SERVICE

The characteristics of service have been summarized in a number of recent works (e.g., Lovelock, 1984; Parasuraman et al., 1985; Mills, 1986). The present discussion draws on a review by Bowen and Schneider (1988) in which the defining attributes of service were developed through an integration of the organizational behavior and marketing literatures. Here, we pursue a related focus on how operations and human resource management must be integrated in the service sector.

Services can be basically differentiated from products as follows:

1. Services tend to be relatively intangible.
2. Services tend to be produced and consumed simultaneously.
3. Services tend to involve consumer participation in their production.

The discussion of these attributes is offered with two qualifications. First, the purpose is *not* to present an exhaustive description of service attributes and their management implications. Instead, the intent is to provide at least a sufficient feel for the context of services so that issues prompting the development of the service design matrix are understood. Second, it should be understood that all services do *not* display the described characteristics to the same extent. Certainly, legal advice, for example, displays these attributes differently from a fast-food restaurant. Indeed, it is largely because services can vary in their mix of attributes that a service design matrix relating alternative service delivery options to variable human resource requirements can be a useful analytical tool.

Intangibility

Services are much less tangible than physical goods or products (Levitt, 1981). Services are primarily experiences whereas products are primarily physical possessions (Berry, 1980; Shostack, 1981). A principal determinant of the intangibility of services is that they typically involve an exchange of information more than the transfer of physical objects.

Operations and HRM Implications.   Intangibility forces customers to focus on the process of service delivery (e.g., physical setting and service personnel's attitudes and behavior) in evaluating service quality (Zeithaml, 1981). Underlying operations and HRM practices are important sources of the cues customers attend to in the service environment. In this vein, Schneider and Bowen (1985) have examined the determinants of a firm's service climate (i.e., the cues about service quality that employees display to customers in the act of service delivery). The dimensions of service climate that shaped how employees, in turn, influenced the service experiences of customers included: (a) management behavior, (b) personnel and management information systems support, (c) logistics support in the form of material and machinery, and (d) corporate emphasis on customer attraction and retention. Employee reports of how the firm managed these service climate dimensions have been found to be related to customer perceptions of service quality (Schneider et al., 1980; Schneider and Bowen, 1985) as well as profitability (Moeller and Schneider, 1986).

This research indicated that the service firm's policies and procedures create "a climate for service" that is apparent to both employees and customers. It appears that this climate influences how employees experience their work setting and that employees, in turn, convey their experience to customers in a manner that influences their perception of service quality. Consequently, service firms need to be cognizant that the climate for service fostered by their operations may impact the attitudes and behavior of both employees *and* customers.

Other operations and HRM implications stem from service intangibility making it difficult to specify valid output measures. It is usually not possible to use the same methods of productivity improvement that are effective in manufacturing because the intangibility of service output makes it difficult to establish the performance measures needed to validate the productivity improvement effort. Additionally, these same difficulties in defining and measuring service output complicate the use of goal-setting to guide service employee behaviors (Mills et al., 1983). In other words, although sound human resource management informs us that setting specific goals leads to higher performance (Locke and Latham, 1984), it is more feasible to set explicit production quotas for, say, a machine operator than it is to specify how much of a quality education a teacher is to provide her students.

Simultaneous Production and Consumption

In services, there typically are no middlemen between production and consumption, but rather services involve direct face-to-face interactions between the customer and employee to complete the service exchange (Fuchs, 1968; Chase, 1978; Mills and Margulies, 1980; Czepiel et al., 1985). Overall, the difference in the relationship between production and consumption for goods versus services can be stated as: Goods tend to be produced, inventoried, sold, then consumed; services are usually sold first, then produced and consumed simultaneously because they cannot be inventoried (Berry, 1980; Maister, 1982).

Operations and HRM Implications. Quality assurance is focused very differently in goods versus services. For goods, quality is engineered at the plant; in services, quality occurs during service delivery (Parasuraman et al., 1985). Simultaneity makes it difficult to decouple production, distribution, and sales in service operations. It also means that services cannot be inventoried, making it difficult to balance the supply and demand sides of the service operation (Sasser, 1976). Simultaneity dictates that when the demand for service is present the service must be produced, thus making staffing difficult since staffing to meet customer demand is less predictable than staffing to fit the pace of the assembly line (Chase, 1978). Simultaneity may also require that service operations be physically located close to customers, in marked contrast to the distance between physical plant and customers in the manufacturing sector.

The HRM implications of simultaneity center on the problem of what mechanisms can be used to control employee behavior in the service encounter. When employees are delivering services that are produced and consumed simultaneously, they are essentially acting alone. Typically, no supervisor is present in the employee-customer dyad who can exercise ongoing, immediate quality control. Additionally, the more intangible the service, the more complicated it becomes to set measurable performance goals for employees. Moreover, simultaneity together with customer participation, makes it impossible for service management to specify in advance appropriate employee responses to the unpredictable, diverse range of customer demands that may arise in the service encounter.

Core cultural values (e.g., "the customer is always right") may be important guides for service employee behavior, given the above limitations on the applicability of conventional mechanisms. In turn, HRM practices are critical in creating and sustaining a service-oriented culture. Many service firms need to invest more in developing selection and training techniques for improving the interpersonal skills of their customer-contact personnel. The majority of validated selection tests tap cognitive and motor aptitudes, to the relative exclusion of interpersonal skills. Furthermore, most interpersonal skill development training programs have been used with managers not first-line employees. Overall, many personnel practices are still geared to the needs of manufacturing firms where it is less important for lower-level employees to possess interpersonal skills to perform their production tasks well (Bowen, 1986).

In a related vein, the nature of services suggests that front-line employees should participate in decisions about what new services to offer and how to deliver them (Schneider and Bowen, 1984). Research indicates that participative decision making is appropriate when (a) employees possess relevant information the manager lacks, and (b) employee acceptance of the decision is critical for its implementation (Vroom and Yetton, 1973). Research and current thought on service yields two conclusions that seem to satisfy these prerequisites for employee participation in decision making: (1) front-line employees and their customers share similar views of service (Schneider et al., 1980; Schneider and Bowen, 1985), but bank branch managers were found to be unable to accurately identify customer service preferences (Langeard et al., 1981), and (2) services are often evaluated by customers based on how employees behave in delivering them. Consequently, it would seem that involving front-line employees in decisions about what services to offer would utilize the information they have about customers and build a sense of ownership of the new service that would heighten their enthusiasm in delivering it.

There are multiple returns to the service firm that invests in the proper mix of HRM practices and cultural norms and values. For example, when bank branch employees thought positively of how well they were trained, supervised, and so on, customers also had favorable views of the quality of service they received (Schneider and Bowen, 1985). This suggests that a service-oriented culture can be enhanced by treating front-line employees as "partial customers," individuals deserving the same courteous treatment that management wants the organization's customers to receive (Schneider and Bowen, 1984; Bowen and Schneider, 1985; Bowen, 1986).

Customer Participation

Many service operations involve customers not only as customers but as producers as well. Customers supply both information and physical effort to the service production process (Mills and Moberg, 1982). This can be seen in service settings ranging from customers busing their own tables in a fast-food restaurant to patients describing their symptoms to a doctor and then taking their medicine as prescribed. The production roles customers fill suggests that customers be viewed as "partial employees" of the service organization (Mills et al., 1983; Bowen, 1986; Mills, 1986), extending earlier thinking by Barnard (1948) and Parsons (1956) that customers should be included within the boundaries of organizations. Customers can fill partial employee roles during the input, transformation, and output stages of service production (Mills and Morris, 1986). Customers can function in their service encounters either as "co-producers" with the service employee or as "sole producers" in the case of self-service alternatives (Bowen, 1986).

Operations and HRM Implications. Customer participation in service operations is frequently depicted as an organizational constraint in the literature. Customer involvement has been depicted as limiting the potential operating efficiency of the firm (Chase, 1978; Chase and Tansik, 1983), disrupting organizational routines (Danet, 1981), and leading to service employees relating more closely to customers than the organization. Overall, service systems with high customer contact have been viewed as more difficult to control and rationalize than those with low customer contact, in which the technical core is buffered allowing the application of closed-system logic (Thompson, 1967; Chase, 1978). More generally, customer participation coupled with the labor intensiveness typical of many service operations, makes it difficult to maintain quality control.

However, totally sealing off the core technology may be impossible, as well as undesirable, given that it may limit the interactive exchange of information necessary for a quality service to be provided (Mills and Moberg, 1982). Consequently, the issue becomes one of how to best manage customer contact, particularly when the contact involves the customer filling a role as a partial employee.

When customers participate in service operations, both employees *and* customers constitute the human resources of the service organization (Bowen, 1986). As a result, service organizations face the unique human resource challenge of discovering what management practices can lead to customers being both satisfied and productive during the time they spend with the company.

Relative to customer satisfaction, we have described how management's service and HRM-related practices can help create the kind of climate for service that is satisfying to customers. Relative to customer productivity, service firms need to shape the individual-level performance determinants of motivation, role clarity, and ability of *customers* for any "partial employee" behaviors expected of them. That is, customers perform the way they do based largely on three considerations (Bowen, 1986):

1. Do they understand how they are expected to perform?
2. Are they able to perform as expected?
3. Are there valued rewards for performing as expected?

The service firm needs to put in place practices and personnel that influence customers to answer these questions with a "yes." For example, before customers can be expected to perform well in using an ATM, they may require clear operating instructions posted at the ATM, bank personnel accessible for demonstrating the machine's use, and a clear indication that the ATM is a time-saving alternative to a personal teller.

Overall strategies need to be developed for recruiting, selecting, training, and rewarding customers as partial employees. When customers are managed in this way they become a unique source of productivity improvement for service operations.

This brief review of the attributes of service suggests that the literature has, over the past decade, progressed greatly in identifying the unique nature of service and its influence on organizational dynamics. Services differ from goods—and from one another—relative to intangibility, simultaneity, and customer participation. In turn, these attributes influence the nature of operations and human resource management in the service sector.

The literature lacks, however, an operational taxonomy of service delivery options that takes these unique attributes into account and then suggests the organizational resources necessary to support alternative service delivery options. In the next section, we step onto more exploratory turf and present such a taxonomy that is being developed by Chase and his colleagues (Chase et al., 1984; Chase, 1986).

THE SERVICE DESIGN MATRIX: INTEGRATING OPERATIONS AND HUMAN RESOURCE MANAGEMENT

In this section, we present an operational taxonomy that relates alternative service delivery options to production efficiency, sales opportunity, and human resource requirements. The matrix also helps illustrate how the defining attributes of service are managed across different service offerings. That is, we move beyond a simple typing of services as defined by intangibility, simultaneity, and customer participation, and begin working through issues such as: What are the alternative levels and mechanisms of information exchange in a service encounter? What organizational conditions and strategies favor face-to-face exchange rather than automated exchanges? In what service delivery options is the customer an active rather than passive participant? The service design matrix described below addresses these and related issues.

The Basic Tradeoff: Production Efficiency versus Sales Opportunity

The starting point for introducing design options is to first describe a key strategic issue in service operations that needs to frame design choices. As previously mentioned, several years ago, Chase (1978, 1981) proposed that service systems could maximize their efficiency by limiting the amount of face-to-face contact they had with the customer. The logic behind this suggestion was that customers—people—constitute a highly variable input to a service system. From a purely production perspective, such variability of input can lead to disruptions of the service delivery process. In contrast, the "back office" of a service entity is potentially more efficient than the "front office" since the former processes customer surrogates—papers and forms—rather than people. This reduces uncertainty and permits the use of factory-type production planning and scheduling.

In the past few years, Chase and his colleagues have been investigating the complement to this theory—namely, the benefits accruing to the service firm from regarding the customer as *part of* the system. We have observed the obvious marketing phenomenon that for certain services, the longer the customer is in the system, the greater the potential for sales. Retail businesses such as department stores and car dealerships commonly seek ways to keep customers on the premises to bring into play all of their sales-boosting repertoire. Indeed, for many retail businesses, access to the customer is the name of the game.

When these two notions are brought together (low contact => higher efficiency and high contact => higher sales), an important tradeoff for any service business becomes clear: *Find the form and amount of customer contact that balances the efficiency potential from low contact with the sales opportunities from high contact. Form* refers to the nature of the interaction between the customer and system; *amount* refers to the length of time of the interaction. The practical objective of this tradeoff is to achieve the most profitable combination of *service delivery options* for the service firm.

Table 1. Definitions and Implications of Service Delivery Options

Mail contact refers to both hard documents and electronic mail. This involves no face-to-face interaction and hence low immediate sales opportunity. However, since mail can be processed in the customer's absence its efficiency is high.

On-site technology refers to devices such as "sales robots" and automatic teller machines which are located on the premises of the service branch. Such technology offers little opportunity for human contact-based sales, although depending upon its physical location (e.g., an ATM inside a bank), contact personnel may be required to assist customers in its use.

Phone contact varies greatly in its sales opportunity but is seen as being generally lower in this dimension than any form of face-to-face contact. Its efficiency potential is quite high since calls can be responded to in any order through the magic of the hold button. Of course, phone contact can be highly disruptive and therefore inefficient when carried out by front-line personnel.

Face-to-face tight spec[ifications] refers to those situations where there is little variation in the service process—neither customer nor server has much discretion in creating the service. Fast-food restaurants and automated rides in amusement parks are two examples.

Face-to-face loose spec[ifications] refers to situations in which there is a general understanding of what the service process is to be, but there are options in the way it will be performed and/or the physical goods that are part of it. Full-service restaurants and car sales agencies have such characteristics.

Face-to-face total customization refers to service encounters where specifications of the encounter must be developed through some interaction between the customer and server. Consulting and medical services are of this type. Examples would be the mobilization of an advertising firm's resources in preparation for an office visit by a major client or an operating team scrambling to prepare for emergency surgery.

Specifying the Delivery Options

All services require some form of information exchange even when the primary product is tangible. In light of this fact, a set of six options representing discrete forms of information exchange is proposed for classifying how service firms interact with the customer (see Table 1). These options are hierarchically related, in a parallel fashion, to what has been called "richness of information transfer" in information exchange (Daft, 1981)—highest for face-to-face discussion, high for telephone conversation, moderate for informal letters, low for (impersonally addressed) formal documents, and lowest for formal numeric documents.

Service Design Matrix

To fully exploit the sales-efficiency tradeoff, we must anchor these options to the contact dimension in a meaningful and practical way. The anchoring

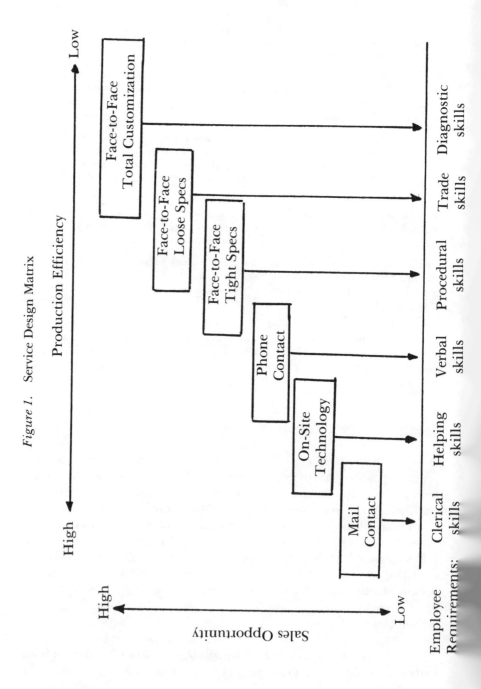

Figure 1. Service Design Matrix

mechanism uses a multidimensional matrix similar to the one developed by Hayes and Wheelwright (1979) for analyzing manufacturing. The Hayes-Wheelwright matrix describes the relationship between production volume and process technology. It shows how the various production options (job shop, flow shop, continuous production) come into play as product demand increases. This process allows management to evaluate its manufacturing strategy and to look at the implications of alternative production options. The Hayes-Wheelwright matrix has become the standard framework for analyzing production systems, and it is hoped that the one developed here will prove equally beneficial for service systems.

The matrix shown in Figure 1 arrays the six options noted above according to degree of production efficiency (horizontal axis) and sales opportunity (vertical axis). Along the bottom of the matrix are listed the employee requirements logically associated with each option. To elaborate on these, the relationships between mail contact and clerical skills, and phone contact and verbal skills, are self-evident. On-site technology requires helping skills on those occasions where the customer is unfamiliar with how the equipment works. Face-to-face "tight specs" require procedural skills because the worker must follow the routine in conducting a generally standardized, high-volume process. Face-to-face "loose specs" frequently call for trade skills (e.g., shoemaker, draftsman, maitré d', dental hygienist) to "finalize" the design of the service. Face-to-face total customization tends to call for diagnostic skills of the professional to ascertain the needs of the client. Note that this approach, unlike traditional industrial engineering approaches, humanizes the job by telling us in general terms the nature of the relationship that the service employee has with the customer. Industrial engineering techniques, such as flow charting and work methods analysis, focus on material transformation and thus ignore behavioral and marketing dimensions. (In fact, the term "robot" could be substituted in place of "worker" in an industrial engineering analysis without changing the character of the information conveyed.)

Application to a Savings and Loan Firm

The following case describes how the service matrix was applied in a large savings and loan (S&L) company in the West. This particular S&L was interested in answering two questions: (1) "How do we attract big depositors to our 'sales machine'?" and (2) "How do we keep the small depositors from using up our 'machine capacity'?" The design matrix was useful in determining the answers to these questions.

Analyses. The first step was to identify a representative branch and to list all of the major services it offered. A representative branch was one that

Table 2. Partial Listing of Savings and Loan Branch Services

Service	Dominant Contact Mode at Branch				
	Mail	*Technology*	*Tight Specs*	*Loose Specs*	*Total Customization*
Opening a Checking Account			X	△	
Opening a Savings Account			X	△	
Discount Movie Tickets		△	X		
Travelers Checks		△	X		
Financial Planning				X	△
Savings Withdrawal			√		
Savings Addition			√		
Checking Addition			√		
Checking Withdrawal		√			
Loan Payment	√				
Safety Deposit Use			√		
Closing Account				√	

√ = OK as is
X = Candidate for change
△ = Proposed change

Table 3.   Outcomes of Contact Matches and Mismatches

	High Contact Required for Selling Purposes	Low Contact Required for Efficiency Purposes
High Contact Provided		
Customization	High Sales Opportunity	High Operating Cost
Loose Specs		
Tight Specs		
Low Contact Provided		
Phone		
Technology	Low Sales Opportunity	Low Operating Cost
Mail		

provided the complete range of S&L services and had a representative mix of customers. A service was defined as a product being delivered in either tangible or intangible form. A partial listing of these services is shown in the Service column of Table 2. The next step was to specify the dominant mode by which each of these services currently was delivered (i.e., mail, phone, on-site technology, tight specs, loose specs, or total customization). This information was obtained by observing and recording the processes performed by branch personnel throughout the study period and by pulling transaction data from ATM records. Next, as also shown in Table 2, the data were tabulated to identify mismatches between the S&L's use of productive capacity and its sales opportunities and the production efficiency of each product (i.e., service). Here we brainstormed with management on precisely what constituted such mismatches. The conceptual model was simple: If high-contact options were provided, and if high contact was required to sell more services, a real sales opportunity existed. Likewise, if low-contact options were provided, and low-contact modes were made available (and used), low operating costs could be achieved (see Table 3). The obvious mismatches were those situations where a service fell in the high operating cost or low sales opportunity cells in Table 3.

Out of the total set of mismatches identified in Table 2, our analysis suggested that travelers checks, movie tickets, checking and savings account openings, and financial planning were areas where significant improvements in delivery mode could be made. Discount movie tickets and travelers checks were inviting targets for three reasons. First, they could have been performed by low-contact modes, particularly on-site (or off-site) technology. Second, the valuable sales capacity of the S&L was essentially wasted on low-sales-opportunity interactions (interactions with customers who are unlikely to buy additional services). A customer who falls into this category typically is one who has a small balance in his or her account. (As part of our data gathering, we observed the classic 80-20 rule in operation: 80% of the people accounted for only 10-20% of the deposits. We also discovered through sampling that the same 80% accounted for about 90% of face-to-face interactions with the branches.) Third, and most startling, over 40% of the average teller's day was spent tending to movie ticket sales.

Opening checking and savings accounts, on the other hand, was seen as being overly routinized. Branch practice had been to make the entire process a tight-spec operation where the customer did practically all of the paperwork on his or her own. However, while this saved the time of branch employees, it also eliminated valuable access to the customer—and hence reduced sales opportunity.

Revising the contact mode for financial planning was viewed as having the highest potential payoff and as being the most expensive of the improvements considered. As currently offered, the closest thing to financial planning was pointing the customer to a rack that contained a list of investment accounts offered by the S&L. If a customer decided to invest, then he or she would walk over to a teller's window or to an officer's desk and specify which account was desired. In the context of our classification, this desideratum was an ill-conceived loose-spec operation.

Changes in the Mix of Delivery Options. First, we recommended that movie tickets and travelers checks cease to be provided via tellers and instead be dispensed through the ATMs. This change was designed to get the lower dollar, more casual customer away from the organizational setting in which more substantial transactions could occur.

Second, we recommended that new account openings be conducted as loose-spec operations, with all of the paperwork being filled out by the branch employee to "help" the client through the process. Such help would include cross-selling of other branch services as well as the opportunity to train customers. This change was introduced to take best advantage of this high-contact encounter.

Third, we recommended that complete portfolio planning capability be made available for the one-third of the customers who accounted for two-thirds of the deposits. While a number of improvements could have been made in delivering this service in its present form (e.g., better promotional signage), we believed that more creative and profitable options were available. From the various choices, we recommended high-tech capability in financial planning through computerized portfolio analysis. This program was to be used interactively by an officer of the branch working with the customer. The purpose of the program was to develop a full financial plan by permitting the customer to allocate funds to all types of stocks and bonds not just the investment instruments offered by the S&L. In essence, it was a new product falling under the heading of face-to-face total customization.

Results and Reflections. Providing travelers checks and movie tickets through the ATM was well received by the branch tellers and branch managers. However, a small percentage of customers surveyed did not like it, and a few stated that they were going to change their S&L because of it. This response brings out an important point inherent in the approach proposed here: Any given operations design cannot please all customers, and management has to be willing to risk some customer turnover to make optimum use of service capacity. The S&L's management held its ground on this change even though it went counter to the prevailing industry philosophy that you should never do anything that may lose a customer, and you should never alter or eliminate a service until at least three competitors identify it as a loser.

The transformation of the account-opening process to a loose-spec operation worked well at the experimental branch. The procedure followed was to route new account prospects to a sales-trained branch manager who guided each customer through all steps of the account-opening process. Though only slightly more CDs and IRAs were sold as compared to the tight-spec procedure, about 20% of the customers tended to place larger amounts in the new accounts than was common in the past. This money was taken away from competitors, since the funds were actually drawn from accounts that customers held at other financial institutions. In view of the fact that most savers hold accounts in more than one place, this resulted in unexpected sales opportunities for the branch personnel.

The portfolio analysis computer program was the most risky of the proposed changes, and while management liked the idea and the demonstration program, it was not willing to commit the level of funding necessary to make it a reality. For the program to operate as we had envisioned would have required significant programming effort and a direct linkage to the S&L's mainframe computer. The latter point was a particular stumbling block because, as we later discovered, the firm's computer systems group was unenthusiastic about virtually any type of point-of-sale computer use. It appeared that in this S&L, as well as in many other service firms, computer systems groups were reluctant to get involved with service marketing innovations. While plenty of systems may be called to record buy-sell transactions at the point of sale, few are chosen to link, say, a customer data base with workstation terminals at the branch (as required by the portfolio management program). Indeed, it seems that automating the payroll, modifying the computerized billing program, or setting up E-mail for executives takes precedence over something creative for point-of-sale marketing.

Table 4.   Some Heuristics for Looking for Sales Opportunities
and Production Efficiencies in High-Contact Services

Look for sales opportunities where ...

1. Quality of the service is in the eye of the beholder
    (The virtues of more expensive services can be advocated)
    "For a really unobtrusive crown, we recommend the porcelain over the gold."

2. Expected service time is slow
    (Customers have more time to listen to a sales pitch)
    "What do you think about our new brochure; you're the first to see it."

3. Service time must take some minimum duration to be credible
    (Sales pitches can be interspersed with the service)
    "Let me tell you about a very intelligent customer I had this morning."

4. Customers have a favorite server
    (Implicit obligation to pay for one's preferences)
    "I told my husband all about your grandchildren."

5. Boy meets girl
    (Customers are likely to buy more from an attractive server [i.e., sex sells])
    "Let's see how this necktie goes with your eyes ... a little closer please."

6. Customization is perceived as necessary
    (A standardized service that looks customized is the best of all possible worlds)
    "Do you want the regular Camaro logo on your pit jacket or the embroidered ... while
    you wait, of course."

7. The customer is uncertain about his or her need for the service
    "Ramon, do you think I need a permanent?"

8. Price reductions can be made on the spot
    "For you, a very special deal today only."

9. Excess capacity exists
    "My next appointment hasn't come in yet, so let's go ahead and do a treadmill test."

10. Emergency situations
    (Not advocated but universal nonetheless)
    "As long as we're replacing your muffler, you can save time and trouble by replacing
    your worn out shocks."

Look for production efficiencies where ...

1. Quality is known in advance of service
    (Find cheapest way to meet customer's expectations)
    "A Big Mac is a Big Mac is a Big Mac."

2. Speed of service is what the customer demands
    (Maximize throughout a la the factory)
    "All clerks to the checkout stands!"

Table 4.   (continued)

---

3. Service cost is all that matters—and all that can be sold
    (Train customers to be servers)
    Sign at convenience store: "No credit cards, pay in advance, tell cashier your pump
    number, 25 cents for use of tire air compressor ..."

4. The service encounter presents no real sales opportunity (see Technology below)

5. Technology permits moving out of the contact business entirely
    (This can be soft technology, such as recorded announcements, as well as hard technology,
    such as ATM's)
    "The white zone is for loading and unloading passengers only ... The white zone is for
    loading and unloading passengers only ..."

6. Facilities and methods obviously need improvement (Even if sales opportunities exist,
    the service system must achieve a basic level of order)
    "Oh, waiter ... waiter!"

On a more positive note, S&L management observed that our contact approach could also be used to define and evaluate the choice of service delivery modes made by competitors. They did this by using their employees as "mystery shoppers" to visit and appraise other S&Ls and banks, and to then report on the modes of contact as well as teller friendliness and expertise. This capability is now being built into the mystery shoppers' checklist used by the S&L.

There were also positive comments on the effectiveness of the approach in evaluating the usefulness of cross-selling. This S&L, like many of its competitors, had tried cross-selling its services to *anybody* who came into the branch. The philosophy of the approach proposed here is clearly that cross-selling should be used only in situations where there is a reasonable sales opportunity—or at the very least where the customer has deep pockets.

In summary, though it is true that other financial institutions have implemented similar modifications in their operations, their interventions are usually piecemeal, lacking a broader framework for analysis. The design approach described here cuts to the heart of the issue: It provides a mechanism for systematically looking at financial service systems to identify the mix of delivery options that best balances production efficiency and sales opportunity. (See Table 4 for some guidelines on where to look for sales opportunities and production efficiencies in any high-contact service encounter.)

The Service Design Matrix: Implications, Refinements, and Extensions

The first obvious extension of the matrix is to include a formal procedure for quantifying the sales opportunity and production efficiency impacts suggested by the guidelines in Table 4. That is, given that the guideline suggests a change in delivery options, how can the potential payoff from making such a change be quantitatively determined? One possible approach is to use the following simple cost-benefit formula: Cost-Benefit Ratio = (Sales + Efficiency) ÷ Cost of the Change.

For example, suppose that the opening of a checking account is shifted from tight spec to loose spec, and suppose further that on average 750 customers will buy $10.00 more of the S&L's services but at a cost of $5 each in "lost" efficiency. If it costs $500 to retrain the tellers, then the cost-benefit ratio would be ($7500 − $3750) ÷ $500 or 7.5. This ratio could then be compared to ratios for other proposed changes, and/or target ratio, and a go/no-go decision made. (Obviously, change candidates with cost-benefit ratios of less than one would be rejected out of hand.)

Second, the arraying of employee requirements across service delivery options can guide the development of selection tests and training programs for staffing and developing employees in alternative service positions. At a very general level, the matrix highlights the importance of interpersonal requirements in service production and delivery. Service firms often pay little attention to the issue of whether their customer-contact people have adequate interpersonal skills. For example, training programs for newly-hired bank tellers or store clerks may place great emphasis on how to "cost-out" at the end of the day but largely ignore training in how to interact with customers (Burstiner, 1975). In those service firms that *do* have an appreciation of the importance of interpersonal skills, the question of which interpersonal skills are most important is often not rigorously addressed. The matrix suggests, for example, the jobs for which alternative interpersonal skills, such as helping skills or diagnostic skills, are most important.

Third, a related issue is whether the array of employee requirements is essentially cumulative. That is, it might be more appropriate to think of phone contact as involving not just verbal skills but helping and clerical skills as well; indeed, face-to-face customization may be a delivery option that requires *all* the requirements listed of the service provider. Future applications of the matrix need to address this point.

Fourth, a logical next step in the development of the matrix would be to work through the *customer* requirements of the six delivery options. Again, since customers can be viewed as "partial employees" and co-producers, they too are employees of the service delivery system. For example, customers must possess certain skills to effectively use ATMs (on-site technology) or at least need to be motivated to acquire the necessary skills. The extent to which customers are skilled or motivated in this regard will strongly influence the extent to which service personnel need to have helping skills.

Considering the face-to-face customization delivery options, the matrix emphasizes the importance of diagnostic skills. At the same time, though, it is accepted that the ease and reliability of a doctor's diagnosis is, in part, a function of the patient's ability to describe his or her symptoms fully and accurately. The notion, then, of working through the human resource requirements of customers for alternative service delivery options is a promising avenue of future thought and research that can build on the consumer behavior literature on the socialization of customers (e.g., Ward, 1973) and techniques for the recruitment, selection, and training of customers as partial employees (Bowen, 1986; Mills, 1986; Mills and Morris, 1986).

Fifth, future applications of the matrix will help establish the extent to which the tradeoff between sales opportunity and production efficiency captures the advantages and disadvantages of customer contact. Sales opportunity certainly seems to be a strong contender for the lead benefit of contact. However, if there are additional benefits, then the case grows stronger for delivery options involving high customer contact. In that regard, there is some evidence to suggest that employees consider customer contact and feedback an enriching characteristic of their jobs (Hackman et al., 1975) and that employees obtain satisfaction from customers' praise as well as from their immediate supervisor's praise (Bowen, 1983). Additionally, service employees who have close contact with the customer are reliable sources of information for service management about customer perceptions of the firm's climate for service and overall service quality (Schneider and Bowen, 1985). On the other hand, customer contact can be a source of emotional strain for employees (Parkington and Schneider, 1979; Hoschild, 1983). The point is that future work in the services area needs to be generally attentive to the tradeoffs involved in customer contact and, specifically, the behavioral implications of the service employee-customer interface.

Sixth, service delivery strategies and issues need to be researched from the customer's point of view. That is, how do customers assess the tradeoffs involved in *employee contact?* Central, here, would be research on the customer's "service ideal"—the expectations and assumptions about what constitutes quality service that customers use in evaluating the service they receive (Shamir, 1980; Schneider and Bowen, 1985). Do customers value speed or friendliness in service delivery? Relative to sales opportunity, do some customers respond more positively to marketing via the mail than being approached by a salesperson in the showroom? Even more basic to the contact issue, do customers value an automated or interpersonal service encounter? If interpersonal, the firm may need to use loose-spec or customized service delivery options even though it may compromise production efficiency.

Seventh, a focus on the customer-contact dimension of service operations should not deemphasize the importance of "back-office" operations (preparing bank statements, laboratory testing in hospitals, etc.). The focus of this chapter was on customer-contact operations because there has been only limited development of the appropriate operations and human resource principles in this area. Alternatively, the nature of back-office operations renders more fully-developed manufacturing procedures appropriate (Chase, 1978; Chase and Tansik, 1983).

Eighth, while the service design approach was demonstrated here in financial services, it can be used in many other settings including, for example, retailing. Here its benefits lie in fine-tuning several dimensions of retailing and support operations: (a) deciding upon the specific nature of contact appropriate to each department (e.g., tight specs for low-margin, low-volume departments); (b) specifying the kinds of skills required by contact personnel on a department-by-department basis; and (c) providing another basis for evaluating departmental sales and expense performance beyond simple comparisons with industry norms or past performance.

Ninth, this design approach can also be extended to designing the internal operations of an organization, service or manufacturing. For example, contact between departments of manufacturing firms is frequently ill-defined, with no thought given to how interactions between personnel should be designed. Consider staff interactions with line personnel. Staff functions such as HRM and MIS can be conceived of as service operations whose customers are internal "clients" of the organization such as senior executives and line managers (Bowen and Greiner, 1986). Thus, the service design matrix could be used to guide these internal operations. Surely, some internal total customization interactions would be more productively performed as tight-spec encounters and vice versa. Similarly, it seems likely that better decisions regarding MIS could be achieved if each application is considered in the context of the contact issues addressed in the service design matrix.

Last, the service design matrix can be usefully extended to the manufacturing sector as well. The importance of a service component to product strategy is receiving increased emphasis (Peters and Waterman, 1982). Yet, how can these services be best delivered so that efforts directed toward "staying close to the customer" do not outweigh production efficiency? The matrix and its key tradeoff can help to frame answers to this question.

CONCLUSION

We have described how the unique character of the service sector requires fresh approaches to issues of strategy, design, and human resource management. Particularly compelling is the need to integrate operations and human resource management in the design of service systems. We described some of the organizational issues concerning this integration and introduced a service design matrix of alternative forms of customer contact supported by different human resource requirements. This matrix represents one of the first efforts to systematically indicate alternative configurations of service attributes (intangibility, simultaneity, and customer participation) in the production and delivery of service.

In closing, we hope this chapter has helped in the development of concepts and approaches that indeed fit the service sector. The organizational sciences must continue to develop a "language" for services. Unlike the language of manufacturing firms, the language of services is really a mixture of many dialects drawn from the roughly 2,000 types of services listed in the Standard Industrial Classification code. This heterogeneity of language has inhibited the sharing of ideas and experiences which would otherwise be facilitated if services spoke the same mother tongue. And, in the absence of a common set of concepts that pertain directly to services, service organizations have resorted to force-fitting manufacturing and industrial engineering terms and solutions to environments where they simply do not apply. Isn't it time that the largest sector of the economy breaks away from this factory mind-set and develops better ways of specifying what happens when the customer walks through the door?

ACKNOWLEDGMENT

The first author gratefully acknowledges the work of his former colleagues, Gerrit Wolf, Greg Northcraft, and Nicholas Aquilano, on the savings and loan study cited in this chapter.

REFERENCES

Barnard, Chester I. (1948). *Organization and Management.* Cambridge, MA: Harvard University Press.

Berry, Len L. (1980). "Service Marketing is Different." *Business* May-June:24-28.

Bowen, David E. (1983). Customers as Substitutes for Leadership in Service Organizations. Doctoral Dissertation, Michigan State University.

———— (1986). "Managing Customers as Human Resources in Service Organizations." *Human Resource Management* 25:371-383.

Bowen, David E., and Benjamin Schneider (1985). "Boundary Spanning Role Employees and the Service Encounter: Some Guidelines for Management and Research." In John A. Czepiel, Richard Solomon, and Carol Surprenant (eds.), *The Service Encounter.* Lexington, MA: D.C. Heath, pp. 127-147.

Bowen, David E., and Larry E. Greiner (1986). "Moving from Production to Service in Human Resources Management." *Organizational Dynamics* Summer:35-53.

Bowen, David E., and Benjamin Schneider (1988). "Services Marketing and Management: Implications for Organizational Behavior." In Barry Staw and Larry L. Cummings (eds.), *Research in Organizational Behavior,* Vol. 10. Greenwich, CT: JAI Press, pp. 43-80.

Burstiner, Irving (1975). "Current Personnel Practices in Department Stores." *Journal of Retailing* 51:3-14.

Chase, Richard B. (1978). "Where Does the Customer Fit in a Service Operation?" *Harvard Business Review* 56:137-142.

———— (1981). "The Customer Contact Approach to Services: Theoretical Bases and Practical Extensions." *Operations Research* 29:698-706.

———— (1986). A New Approach to Service System Design. Working Paper, University of Southern California.

Chase, Richard B., and David A. Tansik (1983). "The Customer Contact Model for Organizational Design." *Management Science* 49:1037-1050.

Chase, Richard B., Greg Northcraft, and Gerritt Wolf (1984). "Designing High Contact Service Systems: Applications to Branches of a Savings and Loan." *Decision Sciences* 15:542-555.

Czepiel, John A., Richard Solomon, and Carol Surprenant (eds.) (1985). *The Service Encounter.* Lexington, MA: D.C. Heath.

Daft, Richard L. (1981). *Organization Theory and Design.* St. Paul: West Publishing.

Danet, Brenda (1981). "Client-Organization Relationships." In Paul C. Nystrom and William H. Starbuck (eds.), *Handbook of Organizational Design.* New York: Oxford University Press, pp. 382-428.

Fuchs, Victor R. (1968). *The Service Economy.* New York: National Bureau of Economic Research.

Hackman, J. Richard, Greg Oldham, Robert Janson, and Kenneth Purdy (1975). "A New Strategy for Job Enrichment." *California Management Review* 17:57-71.

Hayes, Robert H., and Steven Wheelwright (1979). "Link Manufacturing Product and Process Life Cycles." *Harvard Business Review* 57:133-140.

Hoschild, Arlene (1983). *The Managed Heart: The Commercialization of Human Feeling.* Berkeley: University of California Press.

Langeard, Eric, John E.G. Bateson, Christopher H. Lovelock, and Pierre Eiglier (1981). *Services Marketing: New Insights from Consumers and Managers.* Cambridge, MA: Marketing Science Institute, pp. 81-104.

Levitt, Theodore (1981). "Marketing Intangible Products and Product Intangibles." *Harvard Business Review* 52:94-102.

Locke, Edwin A., and Gary P. Latham (1984). *Goal-Setting: A Motivational Technique that Works!* Englewood Cliffs, NJ: Prentice-Hall.

Lovelock, Christopher H. (1981). "Why Marketing Management Needs to be Different for Services." In James H. Donnelly and William R. George (eds.), *Marketing of Services.* Chicago: American Marketing Association, pp. 5-9.

———— (1984). *Services Marketing.* Englewood Cliffs, NJ: Prentice-Hall.

Maister, David H. (1982). "Managing Service Enterprises in the Eighties." In E.E. Scheuing (ed.), *The Service Economy.* New York: KCG Productions.

Mills, Peter K. (1986). *Managing Service Industries: Organizational Practices in Post-Industrial Economy.* Cambridge, MA: Ballinger.

Mills, Peter K., and Newton Margulies (1980). "Toward a Core Typology of Service Organizations." *Academy of Management Review* 5:255-265.

Mills, Peter K., and Dennis J. Moberg (1982). "Perspectives on the Technology of Service Operations." *Academy of Management Review* 7:467-478.

Mills, Peter K., Richard B. Chase, and Newton Margulies (1983). "Motivating the Client/ Employee System as a Service Production Strategy." *Academy of Management Review* 8:301-310.

Mills, Peter K., and James H. Morris (1986). "Clients as Partial Employees of Service Organizations: Role Development in Client Participation." *Academy of Management Review* 11:726-735.

Moeller, Nancy, and Benjamin Schneider (1986). Climate for Service and the Bottom Line. Paper presented at AMA Services Marketing Conference, Chicago.

Parkington, John J., and Benjamin Schneider (1979). "Some Correlates of Experienced Job Stress: A Boundary-Role Study." *Academy of Management Journal* 22:270-281.

Parasuraman, A., Valerie A. Zeithaml, and Len L. Barry (1985). "A Conceptual Model of Service Quality and Its Implications for Future Research." *Journal of Marketing* 49:41-50.

Parsons, Talcott (1956). "Suggestions for a Sociological Approach to the Theory of Organizations." *Administrative Science Quarterly* 1:63-85.

Peters, Thomas J., and Robert H. Waterman, Jr. (1982). *In Search of Excellence: Lessons from America's Best-Run Companies.* New York: Harper & Row.

Sasser, Earl (1976). "Match Supply and Demand in Service Industries." *Harvard Business Review* 54:133-148.

Schneider, Benjamin, John J. Parkington, and Virginia M. Buxton (1980). "Employee and Customer Perceptions of Service in Banks." *Administrative Science Quarterly* 25:252-267.

Schneider, Benjamin, and David E. Bowen (1984). "New Services Design, Development, and Implementation and the Employee." In William R. George and Claudia E. Marshall (eds.), *Developing New Services.* Chicago: American Marketing Association, pp. 82-101.

Schneider, Benjamin, and David E. Bowen (1985). "Employee and Customer Perceptions of Service in Banks: Replication and Extension." *Journal of Applied Psychology* 70:423-433.

Shamir, Boas (1980). "Between Service and Servility: Role Conflict in Subordinate Service Roles." *Human Relations* 33:741-756.

Shostack, G. Lynn (1981). "How to Design a Service." In James H. Donnelly and William R. George (eds.), *Marketing of Services.* Chicago: American Marketing Association, pp. 221-229.

Thompson, James D. (1967). *Organizations in Action.* New York: McGraw-Hill.

Ward, Thomas (1973). *The Distribution of Consumer Goods.* Cambridge: MA: Cambridge University Press.

Vroom, Victor R., and Phillip W. Yetton (1973). *Leadership and Decision Making.* Pittsburgh: University of Pittsburgh Press.

Zeithaml, Valerie (1981). "How Consumer Evaluation Processes Differ Between Goods and Services." In James H. Donnelly and William R. George (eds.), *Marketing of Services.* Chicago: American Marketing Association, pp. 191-199.

STRATEGIC RESPONSES TO GLOBAL COMPETITION:
ADVANCED TECHNOLOGY,
ORGANIZATION DESIGN, AND
HUMAN RESOURCE PRACTICES

James W. Dean, Jr. and Gerald I. Susman

This chapter discusses the new strategies manufacturing firms are implementing to respond effectively to domestic and international competitive trends. Advanced manufacturing technology (AMT), which enhances a firm's ability to simultaneously lower costs, increase quality, and provide rapid delivery of customized products, is the centerpiece of many of these strategies. AMT is being adopted across a broad spectrum of industry and is arguably one of the most important developments in business today. However, the capability of AMT cannot be fully realized nor the new strategies effectively implemented without significant changes in manufacturing practices, organization design, and human resource management.

Our intention is to provide an integrated discussion of the various components of these contemporary strategies. We begin in the first section with a discussion of the relationship between manufacturing strategy and corporate/business unit strategy, and note major trends in the competitive environment of manufacturing firms that necessitate new competitive strategies. This discussion is necessary to set the context in which AMT is being adopted. In the second section, we discuss how AMT can alter the strategic options that have traditionally faced manufacturing, and how firms can use AMT as well as innovative manufacturing practices to respond to the changing competitive environment. The third and fourth sections examine the changes in organization design and human resource practices, respectively, that complement AMT in achieving strategic goals.

COMPETITIVE STRATEGY AND ENVIRONMENTAL TRENDS

Competitive Strategy

Corporate Strategy. An organization's strategy is generally seen as consisting of three levels: corporate, business, and functional (Hofer and Schendel, 1978). Corporate strategy specifies two areas of interest to the firm: (a) the businesses in which the corporation will (and will not) participate, and (b) the acquisition and allocation of resources among these businesses (Hayes and Wheelwright, 1984). The decision by a corporation to participate in a particular business is generally influenced by its dominant orientation, whether toward materials (e.g., glass, aluminum, steel), markets (e.g., consumer, industrial), or technology (e.g., mass or customized production).

Business Strategy. Strategy at the business level specifies the basis on which an organization will achieve and maintain a competitive advantage in a particular product market. Several common or "generic" strategies can be used by a firm to conduct business in a variety of different industries (Porter, 1980, 1985). Underlying the concept of generic strategy is the assumption that while the superficial characteristics of industries may differ, their deep structure is sufficiently similar that certain ways of competing, if effectively implemented, can lead to competitive advantage in many industries. However, the concept of generic strategy may be less useful in new industries created by a major technological or product innovation because competition among firms may be based almost exclusively on product performance. As performance capabilities stabilize and new industries mature, the generic strategies become increasingly relevant.

Porter (1980) has identified three (actually four) generic strategies. The first major distinction between strategies is whether they involve competition in the entire market (broad focus) or only in targeted market segments (narrow focus). The second distinction is whether competition in

Figure 1. Generic Business Strategies

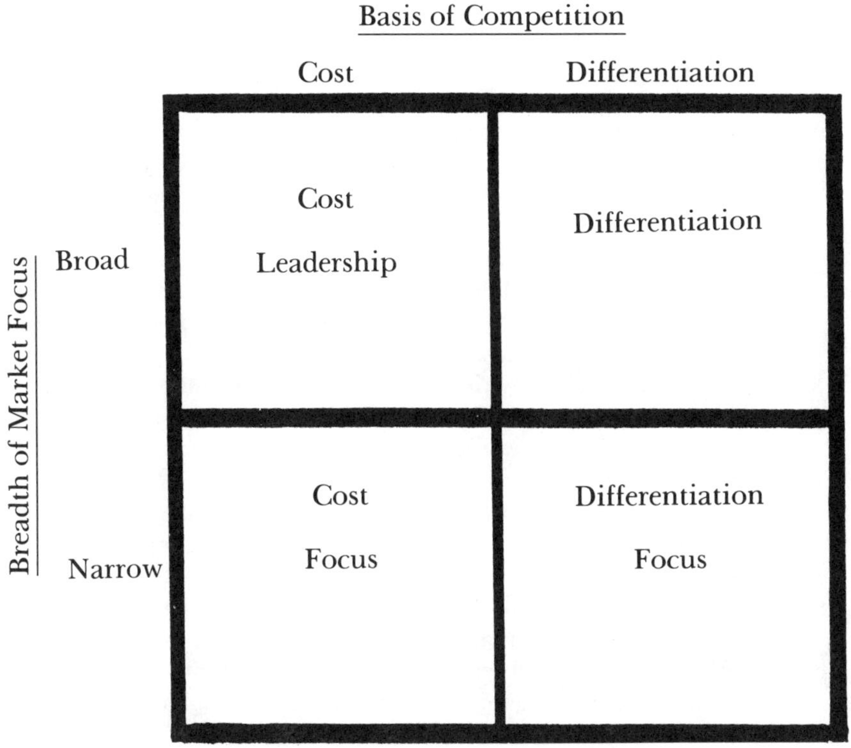

Basis of Competition

	Cost	Differentiation
Broad	Cost Leadership	Differentiation
Narrow	Cost Focus	Differentiation Focus

Breadth of Market Focus

Source: Adapted from Michael E. Porter (1985), *Competitive Advantage.* New York: Free Press, p. 12.

these respective types of markets will be on the basis of cost or differentiation. The four strategies that emerge from these two distinctions are shown in Figure 1.

The first strategy consists of competing in the entire market on the basis of price (and therefore cost). This strategy is based on keeping the firm's cost sufficiently low that it can gain market share by having lower prices than the competition or make greater profits than a competitor which chooses to match prices but has higher costs. This strategy is somewhat self-reinforcing, since large market share (and therefore high volume) tend to lower costs further. Lincoln Electric Company is a good example of a consistently executed low-cost strategy.

The second generic strategy is differentiation, in which a firm competes across the entire market by being different than the other firms in the industry on some dimension that is valued by the market. There are a large number of possible bases of differentiation, including product quality, reliability, delivery, and service. In the computer industry, IBM's consistent emphasis on customer service has constituted a major means of differentiation.

The third and fourth strategies involve an attempt to focus on one or more market segments, and to devote the firm's resources to serving those and only those customers. The assumption of this strategy is that a firm that concentrates its efforts will be more effective with a particular set of customers than a firm that tries to serve a variety of customers. The focus strategy has two variations, cost focus and differentiation focus. In the cost variation, a firm's concentration on a particular market segment allows it to serve those customers at lower cost. In the differentiation variation, concentration allows the firm to provide customers with some added value relative to nonspecialized firms. For example, Cray's focus on very high speed "supercomputers" allows it to concentrate research and development efforts on areas that most computer producers and consumers would consider unimportant but are crucial to the development of computers for Cray's industrial customers.

A fundamental tenet of Porter's (1980) framework is that "no firm can serve two masters." Firms must make a decision to pursue only one of the generic strategies and make operating decisions so as to consistently support this choice. A firm that fails to do this runs the risk of being "stuck in the middle" with higher costs than those which concentrate on cost, less differentiation than those which concentrate on differentiation, and less focus than those which make this their strategic objective. Such a firm will meet this fate due to an inconsistent pattern of decisions: Initiatives to achieve one strategic objective in one part of the firm will be foiled by conflicting initiatives in other parts of the firm. Failure to choose and consistently pursue a single strategy will lead to competitive failure.

This is not to suggest, however, that a firm that chooses one of these generic strategies can ignore the others. On the contrary, a firm that chooses to compete on one basis (e.g., cost) will only be successful if customers believe that the advantage (lower prices) offered by the firm more than compensate for the disadvantages (poorer quality or service) that accompany it. Similarly, a firm that competes by differentiation will only succeed if the added value of its products more than compensates for the higher prices they entail.

A strategy is created when a series of decisions over a period of time forms a pattern (Mintzberg, 1978). The decisions that are the raw material for strategy involve everything from marketing mix and type of process technology to organization design and compensation packages. Some choices that present themselves to a firm will involve tradeoffs between strategic objectives, others will not. When tradeoffs exist, they must always be resolved in the direction of supporting the chosen objective (Porter, 1985).

The greater the number of decisions that involve tradeoffs, the more often a firm will have to sacrifice one objective in favor of another.

Manufacturing Strategy. The third level of competitive strategy is the functional level, including manufacturing, finance, and marketing strategies. To be effective, each functional strategy must support, through a consistent pattern of decisions and tradeoffs between competitive priorities, the competitive advantage being sought by the business unit.

Until recently, manufacturing was widely regarded as involving tactical, not strategic, issues. Production took a back seat to financial, marketing, and legal considerations (Lubar, 1981). But through the efforts of a number of scholars, notably Skinner (1974) and Hayes and Wheelwright (1984), academics have come to recognize the importance of manufacturing for achieving competitive advantage. The currently accepted view is that an organization's manufacturing unit should have a strategy that supports the strategy of the business unit.

Manufacturing can support one or more of the generic business strategies by attempting to achieve low manufacturing cost, high levels of quality (dependability and/or superior performance), or high levels of flexibility (rapid introduction of new products, fast reliable delivery, and product customization). These three strategic manufacturing objectives are important not only because they capture a good portion of what manufacturing managers are trying to achieve but because they map closely onto the generic strategies outlined above. Thus, they are not only strategic objectives for manufacturing but also ways in which the manufacturing function can facilitate the competitive success of the business unit.

Control over manufacturing costs will obviously have an important impact on whether a firm will be able to successfully execute a competitive strategy based on low cost, in either an entire market or market segments. Product quality (performance and dependability) is an important potential contributor to either version of the differentiation strategy. Fast, reliable delivery and frequent new-product introduction also represent means of generic differentiation in either segments or the market as a whole. Finally, product customization as a generic manufacturing strategy supports a business strategy of differentiation in focused market segments. Of course, efforts by manufacturing will need to be supported by other functions in order to assure that any of the chosen generic strategies will be effective.

Like business strategy, manufacturing strategy is enacted by a series of decisions. These decisions involve such issues as capacity, plant size and location, type of technology, vertical integration, and organization of the manufacturing function (Skinner, 1974; Hayes and Wheelwright, 1984). Similar to business strategy, there are tradeoffs to be made in developing manufacturing strategy; some objectives must be sacrificed in favor of others.

JAMES W. DEAN, JR. and GERALD I. SUSMAN

Skinner (1974) has carried this idea to the extreme with the notion of "the focused factory." That is, depending on the competitive strategy of the business unit, a plant should give sole emphasis to the manufacturing objective that is consistent with that strategy, such as flexibility or low cost. If the business unit is emphasizing different capabilities in different market segments, then the firm should produce different types of products in separate plants that focus on specialized abilities or organize a single plant into "plants within a plant" to assure that each product is produced with its appropriate focus. The logic behind this argument is parallel to that of Porter (1980): by trying to achieve several objectives, manufacturing will probably achieve none of them particularly well, thus serving as a millstone rather than a competitive weapon for the firm.

To summarize, firms may seek competitive advantage by pursuing strategies of either cost or differentiation with either a broad or narrow market focus. Manufacturing can facilitate the execution of one or more of these generic strategies by emphasizing cost, quality, or flexibility. However, tradeoffs are an essential component of manufacturing strategy as well as business strategy. Using mass production techniques, for example, will increase productivity and thus lower cost, but will limit flexibility.

Trends in the Competitive Environment of Manufacturing

We see trends emerging in a number of industries that will change and intensify the nature of competition for manufacturing firms into the next century. These trends are to some extent a result of the "globalization" of industry that has profoundly affected many markets. While globalization is a complex phenomenon, two aspects are particularly important for advanced manufacturing technology: (a) the expansion of U.S.-based firms into world markets in many industries, and (b) the entry of many foreign-based firms into American domestic markets. We should note, however, that the trends discussed below are observable even in industries that are primarily domestic in scope. Each of these trends has direct relevance for one of the three strategic manufacturing objectives.

Cost Competition. The first trend is the increasing intensity of cost competition among firms in many industries. This is partially a result of the demonstrated ability of foreign producers to deliver products in the U.S. at prices lower than those that domestic producers can offer. It also has domestic roots in that the current leveling off of inflation or even disinflation in the American economy precludes the passing on of high production costs to consumers (Coopers and Lybrand, 1986).

Organizations have responded to this increased cost pressure with layoffs of unprecedented size in both blue- and white-collar areas as well as cost-cutting moves in virtually every area of operations. Firms have also been quick to pass along cost pressures to their suppliers. For example, American color television manufacturers have demanded substantial price reductions from glass producers that provide them with screens and picture tube funnels. Such widespread attention to costs makes it very difficult for any one firm to dominate the others in its industry by focusing on costs.

Quality. Perhaps the most notable recent development related to manufacturing is the increased emphasis on quality. Throughout the 1970s and 1980s, American consumers have abandoned domestic firms in favor of the higher-quality products of their foreign competitors, notably the Japanese. This has been particularly true for such high value-added products as automobiles and consumer electronics. As consumers have come to expect the level of quality offered by Japanese and other competitors, American firms have undertaken massive programs to attain a level of product quality that will allow them to survive.

The newfound quality emphasis in American producers of consumer goods has increasingly spread to their suppliers. One of the first things a firm focuses on in undertaking a quality program is the quality of the raw materials and components it buys. If component quality is low, the final product cannot be of high quality. Thus, firms have put enormous pressure on their suppliers to not only lower their costs but to raise their quality standards, too. If domestic suppliers do not measure up, foreign-based suppliers may replace them, as is beginning to happen in the U.S. automobile industry (Boyer, 1986). Both the importance and the minimum acceptable level of product quality have substantially increased in consumer and industrial markets.

Market Fragmentation/Short Product Life Cycles. A third important trend affecting the nature of competition in manufacturing industries is market fragmentation combined with shorter product life cycles. We combine these trends because they both increase the need for flexibility in manufacturing. Many firms will be increasingly unable to produce a standard product over a long period of time, needing instead to produce a rapidly evolving mix of customized products. Market fragmentation has come to characterize many industries, including baking, apparel, steel, building materials, tools, medical products, and office equipment (Sabel, 1982; Hirschhorn, 1984). Business in North America, Europe, and Japan expect to be making even more customized products over the next few years (Ferdows et al., 1985). The tendency of many firms to produce for a number of different national markets contributes to this fragmentation as does the increasing diversity of American lifestyles.

A number of observers have noted the increasing brevity of product life-cycles (Skinner, 1978; Jelinek and Goldhar, 1984; Ferdows et al., 1985). One reason for this is the increasing potential for technological breakthroughs to create "dematurity" in a market (Abernathy et al., 1983). Dematurity occurs when new technology so affects the design or manufacture of a product that the market dynamics come to resemble those of a new product. This combination of market fragmentation and shortened product life-cycle places a substantial premium on manufacturing flexibility. In order to be able to compete in many industries today (and presumably even more in the future), firms will need the ability to produce a wide variety of customized products simultaneously and to rapidly abandon production of current products in favor of new ones.

Responding to any one of these three trends would be difficult for a manufacturing firm. But it is the combination of these trends that represents the greatest challenge. Since competitive viability increasingly requires superior performance in terms of cost, quality, *and* flexibility, new strategies that attempt to simultaneously achieve these objectives are needed. Sacrificing cost to attain quality, or flexibility to maintain low cost, will no longer suffice. Thus, firms must find ways to overcome the tradeoffs that constrain their ability to excel on more than one of these objectives.

Responses to Trends in the Manufacturing Environment

Evidence is mounting that firms in several industries have in fact launched a frontal attack on their competition by simultaneously excelling in at least two, if not all three, areas of competitive advantage. Abernathy et al. (1983), for example, provide convincing evidence that Japanese automobile manufacturers hold real competitive advantages over their American competitors in both cost and quality. It would be incorrect, however, to equate this new form of competition with Japanese firms or the auto industry alone. American firms in other industries have begun to demonstrate a capacity to "surround" their competitors by simultaneously amassing multiple competitive advantages. For example, General Electric has strengthened an already strong position in the dishwasher business by producing high-quality machines at very low cost. Also, Allen-Bradley (a subsidiary of Rockwell International) has acquired the capacity to produce 600 varieties of industrial controls, all at the lowest costs in the industry (Bylinsky, 1986).

Our belief is that the simultaneous dominance of these and other firms on two or more dimensions of competitive advantage is an adaptive response to the changing nature of demand and competition in manufacturing industries. In order to be successful, firms in the future will need to achieve patterns of competitive strength similar to those we have mentioned. Furthermore, the apparent contradiction between this multipronged strategy and academic orthodoxy on strategy is really not a contradiction at all. The reader will recall that choosing one type of competitive advantage over another need only be done when decisions force tradeoffs among the various types of advantage. We believe that the firms mentioned, and increasingly many more like them, have come to dominate their competition by discovering ways to avoid making the traditional tradeoffs between cost and quality, cost and flexibility, and quality and flexibility. Thus, advantages can be gained in one area without sacrifices in the others. The execution of these strategies is complex, involving an innovative integration of manufacturing technology and practices, organization design, and human resource policies. We will now elaborate on each of these areas, showing how organizations can gain multiple competitive advantages by successfully combining innovative approaches in all three areas.

ADVANCED MANUFACTURING TECHNOLOGY AND PRACTICES

Firms have developed a number of tactics to respond to the increasingly intense competition that is based both on cost and the various types of differentiation. The second column of Table 1 lists 10 such tactics. Many of these tactics strengthen a firm's capabilities in several areas of competitive advantage, but for convenience we have linked each tactic in the table to the strategic objective to which it makes the greatest contribution. Collectively, these tactics permit a firm to transcend the tradeoffs among cost, quality, and flexibility.

Each tactic involves a combination of advanced manufacturing technology and innovative manufacturing practices (columns 3 and 4 of Table 1). Those practices that develop and utilize human resources more effectively are discussed in detail in a later section. Advanced manufacturing technology and the practices discussed in this chapter are generally complementary rather than substitutes for each other. In fact, Schonberger (1986) has suggested that most of the manufacturing practices listed in Table 1 are prerequisites to the introduction of advanced technology. If such practices are not introduced first, Schonberger suggests, firms may automate the inefficiencies that the practices are designed to eliminate. Nevertheless, there are a few cases where introducing the practices may reduce the need for some types of AMT. Examples are discussed below where applicable.

Advanced Manufacturing Technology

Computer-Aided Manufacturing. Computer-aided manufacturing (CAM) consists of robotics, numerically controlled (NC) machines, computer and direct numerical control (CNC and DNC), and flexible

Table 1.   Tactics, Technologies, and Manufacturing Practices
for Competitive Advantage

Strategic Objectives	Tactic	Advanced Manufacturing Technology	Manufacturing Practice
Manufacturing Cost	Reduce direct cost	CAM	Multiskilling
	Reduce inventory	MRP	Just-in-time
	Simplify coordination	GT	Cellular manufacturing
			Point-of-use manufacturing
			Decentralization
Quality	Simplify products	CAD	Producibility
	Reduce defects	CAM	Problem-solving groups
		CAT	
Fast, Reliable Delivery	Reduce throughput time	CAM	Just-in-time
	Reduce setup time	CAM	Problem-solving groups
	Eliminate bottlenecks	CAPP	
Innovative Products	Reduce product development times	CAD/CAE	Cross-functional teams
Customized Products	Enhance flexibility	CAM/CIM	Multiskilling
			Smaller machines

manufacturing systems (FMS). CAM is the most hardware-intensive of the
technologies that make up AMT and the one that has the most direct contact
with the actual fabrication or assembly of the product. Robots are
"reprogrammable multifunction manipulators designed to move materials,
parts, tools, or specialized devices through variable programmed motions